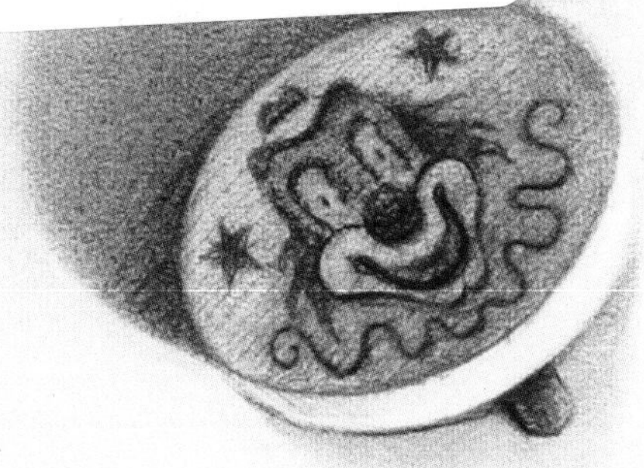

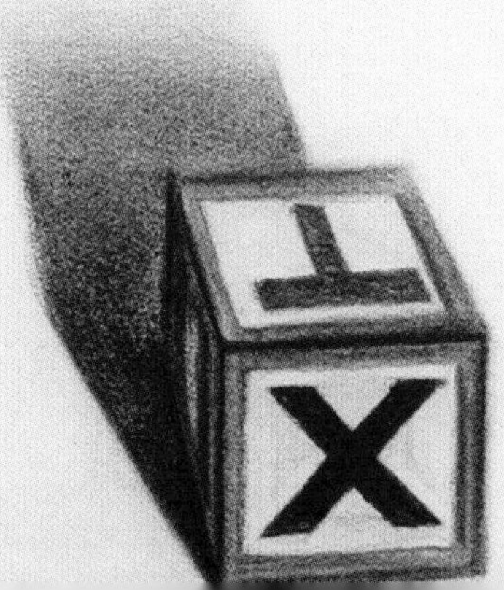

Wayne Thiebaud

ISABELLE DERVAUX

Wayne Thiebaud

Draftsman

THE MORGAN LIBRARY & MUSEUM

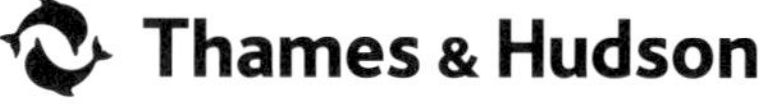 Thames & Hudson

Contents

Director's Foreword

On a page of sketches dated 1981, below the drawing of a luscious bowl of cherries, Wayne Thiebaud wrote *Notes on drawing exhibit (Morgan Library)*. There follows a list of comments on the use of pounce for transfer, black chalk vs. charcoal, the direction of hatching lines, and the presence of pink in the shadows of nineteenth-century French artist Pierre-Paul Prud'hon. The technical aspect of these notes reveals the preoccupations of the expert draftsman carefully studying the methods of his forebears. Whereas Thiebaud may be best known for his mouthwatering paintings of cakes and candy counters, his work covers a much broader range of mediums and subjects, informed by a passion for drawing and the art of the past. It is therefore fitting that the Morgan Library & Museum, renowned for its collection of old-master and nineteenth-century drawings, should organize an exhibition of Thiebaud's works on paper. Despite the artist's popularity and the large number of exhibitions that have been devoted to his work, this is the first comprehensive retrospective of his drawings presented by a museum.

Beginning with Thiebaud's early career as a cartoonist and commercial draftsman in the 1940s and 1950s, the exhibition examines the role this background played in the development of his mature style. In 1962, he became famous almost overnight when his first paintings of pies and hamburgers were shown at Allan Stone Gallery in New York. He was dubbed "the Walt Whitman of the delicatessen" by the *New York Times*, while his everyday subjects and deadpan representation were associated with the Pop Art movement emerging at the time. Although Thiebaud's imagery did share affinities with Pop Art, his attachment to traditional techniques set his work apart from the formal experiments of artists such as Andy Warhol and Roy Lichtenstein. Within a year, Thiebaud was expanding the range of his subjects to include figures and landscapes. Even though he has often revisited the food theme throughout his career, he has also created compelling series of works on subjects such as the San Francisco cityscape and the landscape of the Sacramento River valley.

The exhibition explores the role of drawing during these different phases of Thiebaud's development, with particular attention to his inquiries into the possibilities offered by different mediums, from pencil and charcoal to ink, pastel, and watercolor. Several groups of works show him tackling the same image—a row of candy sticks, for instance—in different techniques. An important section of the exhibition is devoted to Thiebaud's sketches. It comprises a selection of sheets on which the artist tried out ideas for paintings and accumulated graphic notations that reveal the centrality of drawing to his process. The pedagogical aspect of some of the juxtapositions and comparisons is intended to convey Thiebaud's passion for teaching, an activity

he has pursued throughout his career and that has contributed to his immense
influence upon younger artists. In a recent interview, recorded for this
publication, Thiebaud shares some of his teaching methods and expands on
the importance of learning drawing.

A large number of the drawings in the exhibition, including all of the sketches,
belong to the artist. Many have never or rarely been exhibited. I am deeply
grateful to Wayne Thiebaud for his cooperation in the organization of the
exhibition and for his generosity, not only in agreeing to lend many works
but also in graciously devoting so much time to answering our questions and
queries. I also would like to acknowledge the kind assistance of Matthew and
Alex Bult and Colleen Casey of his studio.

The exhibition was conceived and organized by Isabelle Dervaux, Acquavella
Curator of Modern and Contemporary Drawings, to whom I am thankful
for her dedication as well as her thoughtful contributions to this catalogue.
Many others at the Morgan have played an essential role in this project;
they are listed in the Acknowledgments.

The exhibition would not have been possible without the generosity of the
lenders (listed elsewhere in this volume) who have kindly agreed to part with
their drawings for several months. I am extremely grateful to all of them.
Finally, I extend my deepest thanks to the sponsors, whose financial support
has been vital to the success of this project: Acquavella Galleries, Allan
Stone Projects, Agnes Gund, the Wyeth Foundation for American Art, Alan
and Ellen Meckler, and Nancy Schwartz.

Colin B. Bailey

Acknowledgments

It is a great privilege to celebrate the work of such a superb artist and consummate draftsman as Wayne Thiebaud. Working in close collaboration with him was one of the singular pleasures of preparing this exhibition. At ninety-seven, Wayne Thiebaud is actively engaged in making art—when he is not playing tennis. I am immensely grateful to him for his kindness throughout this project, his generosity with his time, his willingness to go through piles of drawings—some of them dating back to many decades— and answering countless questions. I wish to express here my thanks and admiration. At Wayne's studio, I also would like to thank Colleen Casey and Matthew and Alex Bult, who kindly helped with a myriad of tasks, from locating works and having them framed and photographed to providing documentation.

I extend my appreciation to all the lenders who have been extremely gracious and generous in their cooperation. For their assistance in tracking down drawings that have changed hands over the years and facilitating loans from private collections, I am indebted to Wayne Thiebaud's dealers. At Allan Stone Projects, Bo Joseph showed me many works from the collection of Allan Stone, who first exhibited Thiebaud's paintings in New York in 1962 and until his death in 2006 remained Thiebaud's champion. At Acquavella Galleries, Thiebaud's current dealer, I owe special thanks to Eleanor Acquavella Dejoux, Nicholas Acquavella, and Jean Edmonson, who kindly contacted many collectors on my behalf. In San Francisco, I wish to thank Kelly Purcell at Paul Thiebaud Gallery and John Berggruen and Lindsay Snyder at John Berggruen Gallery. For forwarding my requests to collectors who had purchased their works at auction, I am grateful to Sara Friedlander and Corrie Searls at Christie's and Emma Baker, Emily Kaplan, and Emily Miles at Sotheby's.

Museum colleagues have graciously answered queries and assisted in making arrangements for me to view Thiebaud's drawings. I am thankful to Christie K. Hajela at the Crocker Art Museum, Sacramento; Rebecca Tilghman at the Metropolitan Museum of Art, New York; Janet Bishop and Nancy Lim at the San Francisco Museum of Modern Art; Francesca Wilmott at the Jan Shrem & Marie Manetti Shrem Museum of Art, Davis, California; and Jock Reynolds, Suzanne Boorsch, Suzanne Greenawalt, and Theresa Fairbanks-Harris at Yale University Art Gallery. Many individuals also deserve mention for their kind support: Michelle Jones and Karen Saracino at the Anderson Collection; Shannon Carlin; Giampaolo and Monica Catani; Abigail Asher and Jessica Lewis at Guggenheim, Asher Associates; Fred Friedler; Lawrence Markey; and Alan M. Meckler.

For their help in researching archival material, I would like to acknowledge Frank Sternad, who kindly provided images from his collection of documents related to Rexall Drug Company; Elena Smith and Kathleen Correia at the California State Library in Sacramento; Lori Salmon at the New York Public Library; Vivian Woo at College Art Association; Phyllis Graham at the Crocker Art Museum; and Brian Lewis at the San Francisco Museum of Modern Art Library.

At the Morgan, my most heartfelt thanks go to Director Colin B. Bailey and Deputy Director Jessica Ludwig for their continuous encouragement and support. I am very grateful to the many members of the staff who were involved at various stages in the organization of the exhibition: Rachel Federman and Sofia Kofodimos in Modern and Contemporary Drawings; John D. Alexander, Senior Manager of Exhibition and Collection Administration; Winona Packer, Lindsay Stavros, Sophie Worley, Keith Johnson, and Ryan Shreves in the Registrar's office; Marco Bolzoni and Zoe Watnik in Drawings and Prints; Roger S. Wieck in Medieval and Renaissance Manuscripts; V. Heidi Hass and Peter Gammie in the Reference Collection; Lindsey Tyne, Maria Fredericks, Frank Trujillo, and James Donchez in the Thaw Conservation Center; Karen Banks, Patricia Emerson, and Eliza Heitzman in Publications; Marilyn Palmeri, Graham Haber, and Min Tian in Imaging and Rights; Lauren Stakias and Anita Masi in Development. Special thanks are due to the interns who have provided tireless assistance over the years: Sarah F. Cohen, Crystal M. Ferrer, Emma Holter, and Sam Sackeroff.

Finally, I would like to acknowledge David Zaza and Michelle Lee Nix from McCall Associates for the elegant design of this catalogue.

Lenders to the Exhibition

Harry W. and Mary Margaret Anderson

Gretchen and John Berggruen, San Francisco

Karen and Brian Conway

Mia I. Groszkowski

Alan and Ellen Meckler

Private collection, courtesy Acquavella Galleries

Private collection, courtesy of Guggenheim, Asher Associates

Christine and David Provost

The Putt-McCann Art Collection,
in memory of Charlie and Glenna Campbell

Allan Stone Collection, courtesy Allan Stone Projects, NY

Allison Stone Stabile

Wayne Thiebaud

Thiebaud Family Collection

Yale University Art Gallery

And other lenders who wish to remain anonymous

Drawing Keeps You from Cheating

*One day Kathan brought down lunch, which was
a cheese sandwich, a couple of olives, and a beer,
and I said, "Before we eat that, I think I'll draw it."*

—Wayne Thiebaud[1]

One of the most evident and talked-about aspects of Wayne Thiebaud's paintings is his lush and thick handling of paint. From Hilton Kramer—"He really can spread it on!"—to Donald Judd—"The juiciness of the paint is a little gross"—critics have emphasized the materiality of the pigments as a defining characteristic of Thiebaud's art.[2] This property has generated an abundance of clichés on the analogy between his paintings and their most popular subjects: frosted cakes and ice cream cones. In this context, what are we to make of Thiebaud's drawing? What role does it play in this celebration of the sensuous qualities of oil paint?

And yet, Thiebaud was a draftsman before he was a painter. Drawing has been at the core of his practice since he began his career as a cartoonist in the 1940s, and the graphic element has remained essential throughout his development as an artist. "Drawing, to me, is a kind of inquiring research tool that painting rests upon," Thiebaud said. Following a traditional classification, he divides his drawings into two basic categories. "There's a sort of public aspect of drawing, where drawings are made to be shown. . . . And [there are] private drawings, where they're made mostly for research and you don't even care whether they're ever seen or not."[3] The first group includes the finished drawings in pencil, ink, pastel, and watercolor that Thiebaud has exhibited regularly. Some may be studies for paintings, but most were done primarily to satisfy his inquisitive mind. What would the same subject look like in a different medium?

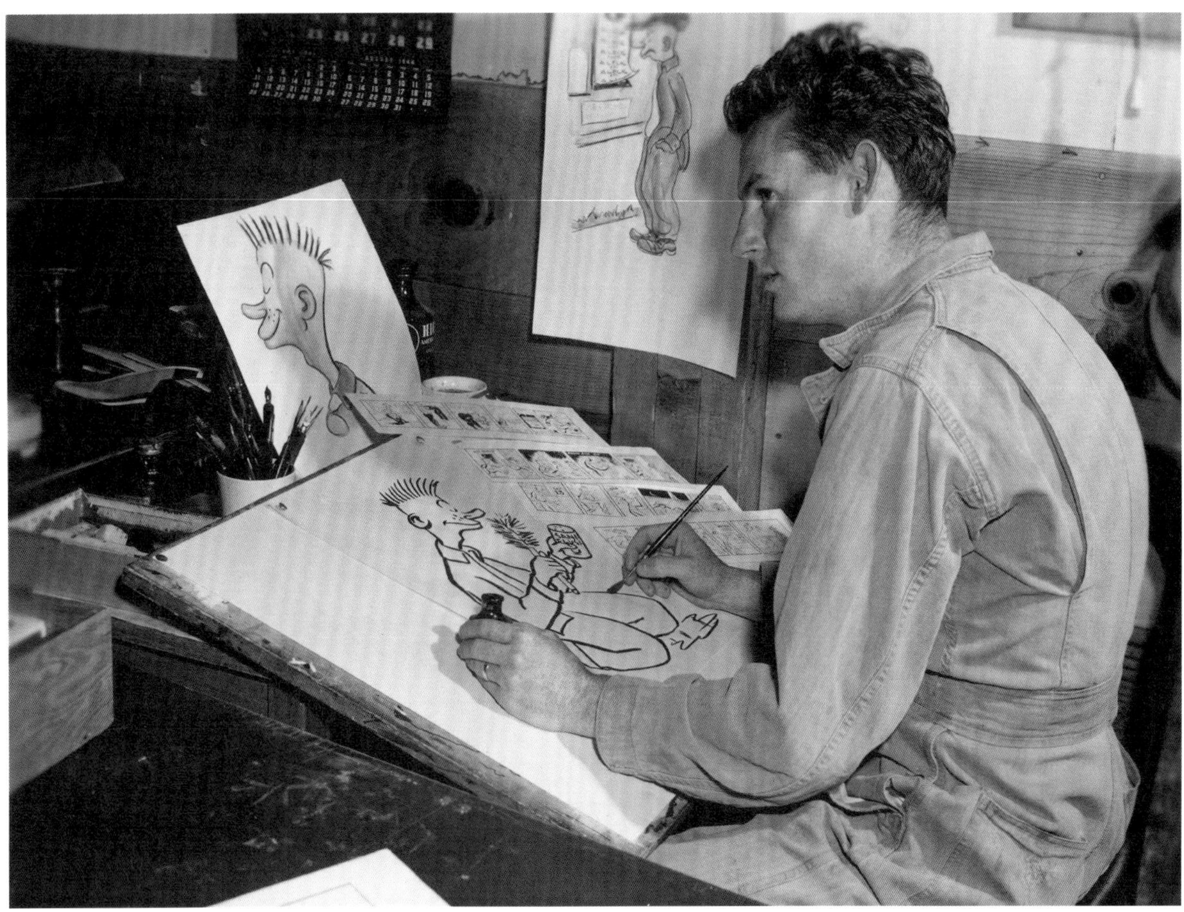

"What sorts of things occur," he wonders, if you "transpose say a thick, rich colorful painting into black and white in a sparse or less sensual medium?"[4] The second group consists of sketches in various degrees of finish, ranging from thumbnails of ideas for compositions to quick studies made from observation. The present essay will focus on the first group. The sketches are the subject of a separate study (see p. 110).

FIG. 1.
Thiebaud working on Aleck cartoons,
Mather Army Air Field, 1944.
Courtesy of Wayne Thiebaud.

I. I WANTED TO BE A CARTOONIST FIRST

Thiebaud was forty-one years old in 1962, when his first exhibition of pie and cake paintings at Allan Stone Gallery, New York, launched his reputation. Before that, he had worked primarily as a commercial draftsman. "I didn't ever think about being an artist or becoming an artist," he recalled. "I wanted to be a cartoonist first."[5] For about fifteen years, he earned his living as a cartoonist, designer, illustrator, sign painter, and advertising art director. Early experiences

included a brief stint, at age sixteen, as an "in-betweener" (drawing the
intermediate frames between the main images) in the animation department
of Walt Disney Studios—"the low life of animation," as Thiebaud put it.[6] Fired
after a few months for participating in union activities, he retained the ability
to draw Mickey Mouse or Jiminy Cricket using either hand.[7]

Thiebaud did not go to art school but studied commercial art at Frank Wiggins
Trade School, Los Angeles, in 1937–38. During the Second World War, he
enlisted in the U.S. Army Air Forces with the hope of becoming a pilot
but ended up making posters and drawing cartoons for the army weeklies
(Figs. 1–3). After his discharge, he moved to New York, where he tried to
establish himself as a freelance cartoonist. This was a common experience of
many artists at the time—Franz Kline and Tom Wesselman, for instance, also
started as cartoonists. In the commercial world of the postwar era, the type
of drawing associated with the genre—slick and highly stylized contour
drawing—was very much in demand, owing to the popularity of comic books.
"In the mid-1940s," critic David Hajdu wrote, "the comic book was the most
popular form of entertainment in America. Comics were selling between
eighty million and a hundred million copies every week . . . reaching more
people than movies, television, radio, or magazines for adults."[8] Thiebaud,
however, was unable to break into the field. He turned to sign painting and
illustration and, after a year, headed back to Los Angeles, where he worked
for a while at Universal Studios, designing movie posters and publicity sets,
before being fired again for his participation in a labor strike. Finally he landed
a job as layout art director and cartoonist for Rexall Drug Company. He later
described the three years he spent there, from 1946 to 1949, as a critical time.[9]

In many respects, the training Thiebaud received in the field of commercial
drawing was essential to the artist he later became. He has always expressed
admiration for the illustrators, sign painters, and graphic designers he encoun-
tered during this phase of his career, stressing the debt he owed them. "I'm
not too comfortable with that easy categorization of fine and commercial art,"
he said. "Both are precisely the same thing, it's the same language, with various
emphasis and syntaxes."[10] Having taken fashion design courses at Frank Wiggins,
Thiebaud remembered his admiration for Dorothy Hood, the influential
Lord & Taylor illustrator whose wash drawings were highly popular in the 1940s.
"I thought she was better than Matisse," he said.[11]

Drawing for advertising stimulates a pragmatic approach, in which clarity
and efficiency rule. The sense of order prevalent in Thiebaud's later paintings
and drawings derives from the placement strategy essential to advertising
layout, with its emphasis on focal points and directional lines that guide the

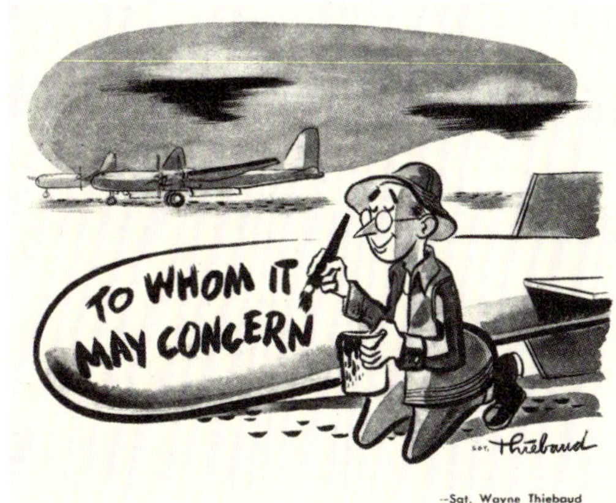

—Sgt. Wayne Thiebaud

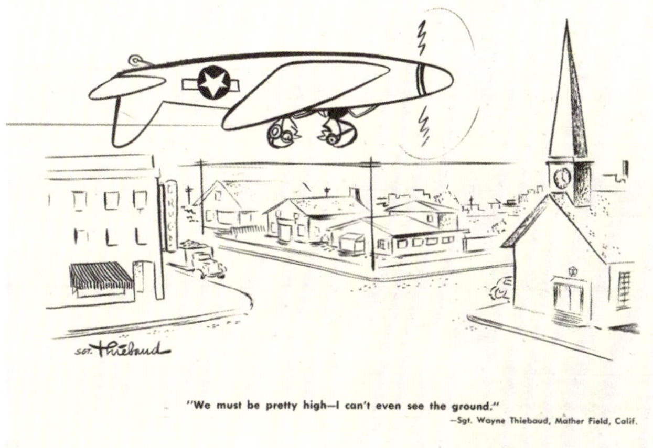

—Sgt. Wayne Thiebaud, Mather Field, Calif.

viewer's eye. Thiebaud learned advertising design when the field was heavily influenced by the International Style. "Less is more" was the dogma. This minimal aesthetic, with its predilection for the grid system, can be detected behind Thiebaud's rows of pies, which owe more to this method than to direct observation of deli counters. Other visual strategies familiar to advertising that Thiebaud exploited include exaggerated perspective, foreshortening, and bird's-eye views—which Thiebaud often adopted in his depictions of lunch counters and buffets (Nos. 24–25)—as well as bold layouts relying on vivid contrasts and generous use of white space to make an object stand out.

Also essential to commercial drawing is the use of graphic conventions and clichés—tricks, as Thiebaud calls them. Commercial draftsmen learn simple, effective ways of depicting objects and people. "Rather than having an actual lipstick pose here, which is going to give you endless amounts of information, you have an already simplified thing to make a structure from," Thiebaud explained. "Those clichés are very much a part of the shapes I use, that I learned in commercial art. There's a certain way to do crystal . . . a certain way to do a glass of water . . . something that looks like a bottle of milk."[12] Although Thiebaud is frequently described as a realist, his representation of foodstuff is not based on observation, not even on memory of actual objects, but rather on the idea of what a cupcake, a cream pie, or a hamburger looks like to the imagination. His pictures look real, not because they are realistic but because they match everyone's conception of the perfect hamburger or ice cream cone—a conception largely formed through visual advertising.

FIGS. 2–3.
Wayne Thiebaud, cartoons published in *Yank: The Army Weekly*, 27 April 1945, p. 24, and 19 October 1945, p. 15.

The evocative power of graphic stylization is central to cartoon and comic imagery, another major influence on Thiebaud's drawing style. "I have always loved cartoons," he said. "The power of the cartoon's graphic energy is something that has always struck me."[13] Like advertising design, cartoon aesthetic rests on economy and efficiency. It uses dramatic simplification and attention-grabbing strategy to attract the reader and convey a message in a limited space. Cartoons and comic strip artists are forced to rely on visual formulas and graphic shorthand to condense a story into a single image or a few panels. Standardization is essential to the effectiveness of communication, while sharp tonal contrasts are imposed by the rudimentary printing techniques of newspapers.

Thiebaud made hundreds of cartoons during the 1940s and 1950s (Nos. 1–2 and Figs. 2–3). Most relate to the "cute" vein that developed in American comics illustration around 1900 and reached its epitome in the Disney style—with which Thiebaud was familiar from his teenage apprenticeship.[14] A transformation is noticeable, however, in the evolution of the *Ferbus* comic strip that he created for *Rexall Magazine*. The somewhat stiff, diagrammatic outline of the early ones, done in 1947 (Fig. 4), gives way to a freer type of drawing with looser contours and greater fluidity in the later ones (Fig. 5). In addition, shadows rendered in washes add a sense of volume and enliven the scenes. This stylistic change may be linked to Thiebaud's growing interest in the fine art tradition. To make up for his lack of art school training he turned to a popular drawing method, *The Natural Way to Draw: A Working Plan for Art Study* by Kimon Nicolaïdes. Published in 1941, the book outlines a rigorous regimen of drawing based on fifteen-hour sessions. For the first half-hour, for instance, the student is to make twenty-five gesture drawings; in the next half-hour, one contour drawing, and so on. With this method, Thiebaud learned the basics of academic drawing, which led him to loosen his taut line and refine the crude quality of his comics style.

"It's a good trick book," Thiebaud said of Nicolaïdes's method, establishing a correspondence, which would remain central to his work, between the academic and commercial traditions in the study of expedient devices.[15] Indeed, art historian Albert Boime has shown the connection between the art of the comic strip and nineteenth-century neoclassicism, the touchstone of academic artistic instruction. "The drawing of neo-classicists and comic strippers reveals the same purity of outline and controlled precision, and not uncommonly, the former make use of as many stylistic clichés as the latter."[16] It was by merging elements from both fields that Thiebaud developed his own style. Although the first pie paintings were drawn with the ease of an expert draftsman, they derive their repetition, bold schematization, and use of shorthand from typical cartoon stratagems.

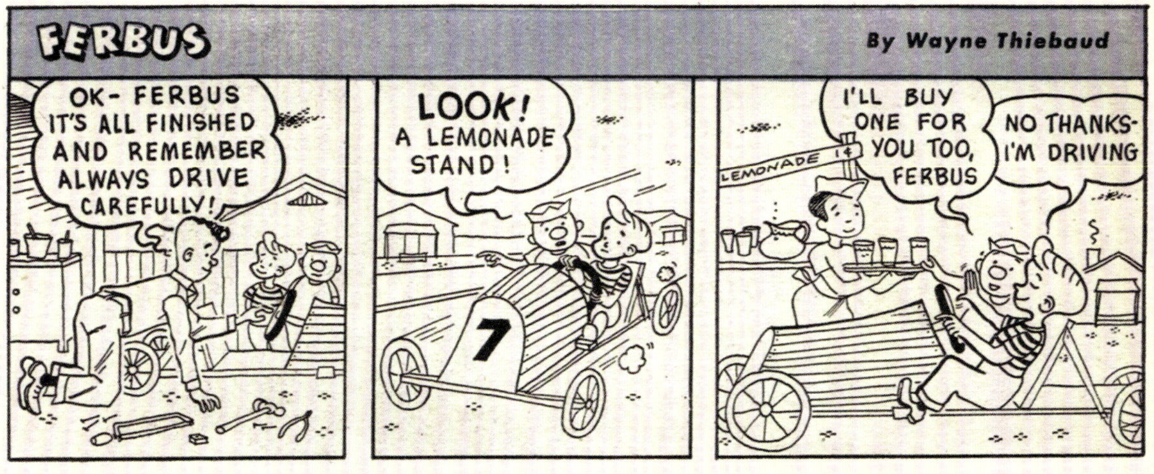

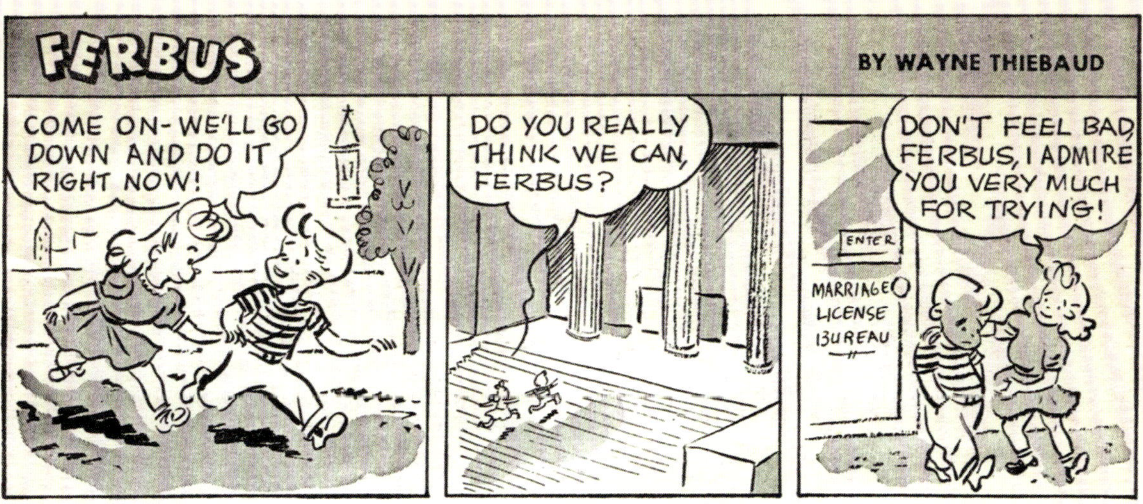

Through his own practice of the genre, Thiebaud was drawn to the work of famous cartoonists, among whom George Herriman deserves special mention. Like Picasso, Willem de Kooning, and Philip Guston before him, Thiebaud found inspiration in the combination of fantasy, poetry, and irony that gives *Krazy Kat*'s scratchy drawings their exceptional appeal. "A lot of the landscapes come out of *Krazy Kat* . . . clouds, mesa, and things," Thiebaud said. Herriman "has these clouds that look sort of like potato chips, or God knows what."[17] Thiebaud, who was born in Arizona, was particularly taken with the backgrounds of *Krazy Kat*, with their sweeping perspectives, at once spare and expressionistic, inspired by the Arizona desert. Thiebaud's massive hill in *Ridge with Clouds* is reminiscent of the tall butte that appears frequently in *Krazy Kat*'s panels

FIGS. 4–5.
Wayne Thiebaud, *Ferbus* comic strips published in *Rexall Magazine*, August 1947 and November 1948.

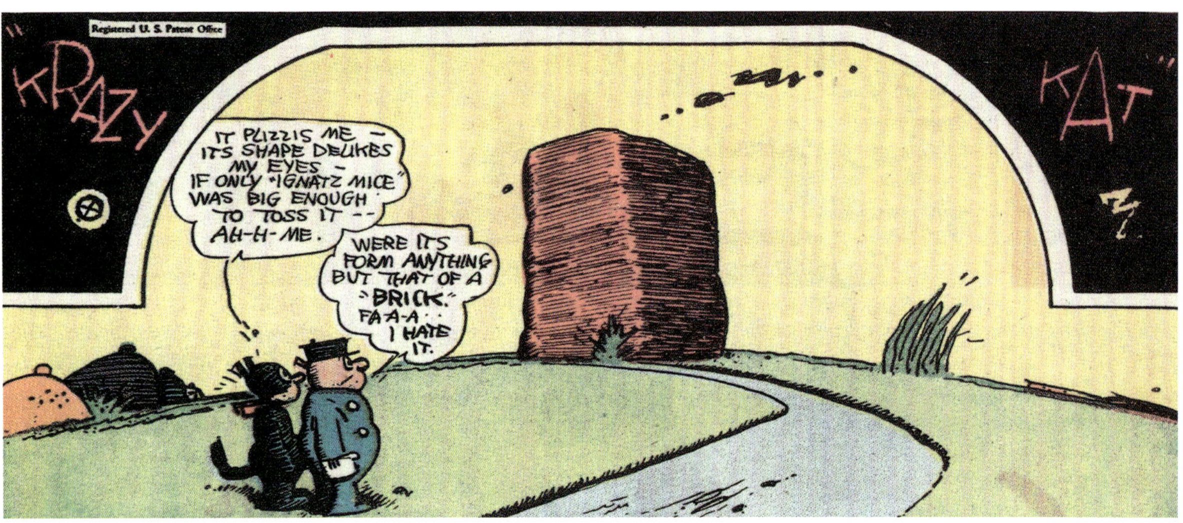

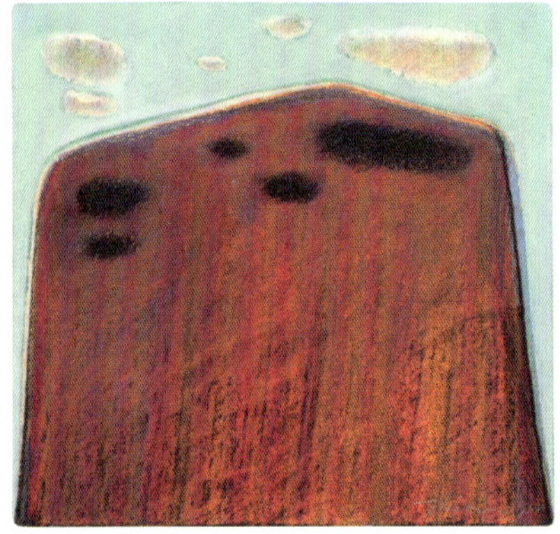

FIG. 6.
George Herriman, *Krazy Kat*,
1 June 1940.

Wayne Thiebaud, *Ridge with Clouds*,
1967–68 (No. 30).

(No. 30 and Fig. 6). Other landscapes from the 1960s, composed, for instance, of a single tree and a small house reflected in a pond or a basic row of palm trees, have the simplicity and immediacy of cartoon drawings (Nos. 26–29). To Thiebaud, the cartoon reference offered a way to deflate the traditional sentimentality of landscape: "Cartoons allow the silly to sit with the sublime."[18]

II. TRYING TO BECOME A PAINTER

Thiebaud discovered modern painting through his work in advertising. "The more I got interested in layout and design, the more I was led to those examples in fine art from which they derived. The most interesting designs were influenced by Mondrian or Degas or Matisse. That revelation really transfixed me. I started drawing a lot and read continually about it and slowly decided . . . that I was going to try to become a painter."[19] Another factor in this decision was his meeting with Robert Mallary, a sculptor who worked as a typographer for Rexall Drug Company in the late 1940s. An intellectual who embraced liberal causes, Mallary had been involved in the Communist party and studied with the politically committed muralists José Clemente Orozco and David Alfaro Siqueiros in Mexico City in the 1930s. He introduced Thiebaud to Karl Marx, the philosophy of Jean-Paul Sartre, and the writings of art historian Erwin Panofsky, among others—opening up a whole new dimension to what being an artist meant. Following Mallary's advice, Thiebaud went back to college, where his studies focused on art history and art education and theory. During the 1950s, he earned his living through a variety of occupations: serving as designer for art fairs and theatrical events, creating public art, teaching television production and film, and establishing a film company that produced educational shorts on art.[20]

Meanwhile he was determined to become an artist and striving to find his own style. Abstraction was the dominant mode of the period, with Abstract Expressionism the most influential avant-garde movement. Although Thiebaud was more interested in representational art, he nevertheless followed the trend and developed what he called abstract expressionist mannerisms, behind which he would hide his subjects—"trying to make a sort of artful, Jackson Pollock-surface."[21] Attracted to thick paint and unctuous strokes, he admired gestural painters such as de Kooning and Franz Kline, both of whom he met and befriended during a year he spent in New York, in 1956–57. A portrait drawing of Kline that Thiebaud made at the time presents the graphic equivalent of the lively brushwork he was drawn to in painting (No. 5). The short pencil strokes, broken outlines, and brisk hatching convey the resemblance and catch the expression of the eyes and mouth without relying on naturalistic depiction. Thiebaud shared with Kline an interest in sports and caricature. Like Thiebaud, Kline had considered a career as a cartoonist and was primarily a draftsman until he began enlarging details from his figurative sketches to create the large paintings for which he became famous, around 1950.

In New York, Thiebaud created a group of ink drawings of market scenes and store windows in which he flirted with abstraction. *New York City Winter* (No. 6) combines a geometric structure, marked by the squaring of the ground and the rectangular panels of the shop front, with a fluid handling of the brush. Although the items in the window are hard to identify—a related painting entitled *Banana Window* gives a clue[22]—Thiebaud's fondness for the accumulation and repetition of objects is already evident in this crowded display. The expressivity of the drawing derives primarily from the stark black-and-white contrast, softened by touches of gray wash that provide a few intermediary values. While the sense of structure brings up echoes of geometric abstract art, the furtive silhouette of a dog running toward the door is reminiscent of cartoon imagery.

Despite Thiebaud's admiration for the broad, dramatic gesture of de Kooning and Kline, his short strokes and deliberate handling imbue his drawings with a lyricism and delicacy that are closer to the work of another artist he met in New York, Philip Guston. At the time, Guston was going through an abstract phase, but, like Thiebaud, he was fundamentally more interested in representation and would soon reintroduce the figure in his pictures. He too was fascinated with cartoons and comics, which would become a major source of inspiration in his later work. In the early 1950s, Guston was making

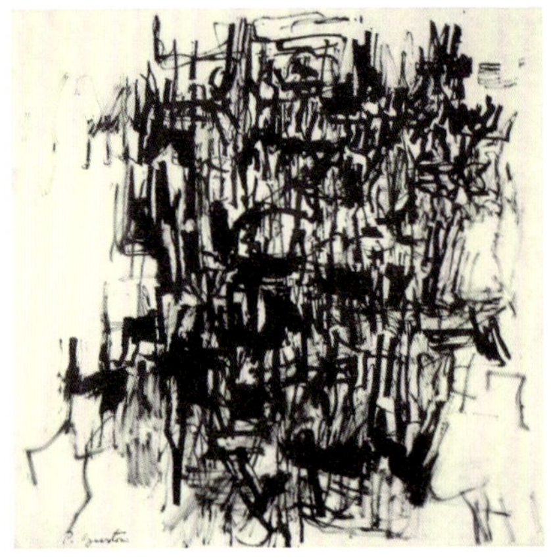

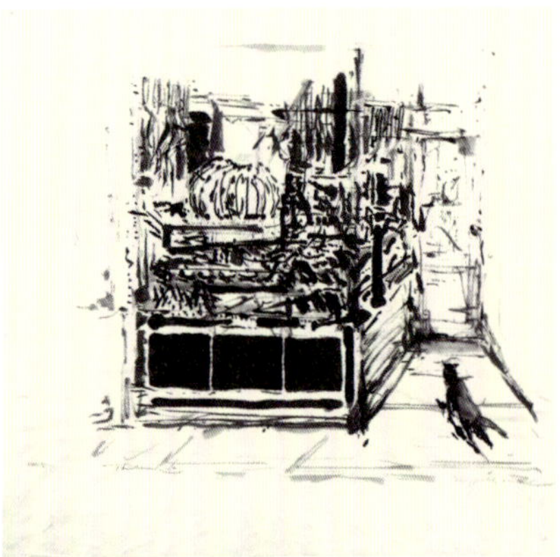

black-and-white ink drawings characterized by clusters of marks that derived their sense of rhythm from the varying length and thickness of the strokes (Fig. 7). Thiebaud emulated Guston's restraint and control as well as the softness and sensitivity of his touch.

Thiebaud's experiments during the 1950s were not only stylistic but also iconographic. Since abstraction did not appeal to him, he had to find the right subject. Shop windows were a recurrent theme throughout the decade, no doubt derived from his early engagement with the world of advertising. An unexpected subject popped up in a group of works of 1957: the electric chair (Fig. 8; this was five years before Warhol took up the subject as part of his Death and Disaster series). Thiebaud's rendition combines realism in the details of the electric paraphernalia with symbolism in the striking viewpoint. Seen up close and from below, the chair resembles a throne. The bright white and blood red of the background contribute to the sense of drama. Although the drawing is unremarkable in its fashionable, brushy style, its unusual subject marks the emergence of two notions that would have bearing on the direction his art was to take in the 1960s. One is the reference to American culture: the electric chair was an American invention, used as a mode of execution almost exclusively in the United States. The other is the left-leaning implication. During the 1950s the electric chair was associated with a major leftist cause, the fight against the controversial 1953 execution of Julius and Ethel Rosenberg following their conviction of espionage. Thiebaud's liberal inclinations date back to his youth, when, as a skilled debater, he had considered becoming a labor lawyer.[23] The electric chair remains an oddity in his work, but it does point to some of the preoccupations that would inform his later development.

III. NOW I HAVE FLIPPED OUT!

When asked about the genesis of his first pie paintings, Thiebaud invariably replies in formal terms, recalling his desire to move away from his "abstract expressionist mannerisms" in favor of greater formal clarity. "I began to feel that I wanted to get rid of the expressionist brushstroke, which jazzes up the surface, making everything active and busy. I decided to go back to very basic, formalist concerns. I took three basic shapes to work with: a rectangle, an ellipse or a circle and a triangle. Well, that's a piece of pie."[24] The disingenuous account seeks to downplay the significance of the subject matter, as if a row of meringue pies on a deli counter was the most obvious motif for the pursuit of geometric investigations. At the same time, however, Thiebaud relishes the memory of his own reaction to these new works. "When I painted the first row of pies, I can remember sitting and laughing . . . 'Now I have flipped out!'"[25]

The food displays derived from the shop windows of the previous decade. By zooming in on the foodstuff, Thiebaud was calling attention to one of the most vivid images of postwar America. As Sidra Stich noted, "With the postwar proliferation of brand-name promotions, convenience foods, fast-food chains, national distribution networks, and giant supermarkets, food became a paramount part of America's image."[26] Rows of food items were symbols of an emerging society of abundance after the privations of the Depression. But deli and cafeteria counters also carried social implications, as they were considered working-class venues. At the same time as he made his first pie pictures, Thiebaud was exploring subjects such as *Trucker's Supper* (Fig. 9). The proletarian references of Thiebaud's paintings were not lost on the critics who reviewed them when they were first exhibited in 1962. Max Kozloff described them as "the truck-driver's dream." Thomas B. Hess was the most explicit: "This is major social criticism made visual."[27] His assumption, however, that Thiebaud was making fun of the American food habit—the way Daumier's caricatures made fun of lawyers—was at odds with the artist's attachment to everything American. "These foods," Thiebaud declared, "are only revolting to a gourmet, others of us lap them up with considerable enjoyment. . . . I believe anyone who doesn't like hamburger is a food snob."[28] To be sure, the period saw an extension of the popularity of the diner beyond the workers' lunch spot into a middle-class family restaurant. Historian Andrew Hurley noted the reversal of the usual cultural flow that such a development signaled: "What seems to be exceptional about the post–World War II years is the extent to which cultural forms with working-class origins percolated up into the middle majority mainstream."[29] Thiebaud's paintings illustrate the "visual garishness" that Hurley saw as a consequence of this social phenomenon. "Perhaps we can detect evidence of the anxieties associated with border crossings in the visual garishness of much mainstream postwar consumer culture. The flashy and often gaudy displays of abundance—the Las Vegas architecture of the commercial strip, . . . the mounds of whipped cream on pies in diner pastry display cases—may have served the psychological needs of working-class families anxious to assert social mobility through consumption."[30]

Thiebaud's engagement with Marxist philosophy and left-leaning causes can be detected behind his assembly-line arrangements of mass-produced pies and hamburgers. Although he didn't spell it out, the artist was acknowledging the social meaning of his subjects. "It seemed to me that there are certain objects that contain telltale evidence of what we're about as a people or as a society."[31] The postwar years corresponded to a period of philosophical inquiry into everyday life, stimulated by Marxist critique. Philosophers trained in this school of thought—most notable among them Henri Lefebvre—turned their attention to the facts of daily existence as subjects of investigation, promoting

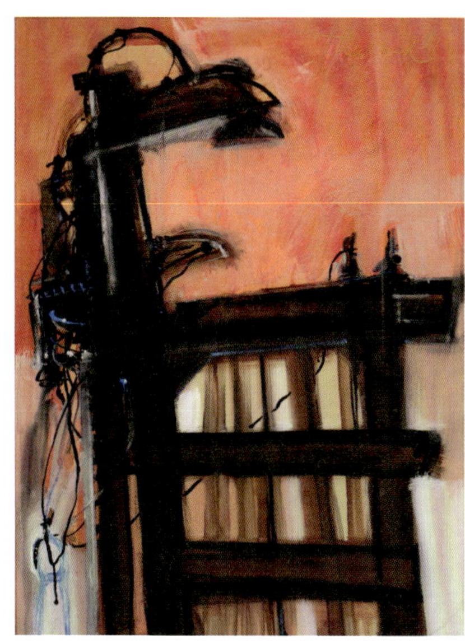

FIG. 8.
Wayne Thiebaud, *Composition*, 1957, watercolor on paper. Smithsonian American Art Museum, Washington, DC, Bequest of Edith S. and Arthur J. Levin; 2005.5.70.

a revaluation of the quotidian as opposed to privileging the exceptional and extraordinary. The imagery Thiebaud began exploring in 1959–60 fits within this broader movement. "Concerted thinking about the everyday arguably gets fully under way at the turn of the 1960s," wrote literary critic Michael Sheringham, who connected the phenomenon to "the emergence of the figure of the consumer in the context of rapid modernization."[32] Lefebvre, like Roland Barthes after him, focused on banal occurrences of daily life in an attempt to rescue the everyday from its negative associations and uncover a field of possibilities behind the notion of sameness and repetition. Barthes's *Mythologies*, published in the mid-1950s, centered on subjects such as plastic, Citroën, detergents, and steak-frites. One can trace parallels between his emphasis on the symbolic significance of everyday items and Thiebaud's attraction to the rituals that govern displays of ordinary food. "I am interested in foods generally which have been fooled with ritualistically," he said, "displays contrived and arranged in certain ways to tempt us or to seduce us or to religiously transcend us. There's something I find fascinating about making a circle of butter, hollowing a cantaloupe. . . ."[33] Thiebaud's depictions of food imply a social space—cafeteria, diner, coffee shop—and its associated rituals.

FIG. 9.
Wayne Thiebaud, *Trucker's Supper*,
1961, oil on canvas. Private collection.

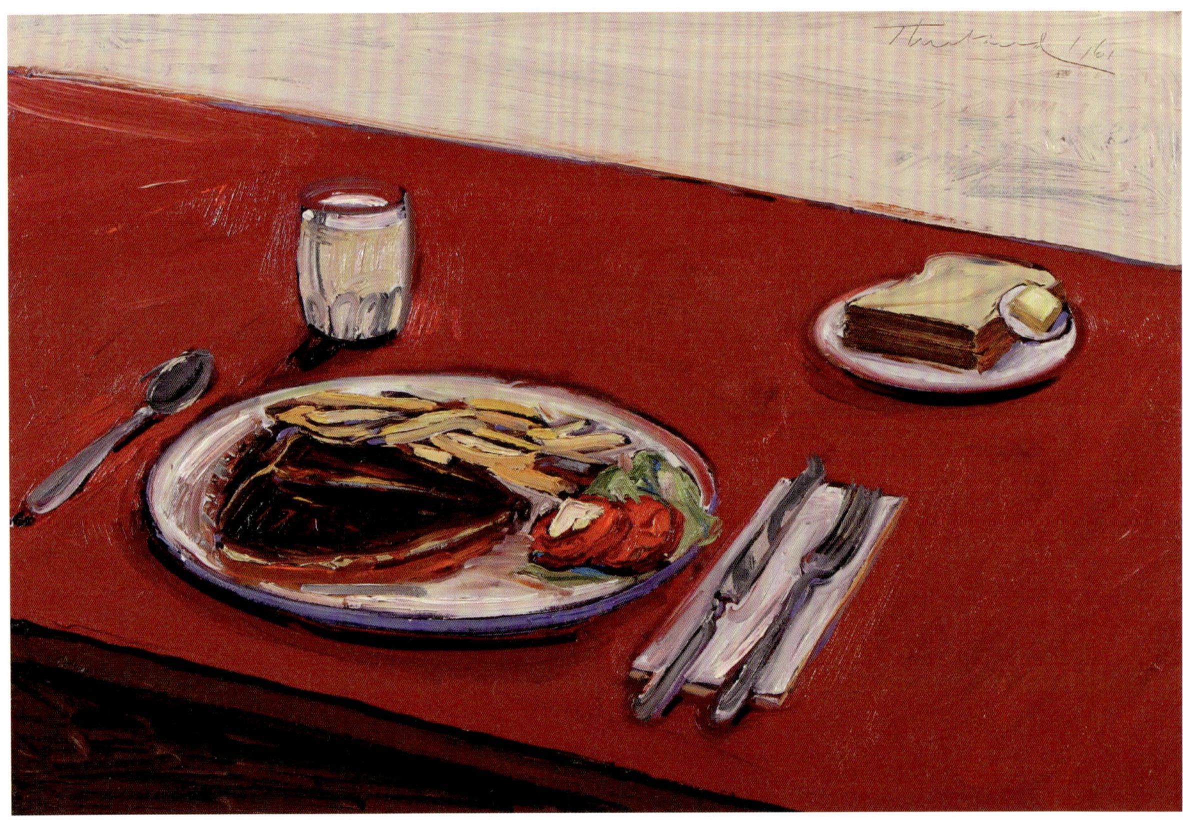

In *Trucker's Supper,* for instance, the ritual is highlighted in the carefully folded napkin under the silverware or in the pat of butter resting on its circular wrapping. Thiebaud is captivated by ornamental details, such as the cherry on a slice of cake or two olives on top of sandwiches (No. 24). He recorded the arrangement of fish into decorative circles at fish markets, presumably intended to make the sight of dead animals more palatable (No. 42 and Fig. 10). "Fish, laid out on a plain white surface, are very moving, a kind of tragedy, actually," Thiebaud remarked.[34] Despite the mood of celebration that cakes and ice cream cones evoke, and the comfort that the artist appears to find in the repetition and consistency of lunch counters across America—"Same buffet spread in almost everywhere"[35]—there remains an ambiguity about what these objects actually tell us about who we are. Thomas Albright reported how, as he was talking with Thiebaud, the latter would "suddenly pause over the reproduction of one of his paintings representing a black lollipop, and muse: 'I wonder if the flavor is death.'"[36]

IV. WHAT WOULD HAPPEN IF . . . : THE CHALLENGE OF THE MEDIUM

Thiebaud's first drawings of pies and cakes were mostly in brush and ink, a medium that allows for deep contrasts of light and dark. The artist acknowledged that at the time he was more interested in value contrasts than color. "The concept of light as a delineating force has always fascinated me—what light sources are about, where they come from, whether they're multiple or variable. The color thing . . . came much later. As I look at the paintings from 1960 up to about 1963, the color is coincidental to the value structure of the picture."[37] In the ink drawings, Thiebaud used a single source of light from the side to create strong cast shadows, which he painted solid black. He left the white of the paper untouched in the brightest areas for maximum contrast (Nos. 7, 10–11). In some of them, a black background heightens the dramatic effect. The artificiality of the concept derives from the technique of low-key lighting used in film and photography to create extreme silhouette, sharply defined shadows, and powerful light-and-shade contrasts. Thiebaud was familiar with cinematographic lighting techniques from his tenure at Universal Studios in the 1940s. "I used to go and watch them light a set. . . . Those were the days of black and white, and they made such rich, beautiful black and white 'paintings' in a sense, on film."[38] Film noir especially exploited bold lighting effects to intensify drama and create unsettling atmosphere. Thiebaud's application of the film noir aesthetic, as it were, to the cafeteria counter, gives his hamburgers and pies a theatrical presence. The progressive refinement of his technique is evident in the difference between *Delicatessen*

Counter of 1961, with its broad scale of grays, and *Food Counter* of 1964, to which the extensive use of deep black in a more stylized composition imparts a mood of mystery (Nos. 8 and 12).

In 1964, Thiebaud developed an interest in color, as is evident from a spectacular group of pastels and watercolors from that year (Nos. 13–14, 22–24). Watercolor presents a particular challenge to an artist who loves his paint "floppy and syrupy."[39] The thinness and fluidity of the medium do not allow for the kind of sculpting of the pigments that is possible with oil paint. Thiebaud had to rely on color itself to evoke the materiality and texture of the objects. As in his black-and-white drawings, he focused his attention on the suggestion of light, exploring the idea that an image can generate its own light through color manipulation in addition to registering the effect of a lighting source outside the frame. He found a model for the combination of the two in Bonnard's paintings. "He'll use a kind of traditional lighting technique, but he'll raise the intensity to such a degree that the color structure is another whole way of creating additional means of lighting the picture without rendering the form."[40] In Thiebaud's *Candy Sticks* (No. 14), for instance, the light source coming from the right produces a bluish shadow to the left of each stick. In addition, the artist played with the juxtaposition of multiple hues to suggest the glistening surface of the candies. Paying special attention to the edges of forms, he avoided sharp lines, replicating instead the phenomenon of halation—derived from photography—by which the edges of a bright area appear slightly blurry to the staring eye. Thiebaud's multicolored edges spread the light that seems to be coming from the candy itself. This buildup of the edge and its resulting fuzziness is an effect he often observed in Vermeer's paintings: "It seems so straightforward," he said while examining one of them at the Metropolitan Museum, "but when you look close, you realize you can't find the edges of anything."[41]

Pastel behaves differently and bears more resemblance to oil painting—perhaps a reason Thiebaud has employed it more often than watercolor. The binder that holds the powdery substance together gives the medium more body. Because pastels cannot be mixed—lest they lose their brilliance—color variations are obtained through a process of juxtaposition and layering that gives more opacity and weight to the resulting image, as opposed to the transparency and lightness of watercolor. Pastel has traditionally been favored for portraits because of its velvetlike quality, which imitates the soft texture of skin. Thiebaud exploited this property to suggest the unctuousness of ice cream and syrup (Nos. 22–23). In addition, the bright colors of pastel provided a match for the food dyes that proliferated in the American food industry of the time. It is noteworthy that the mid-1960s was precisely the

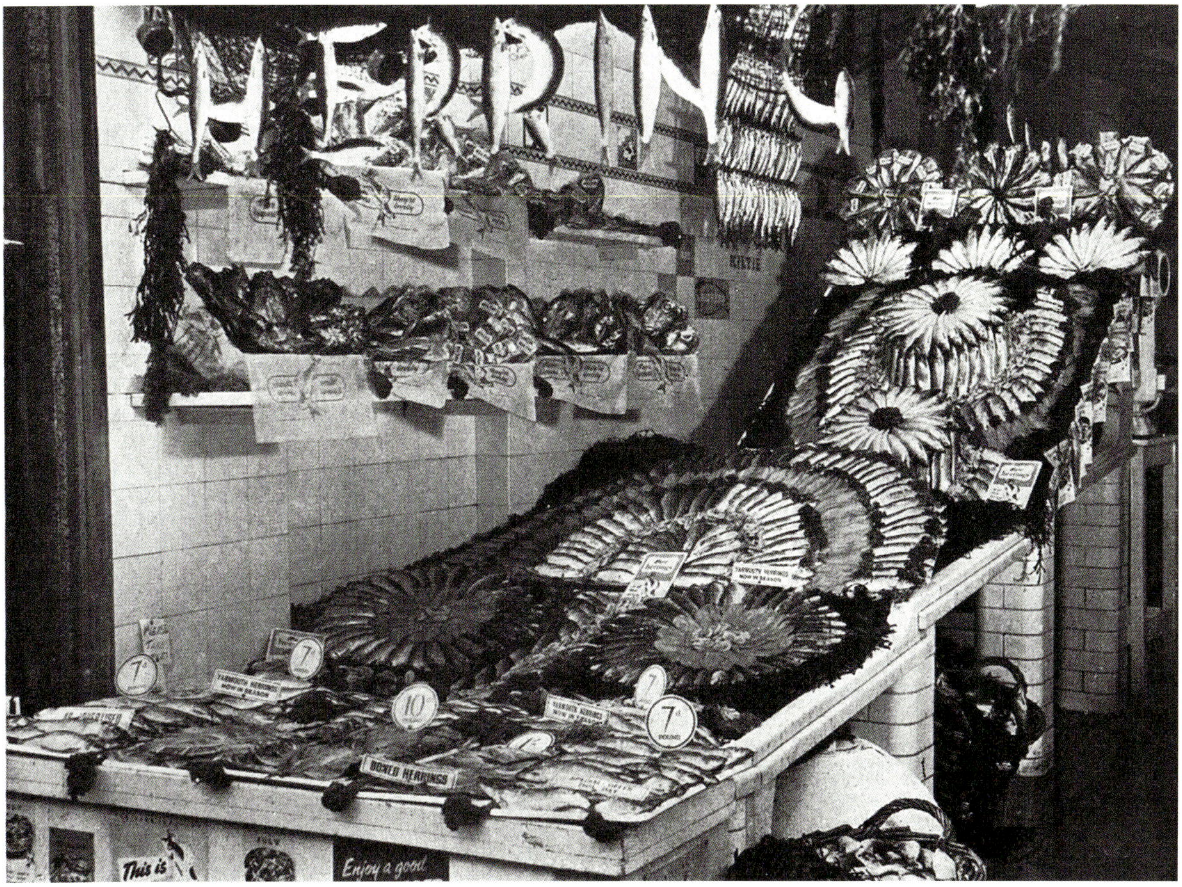

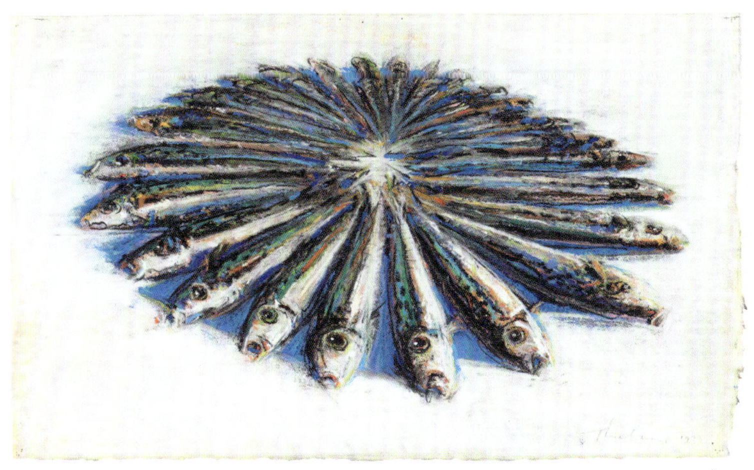

FIG. 10.
Herring display, Mac Fisheries Ltd,
ca. 1954.

Wayne Thiebaud, *Circle of Fish*, 1973
(No. 42).

period during which the growing popularity of color television influenced the development of food coloring to fulfill the demand for visually appealing food in advertising.[42] The vivid colors of Thiebaud's pastels and his sensuous handling of the pigments enabled him to mimic the very consistency of the luscious desserts he was depicting. Pastel allowed Thiebaud to indulge in what he calls his "fixation . . . over object transference, that is, working the paint to look like the substance of the image."[43] He took particular pleasure in the tactile aspect of the process: "You can pretend that you are actually icing the cake."[44]

This tactile quality nourishes Thiebaud's fascination with the properties and reactions of each medium, its unique characteristics, and how they can be in tune with the subject at hand. The relationship between image and medium is one of his persistent subjects of inquiry. "What sort of medium fits your image." "Is there a more legitimate medium for that? . . . The wonder for me is just the challenges."[45] His treatment of a group of jelly apples in different mediums is a case in point. The subject lent itself to such lavish attention. As Roland Barthes noted in an essay on food photography in *Elle* magazine, the prevalence of "smooth coating" in such images, of food buried under "sauces, creams, icing and jellies, . . . comes from the very finality of the coating, which belongs to a visual category, and cooking according to *Elle* is meant for the eye alone."[46] For Thiebaud too, food is for the eye alone. In the painted version of the apples (Fig. 11), he reveled in duplicating the sticky substance of the sugar coating with a thick layer of pigment. In the watercolor (No. 18), he juxtaposed a wide range of hues, from pink to purple, to suggest the luminous surface of the jellied fruit. The black ink version (No. 19) relied on the vivid dark and light contrast to emphasize shininess. The most challenging was the one in pencil (No. 17). Here, Thiebaud shifted the emphasis from the effect of light to the very consistency of the candied apples, suggesting the crispy aspect of hardened sugar—rather than its syrupy quality—by drawing the contours with exacting precision and accentuating the flatness of the top.

Thiebaud has compared this process of transposition to musical arrangements for different instruments, which preserve the form and melody of a piece while changing its timbre and texture.[47] Working in a multiplicity of mediums fuels a cross-pollination among them as methods and processes specific to one technique can be transposed to another. For an artist driven by problems to solve and inquiries to pursue, the phenomenon is particularly productive— which explains the frequency with which Thiebaud revisits some of his favorite subjects, using different techniques and supports.

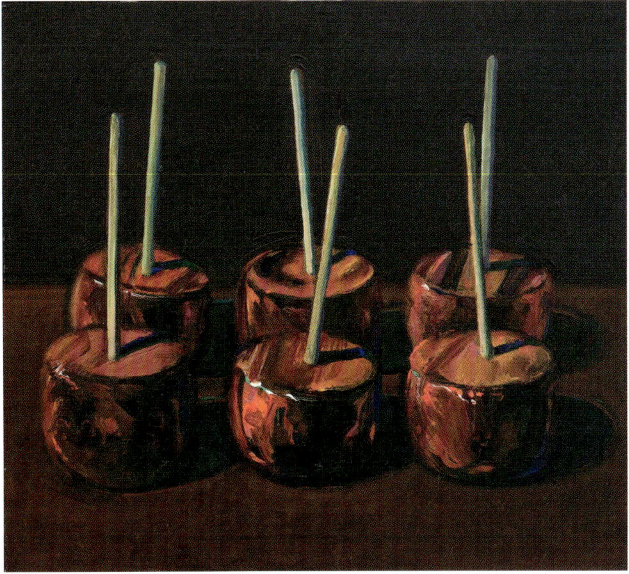

V. COPY PICTURES. ENJOY THE HELL OUT OF IT.

During the 1970s, a shift occurred in Thiebaud's art, stimulated by an increasing engagement with tradition. A group of charcoal drawings from 1971 signals the change (Nos. 35–37). They depict simple objects that belong to a different register from the food still lifes of the 1960s. Their style and composition are also radically different. Made from observation, they carefully reproduce each object according to the conventions of academic drawing, with perspective, modeling, and shading. Disregarding, however, the customary practice of grouping the various components of a still life at the center of the composition, Thiebaud isolated them from each other so they appear randomly strewn on the surface of the sheet or thrown along its edges. The result fuses a traditional approach in the detailed reproduction of each object with a modern sensibility in their unconventional arrangement around an empty center. A tension obtains between the suggestion of volume, on the one hand, and the emphasis on the flat surface of the sheet created by the expanse of white, on the other. This unusual composition derives partly from advertising design but also from Thiebaud's admiration for Degas, a master at creating pictures dominated by an empty floor that takes up most of the space while the various elements (people and objects) are pushed up to and often cut off by the edges.[48]

Thiebaud's charcoal drawings were made in conjunction with his teaching and correspond to assignments he gave his students, stipulating, for instance, the number of objects and their relation to the edges of the sheet.

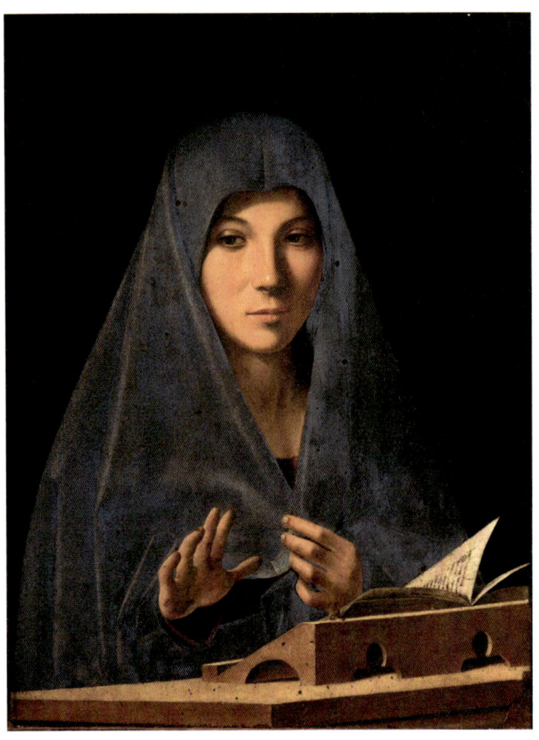
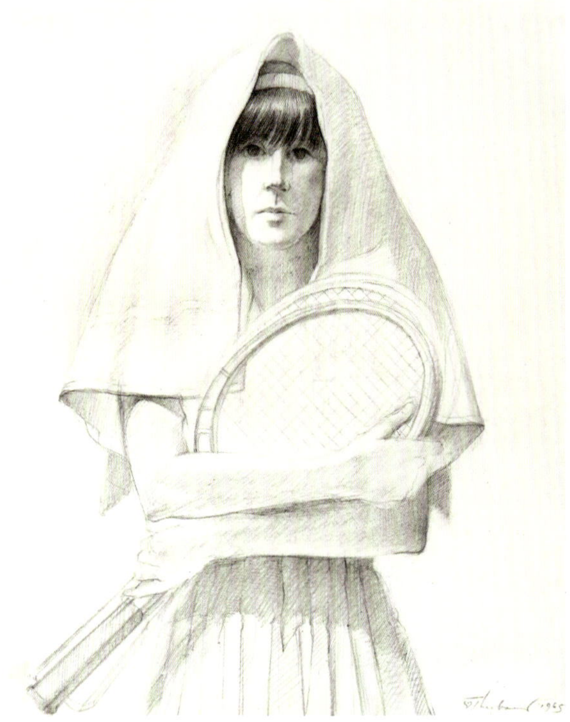

FIG. 12.
Antonello da Messina, *Virgin Annunciate*, ca. 1476, oil on wood. Palazzo Abatellis, Palermo.

Wayne Thiebaud, *Tennis Girl*, 1967 (No. 33).

It was a common practice for him to make a drawing of his own, following the guidelines, as a way of demonstration. Teaching—an essential activity for Thiebaud throughout his career—was for him "a way of experimenting." It "substitutes for a laboratory," he noted.[49] He especially enjoyed teaching drawing classes, in which he encouraged his students to do a lot of drawing from observation. "It is an academic approach," he explained, "I expect lots of drawing from my students . . . I ask for a minimum of expression and creativity. . . . In fact, I tell my students I don't want them to have ideas."[50]

Thiebaud's renewed engagement with tradition fueled his interest in figure drawing, the cornerstone of academic training. He had drawn the human figure during the 1960s, producing delicate, linear pencil renderings of single figures isolated on an empty background (Nos. 31–33). In most of them, the sitter appears aloof or withdrawn, closely guarded, her arms crossed in front of her or, as in *Girl in Striped Sweater*, holding her folded legs close to her chest (No. 31). In *Tennis Girl*, the woman with a towel over her head recalls Renaissance depictions of the Virgin Mary wearing a veil, such as the fifteenth-century *Virgin Annunciate* by Antonello da Messina (No. 33 and Fig. 12). In Thiebaud's modern, profane version, she holds tennis rackets firmly against her. Although he claimed that he was not interested in psychological

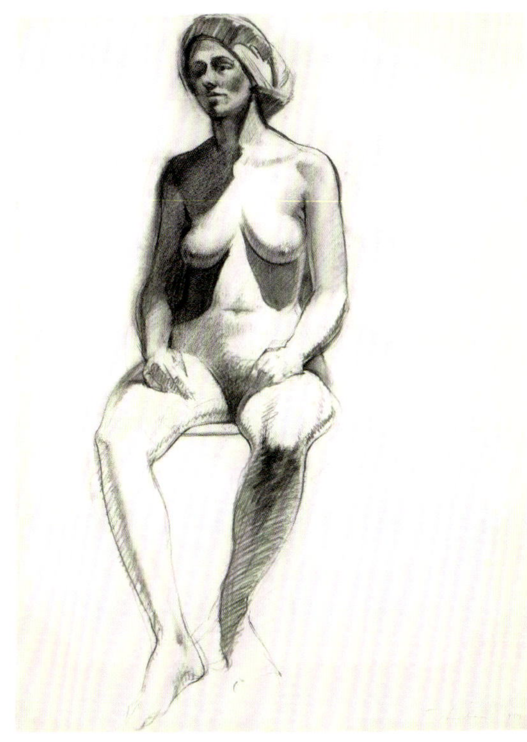

investigation—basically treating a portrait as a still life—the way the woman is looking straight at the viewer gives her an air of defiance, also perceptible in the bold stance of the sitter in *Mallary Ann*, a portrait of the artist's daughter (No. 32).

Thiebaud's figure drawing style changed significantly in the 1970s. Eager to master what he felt was "the most important study the painter can pursue," he devoted himself to drawing from the model.[51] Abandoning the sharp, continuous line of the 1960s drawings, he used charcoal to create a softer line and developed a more academic manner with suggestion of chiaroscuro through extensive hatching and cross-hatching (Fig. 13). Some of the drawings were studies for paintings but most of them were done essentially as a form of practice, following the precept that, like in tennis or golf, a stroke is learned thoroughly through repetition so it eventually comes naturally.[52] Thiebaud held the conviction that the human figure was "a touchstone of so many things." It teaches you "about pressures and balance and rhythmic potential"—elements that can be applied to any subject, including abstract painting.[53] What attracted him also to academic figure drawing was the connection it establishes with earlier artists, who went through the same learning process. "If you keep making some marks, you sort of feel Degas has

FIG. 13.
Wayne Thiebaud, *Seated Woman*, 1977, charcoal on paper. Smithsonian American Art Museum, Washington, DC, Bequest of Edith S. and Arthur J. Levin; 2005.5.71.

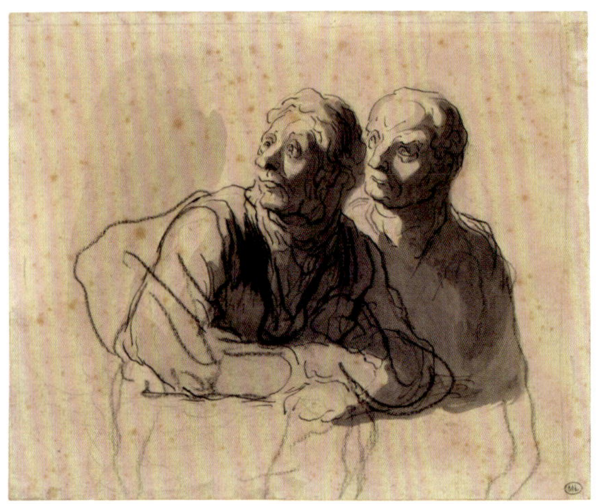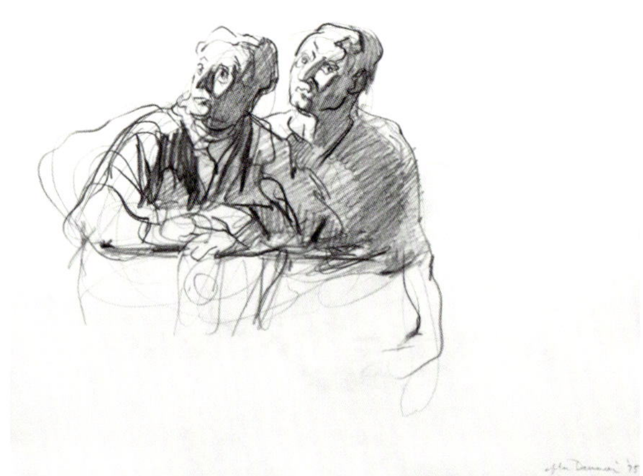

made those marks. And you're making the same kind of marks, however inelegantly. But it's the same sort of experience, and that's, for me, very heartwarming."[54] Thiebaud's deep attachment to the art of the past, especially to the works of nineteenth-century French artists, such as Manet, Degas, or Seurat, who were at once profoundly anchored in tradition and indisputable harbingers of modernity, can be seen in some of his more elaborate figure compositions. The large pastel *Untitled (Reclining Nude)* (No. 59), for instance, with the barely visible silhouette of a male figure in the background, revives some of the sexual tensions found in the paintings of Degas or Gauguin. The rich, multilayered application of pastel and vigorous hatching recall Degas's late pastels of nudes, while the brilliant strokes of pure color and palette of complementary hues—notably the bursts of yellow highlights against the purple shadows—bring to mind Bonnard's depictions of the same subject. Do the French references signal a drastic turn in Thiebaud's art away from American pies and gumball machines? In fact, the group of pastels to which *Untitled (Reclining Nude)* belongs remains unusual in his production and should rather be considered in the context of his practice of another core exercise of academic training: the copy after the old master.

A firm believer that "art comes from art and from nothing else," Thiebaud always placed great emphasis on the study and analysis of the art of the past as an essential pedagogical tool, "an inspirational wellspring and a sort of bureau of standards."[55] He exhorts his students: "Copy pictures. Enjoy the hell out of it."[56] Copies after the old masters had been a staple of artistic instruction for centuries but had lost their currency and significance

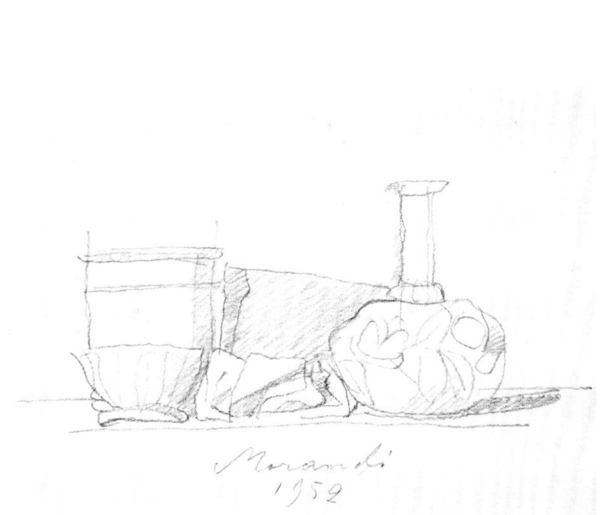 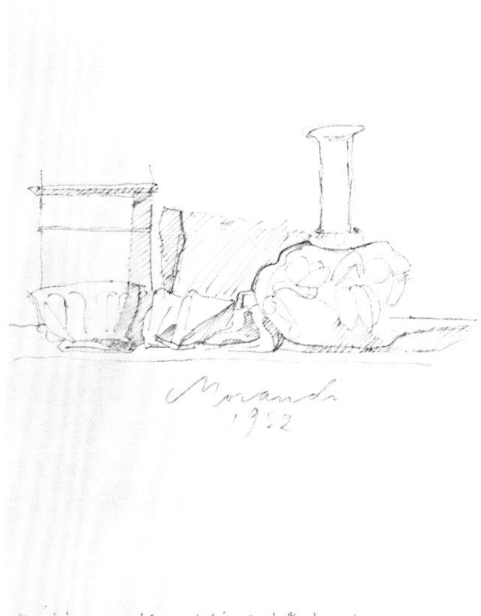

FIG. 15.
Giorgio Morandi, *Still Life*, 1952,
graphite on paper. Museo Morandi,
Bologna.

Wayne Thiebaud, *Untitled
(After Morandi)*, 1979 (No. 43).

during the second half of the nineteenth century with the development of the concept of originality and changes in studio practices.[57] It is therefore noteworthy to find copies after earlier masters among Thiebaud's drawings, and all the more so that they are from the 1970s, when his reputation was already firmly established. They are a testament to his avid quest to keep learning from the artists he held in highest regard. There are no surprises among the names of those he copied. A pencil study after Honoré Daumier recalls Thiebaud's fascination with caricature (No. 44 and Fig. 14). Here, he replicated with uncanny facility the fluid movement of Daumier's drawing style, in which figures emerge from a tangle of swirling lines. Few of Thiebaud's own drawings rely to such an extent on the expressivity of the line. More in keeping with his interest is the marked chiaroscuro of the Daumier, in which the two men are mostly in shadow, while only their face and right shoulder are directly lit.

A copy after a still-life drawing by Giorgio Morandi offers another telling example (No. 43 and Fig. 15). Thiebaud has often expressed his profound admiration for the Italian painter. "We love these little works representing such pure research," he wrote in a moving homage, highlighting the "exquisite tensions" and "tremendous vice-like pressures" of Morandi's compositions.[58] Thiebaud was especially drawn to the "layering of faltering probes," which allow one to see in Morandi's works "the actual birth process of a painting." No wonder his copy—one of several he made after Morandi—reproduces every detail of the drawing with quasi-religious faithfulness, including even the large signature and date Morandi had prominently inscribed at bottom center. Thiebaud followed scrupulously the direction of the lines, applying pressure where Morandi did and imitating the loose pattern of the decorated scent bottle. Such meticulous attention does not only demonstrate a desire to learn from the older artist, it also reflects the belief in "a form of sympathetic magic" to which the academic practice of copying has been linked.[59] Indeed, Thiebaud admitted to an interviewer: "I have taken Morandi paintings and worked with them directly next to my own paintings to try to make mine look more like his."[60]

The attention—empathy even—with which Thiebaud studies the works of earlier masters to unravel their methods and techniques comes through in his numerous comments about other artists' works. In a short preface to the catalogue of an exhibition of drawings by Matisse, Thiebaud offered an illuminating description of Matisse's line, following its movement—animating it, as it were—as if he were re-creating it:

> *The pen makes a pure, clear cutting edge, and the drawing begins. This clean, single silhouette-type line swells and becomes a contour. Suddenly it stops, hops about, crosses back over itself and begins to scribble like a child. Sputtering on awkwardly, the mark slows to a crab-like crawl, ambling along, rocking rhythmically and nervously probing around and over several similar forms. Just when the repetition appears compulsive, the line skips free, picks up great speed and jumps to a full gallop. It then dances out into a large, uninterrupted, open plane expanding the space and scale of the drawing. Finally a tired line halts, slowly turns in on itself and rests. The maker has finished a little world and we can see both the making and what has been made.[61]*

VI. FUSSING AROUND WITH FORM

In the mid-1970s, Thiebaud tackled a new subject in a series of works inspired by the San Francisco cityscape. Drawing played a major role in the development of the theme after the artist realized that painting from nature—setting his easel in the street—did not generate the "dramatic feeling" of the city that he was hoping to replicate.[62] "No one view seemed to get this sense of edges appearing, things swooping around their own edges, that I loved."[63] Prompted by a comment from critic Brian O'Doherty, who pointed out to him that Edward Hopper composed his city paintings by rearranging "like a stage set" the various sketches he made from life, Thiebaud decided to try the same approach. "I began to make a lot of drawings with graphite or charcoal on paper, which I could move around a lot, kind of playing around with them."[64] Starting with quick sketches made from observation or memory, Thiebaud then created larger, more finished drawings, in which he rearranged elements from the sketches into elaborate compositions, some of which eventually served as the basis for paintings. Despite the reference to real places, the final image was worked out like an abstract composition, with Thiebaud moving and adjusting lines and surfaces to achieve the effect he was looking for. "I worked with graphite and an eraser on large sheets of hard-finished Bristol board," he described, "erasing, smudging, and fussing around with form. I thought the drawings were quite abstract, although they showed buildings, cars, and streets. . . . All of them were based on actual scenes, but they became much more interpretive." In the end, "that dialogue between what was actually there and what was made up became the basis of the entire series."[65]

What attracted Thiebaud was not the picturesque architecture of San Francisco but the unusual character of its plunging streets and the feeling of imbalance generated by them. The main subject of his pictures is the strange pattern formed by the streets going up and down. Houses and buildings play a secondary role, filling the space between the large planes of asphalt that project vertically or diagonally. In most drawings, the composition is articulated around an intersection, as can be observed in the sketches for *Cityscape* (No. 45). Thiebaud jotted down the initial idea in a very rough sketch—a rectangle with two sets of lines running through its lower corners. This is the starting point of the picture: the heart of the intersection, seen from above. In a second sketch on the same sheet, the rectangle has become a parallelogram, suggesting a lower viewpoint. The pattern formed by the articulation of the streets around the intersection is now clearly drawn, with each street oriented at a different angle. Thiebaud darkened the roads by filling them in pencil while the buildings are only faintly sketched in. For the finished drawing (No. 46), he adopted a more vertical format, aligned the main street with the vertical axis of the composition, and moved the intersection up on the sheet in order to extend the street in the foreground. As a result, the streets occupy a larger share of the surface, and the space appears flatter. A greater sense of order and symmetry prevails at the expense of the sense of place.

Thiebaud likes to play with extreme spatial configurations. In *Diagonal City*, he divided the sheet along one of its diagonals, revisiting a type of composition he had used earlier in landscapes, such as *Cow Ridge* (Nos. 48 and 28). "*Diagonal City* is a made-up drawing," Thiebaud explained. "It is juxtaposing opposites. There is an attempt in the buildings to apply pressure, to build tensions, or to squeeze in things so that there is not quite enough room for the objects to exist. It creates a marvelous sense of drama."[66] The contrast between the emptiness of the lower half and the crowded, detailed rendering of the upper one heightens the artificiality of the device. In another striking

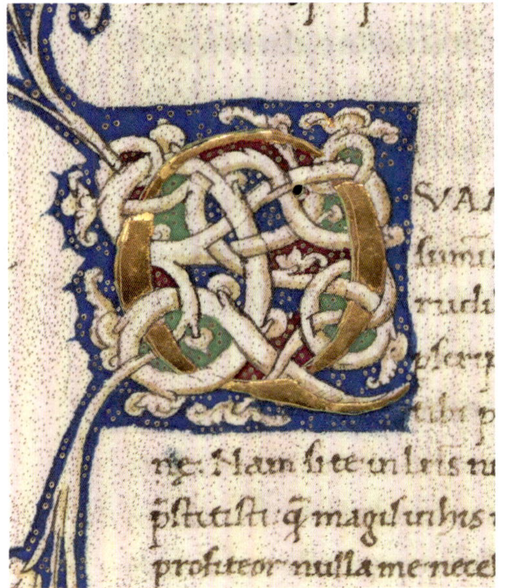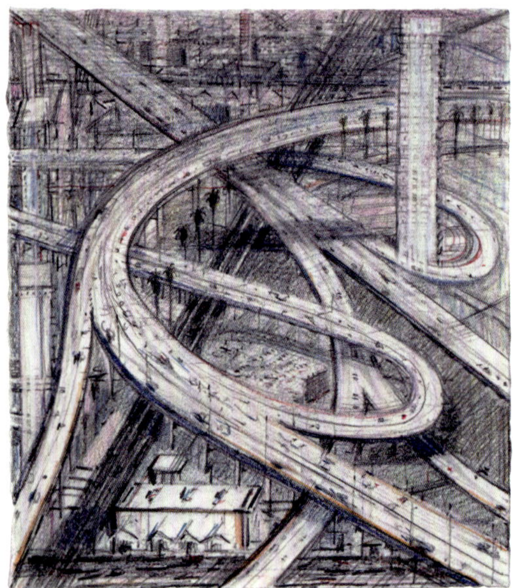

FIG. 16.
Initial *Q* from Lactantius, *Opera*,
Italy, Naples, 1475–99. The Morgan
Library & Museum, New York;
MS M.726, fol. 123v (detail).

Wayne Thiebaud, *Freeways Study*,
ca. 1982 (No. 49).

image, Thiebaud focused on the network of crisscrossing roads in a freeway interchange (No. 49). The small size of the drawing and gracefulness of the linear movement underscore its resemblance to the interweaving patterns of initials in illuminated medieval manuscripts (Fig. 16).

Thiebaud acknowledged that the inspiration for the cityscapes came from Richard Diebenkorn's Berkeley paintings of the early 1960s, such as *Cityscape #1* (Fig. 17).[67] Diebenkorn's urban views were largely informed by his explorations into abstraction from the previous decade and cultivated an ambiguity between observation and invention that appealed to Thiebaud. He was impressed by "the kind of pressure and tension" that held the elements together. "How things are impacted, not just from a cubist, planar standpoint, but more than that: the way things are pushed to the side, or squeezed into areas. . . . "[68] Another source of inspiration for the tension between flatness and illusion that is central to Thiebaud's cityscapes was folk painting. "I'm interested in the way a 'primitive' painter will shoot a street straight up into the air," he said.[69] Folk painters favor bird's-eye views and frequently adopt separate perspectives for different parts of a landscape in an attempt to provide a clearer record of each section (Fig. 18). These contrived manipulations, together with the typical stylization of the genre, endow them with a level of abstraction similar to what Thiebaud achieved in his cityscapes.

If pencil and charcoal lent themselves to the gray palette and grittiness of urban scenes, the brilliant colors of the Sacramento River landscape called for

WAYNE THIEBAUD DRAFTSMAN

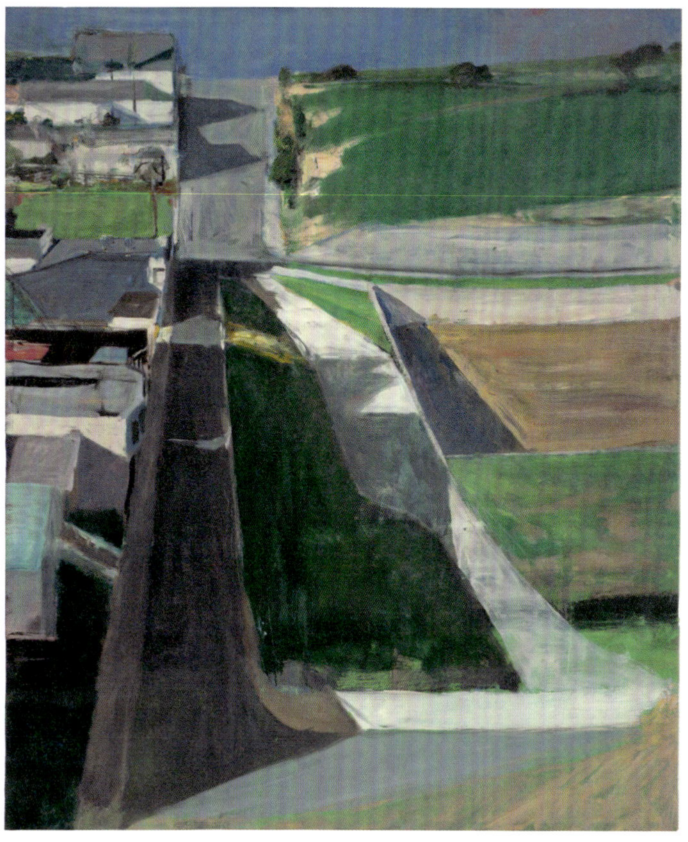

different mediums. Indeed there are fewer drawings of this subject to which
Thiebaud turned his attention in the mid-1990s. The absence of sky, the
flatness of the land, the arabesque of the meandering river, and the repetitive
patterns of the tilled fields create pictures that resemble vast jigsaw puzzles.
Thiebaud worked out the complex arrangements in small sketches done
mostly from imagination (No. 62). "People see them a little too quickly as
aerial views, but they're different in the sense that there are many different
viewpoints simultaneously. I've never gone up and sketched from up high. . . .
It's mostly just invented with perspective structures played around with to try
to bring it together into some sort of cohesive character."[70] The rich agricul-
tural land around the river and its delta offered Thiebaud a perfect subject to
explore a wide range of compositional strategies. He relished the contrast
between the traditional, romantic idea of a river landscape—"It's such a
seductive enterprise, to paint a river, the reflections, the prettiness of it and
so on"[71]—and the amount of maneuvering and scheming with which he
concocted his pictures. In *Study for* Brown River (No. 63), he carefully plotted
echoes across the sheet, from one edge to the other, creating a symmetry

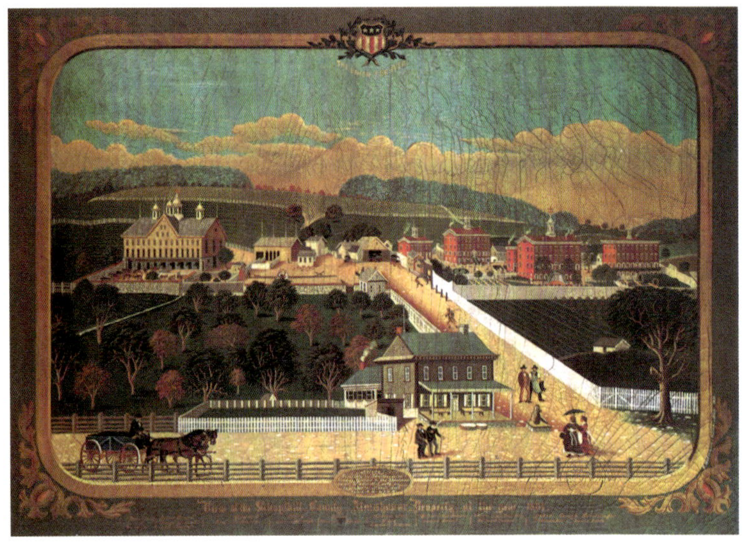

FIG. 18.
Charles C. Hofmann, *View of the Schuylkill County Almshouse Property, at the Year 1881*, 1881, oil on canvas. Formerly collection of Willem J. Wander Hooven.

between the entrance into the picture at bottom and its exit at the top, and playing between repetition and variation among the multiple patterns covering the surface. "I am not just interested in the pictorial aspects of the landscape— see a pretty place and try to paint it—but in some way to manage it, manipulate it, or see what I can turn it into."[72] The result is a highly fabricated image, which, like a folktale that relies on all the tricks and conventions of the genre, retains its power of enchantment.

Thiebaud's cityscapes and landscapes sum up two essential features that highlight the importance of drawing in his art. First, their graphic quality makes evident the role drawing plays in the structure and balance of the composition—in the tension, pressure, and rhythm on which, according to Thiebaud, the success of a picture relies. Drawing "keeps you from cheating," he declared.[73] This is why he has remained deeply engaged in the practice of drawing throughout his career. The second feature relates to the deformations and exaggerations typical of the recent landscapes, their caricatural aspect so to speak, which harks back to the cartoons and comics of Thiebaud's early career. Despite his deepening involvement in the art of the past and the development, over the years, of a more academic strain in his drawing style, Thiebaud has remained infatuated with the graphic energy of cartoon drawings—their tricks and shorthand. This constant reference has allowed him to keep solemnity and sentimentality at bay and ensure that his work stays cool and witty behind the hot, juicy paint.

Notes

1. John Arthur, ed., *Realists at Work*, New York, 1983, p. 128.

2. Hilton Kramer, "Art: Yvonne Jacquette," *The New York Times*, 27 April 1979, p. C21, and Donald Judd, "In the Galleries: Wayne Thiebaud," *Arts Magazine* (September 1962), reprinted in Donald Judd, *Complete Writings 1959–1975*, Halifax and New York, 1975, p. 60.

3. Stephen C. McGough, "An Interview with Wayne Thiebaud," in *Thiebaud Selects Thiebaud: A Forty-Year Survey from Private Collections*, exhibition catalogue, Crocker Art Museum, Sacramento, 1996, p. 8.

4. Constance Lewallen, "Interview with Wayne Thiebaud," *View* 6, no. 6 (Winter 1990), p. 8.

5. McGough, p. 7.

6. Arthur, p. 116.

7. Bill Berkson, "Thiebaud's Vanities," *Art in America* 73, no. 12 (December 1985), pp. 117–18.

8. David Hajdu, *The Ten-Cent Plague: The Great Comic-Book Scare and How It Changed America*, New York, 2008, p. 5.

9. Susan Larsen, oral history interview with Wayne Thiebaud, 17–18 May 2001, Archives of American Art, Smithsonian Institution, transcript, p. 25.

10. McGough, p. 7, and Lewallen, p. 21.

11. Arthur, p. 117.

12. Eve Aschheim and Chris Daubert, *Episodes with Wayne Thiebaud*, New York, 2014, pp. 32–33.

13. Arthur, p. 116.

14. On the "cute" formula that revolutionized American comics around 1900, see Thierry Smolderen, *The Origins of Comics: From William Hogarth to Winsor McCay*, translated by Bart Beaty and Nick Nguyen, Jackson, Mississippi, 2014, p. 108.

15. Conversation with the author, 31 January 2017.

16. Albert Boime, "The Comic Stripped and Ash Canned: A Review Essay," *Art Journal* 32, no. 1 (Autumn 1972), p. 22.

17. Aschheim and Daubert, p. 45, and McGough, p. 12.

18. Wayne Thiebaud, foreword to *Drawn to Excellence: Masters of Cartoon Art*, exhibition catalogue, Cartoon Art Museum, San Francisco, 1988.

19. Mark Strand, ed., *The Art of the Real: Nine Contemporary Figurative Painters*, New York, p. 181.

20. See Steven A. Nash, *Wayne Thiebaud: A Paintings Retrospective*, exhibition catalogue, Fine Arts Museums of San Francisco, 2000, pp. 195–98.

21. Strand, p. 188, and Thomas Albright, "Wayne Thiebaud: Scrambling Around with Ordinary Problems," *Art News* 77, no. 2 (February 1978), p. 84.

22. The painting is reproduced in Aschheim and Daubert, p. 11.

23. Gene Cooper, "Thiebaud, Theater, and Extremism," in *Wayne Thiebaud: Survey 1947–1976*, exhibition catalogue, Phoenix Art Museum, 1976, p. 16. See also Larsen, p. 15.

24. A. LeGrace G. Benson and David H. R. Shearer, "Documents: An Interview with Wayne Thiebaud," *Leonardo* 2, no. 1 (January 1969), p. 66.

25. Arthur, p. 120.

26. Sidra Stich, *Made in USA: An Americanization in Modern Art, the '50s & '60s*, Berkeley, Los Angeles, London, 1987, p. 77.

27. Max Kozloff, "Art," *The Nation*, 5 May 1962, p. 406, and Thomas B. Hess, "Reviews and Previews: New Names this Month," *Art News* (May 1962), p. 17, reprinted in Steven Henry Madoff, ed., *Pop Art: A Critical History*, Berkeley, Los Angeles, London, 1997, p. 341.

28. John Coplans, *Wayne Thiebaud*, exhibition catalogue, Pasadena Art Museum, 1968, p. 24.

29. Andrew Hurley, "From Hash House to Family Restaurant: The Transformation of the Diner and Post–World War II Consumer Culture," *The Journal of American History* 83, no. 4 (March 1997), p. 1307.

30. Ibid., p. 1308.

31. Strand, pp. 188–89.

32. Michael Sheringham, *Everyday Life: Theories and Practices from Surrealism to the Present*, Oxford, 2006, pp. 4–5.

33. Albright, p. 86.

34. Ibid.

35. Larsen, p. 38.

36. Albright, p. 82.

37. Arthur, p. 120.

38. Alessia Masi, "Interview to Wayne Thiebaud," in *Wayne Thiebaud at Museo Morandi*, exhibition catalogue, Museo Morandi, Bologna, 2011, p. 41. On the influence of the theater on Thiebaud's art, see also Cooper's essay cited above.

39. Gwen Stone, "Wayne Thiebaud: In Conversation with Gwen Stone," *Visual Dialog* (Winter 1977–78), p. 15.

40. McGough, p. 11. See also Richard Wollheim, "Matisse at MOMA: Richard Wollheim Talks to Wayne Thiebaud," *Modern Painters* 6, no. 3 (Autumn 1993), p. 58.

41. Michael Kimmelman, "At the Met with Wayne Thiebaud: A Little Weirdness Can Help an Artist," *The New York Times*, 23 August 1996, p. C25.

42. See Karal Ann Marling, *As Seen on TV: The Visual Culture of Everyday Life in the 1950s*, Cambridge, Mass. and London, 1994, p. 221.

43. Coplans, p. 30.

44. Wayne Thiebaud interviewed by Carol Mancusi-Ungaro, 27 June 2001, Artists Documentation Program, Video Interview Transcript, p. 19.

45. Lewallen, p. 17, and Aschheim and Daubert, pp. 38–39.

46. Roland Barthes, *Mythologies*, translated by Annette Lavers, New York, 1972, p. 78.

47. "I've always used a lot of different mediums. . . . That transformation process is something that interests me a lot, how one becomes another, transposes the same way that music transposes." Arthur, p. 128.

48. That Degas was on Thiebaud's mind when he made these drawings is confirmed by the presence of a book on Degas among the still-life elements in one of them. See *Wayne Thiebaud: Charcoal Still Lifes 1964–1974*, exhibition catalogue, Lawrence Markey, San Antonio and Paul Thiebaud Gallery, San Francisco, 2010, p. 48. The current location of the drawing is unknown.

49. Bill Berkson, "Wayne's World," *Modern Painters* 11, no. 2 (Summer 1998), p. 19.

50. Albright, p. 82. Bruce Nauman, who was Thiebaud's teaching assistant at the University of California, Davis, in the 1960s, recalled that Thiebaud "only taught beginning students. . . . He thought nobody was doing a good job with beginning students, really teaching drawing and how to look at stuff. . . . He was a really good teacher." Interview with Bruce Nauman with Kathy Halbreich, 9 January 2012, Museum of Modern Art Archives, Oral History.

51. Dan Tooker, "Wayne Thiebaud Interviewed by Dan Tooker," *Art International* 18 (November 1974), p. 22. From 1976 to 1984, Thiebaud attended weekly sessions of drawing from the model with four other Bay Area artists, Mark Adams, Theophilus Brown, Gordon Cook, and Beth Van Hoesen. See *Figure Drawings: Five San Francisco Artists*, exhibition catalogue, Charles Campbell Gallery, San Francisco, 1983.

52. "In a game like tennis or golf, you have to train a lot in order to no longer think about what you're doing," in Thomas Demand, "Elements of Painting: Wayne Thiebaud in conversation with Thomas Demand," *Frieze Masters*, no. 3 (October 2014), p. 10.

53. Aschheim and Daubert, p. 40.

54. Victoria Dalkey, *Wayne Thiebaud: Figure Drawings*, exhibition catalogue, Campbell-Thiebaud Gallery, San Francisco, 1993, n.p.

55. Wayne Thiebaud, "As Far As I'm Concerned, There Is Only One Study and that Is the Way in which Things Relate to One Another," *Untitled* (Friends of Photography, Carmel, CA) 7/8 (1974), p. 23, and Strand, p. 192.

56. Aschheim and Daubert, p. 77.

57. Albert Boime, *The Academy & French Painting in the Nineteenth Century*, New Haven and London, 1971, pp. 128 and 132.

58. Wayne Thiebaud, "A Fellow Painter's View of Giorgio Morandi," *The New York Times*, 15 November 1981, pp. D37–D38.

59. Boime 1971, p. 123.

60. Stone, p. 12.

61. Wayne Thiebaud, "Matisse—A Personal View," in *Henri Matisse: An Exhibition of Drawings*, exhibition catalogue, John Berggruen Gallery, San Francisco, 1982, p. ix.

62. Richard Wollheim, "An Interview with Wayne Thiebaud," in *Wayne Thiebaud: Cityscapes*, exhibition catalogue, Campbell-Thiebaud Gallery, San Francisco, 1993, n.p.

63. Quoted in Adam Gopnik, "An American Painter," in Nash, p. 58.

64. Wollheim, *Cityscapes*, n.p.

65. Arthur, pp. 125 and 128, and Wollheim, *Cityscapes*, n.p.

66. Frank Gettings, *Drawings 1974–1984*, exhibition catalogue, Hirshhorn Museum and Sculpture Garden, Washington, DC, 1984, p. 230.

67. Richard Wollheim, "On Thiebaud and Diebenkorn: Richard Wollheim Talks to Wayne Thiebaud," *Modern Painters* 4, no. 3 (Autumn 1991), p. 66.

68. Ibid.

69. Albright, p. 86.

70. Larsen, p. 43.

71. McGough, p. 12.

72. Gail Gordon, "Thiebaud Puts a Visual Feast on Canvas," *The California Aggie*, 9 February 1983, p. 2.

73. Aschheim and Daubert, p. 40.

Plates

1. **UNTITLED (MAN WITH BANJO)**, 1940s
Pen and ink and wash
11 × 8½ inches (27.9 × 21.6 cm)
From the artist's studio

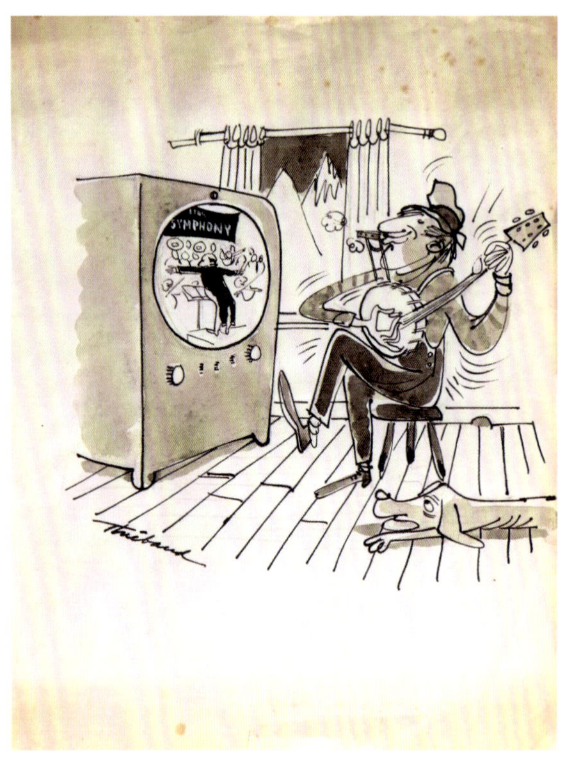
SYMPHONY

2. **"STEP UP PLEASE!"** 1940s
   Pen and ink and wash
   11 × 8½ inches (27.9 × 21.6 cm)
   From the artist's studio

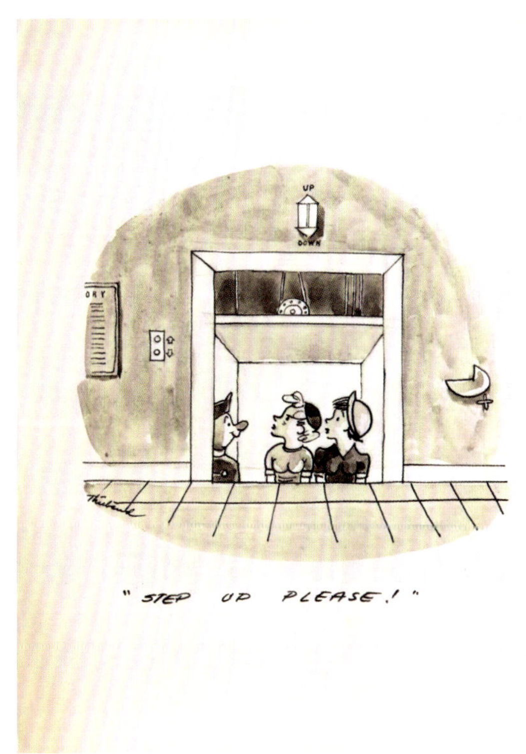

3. **RAILWAY CARS**, 1949
    Watercolor, wash and ink
    11 × 13¾ inches (27.9 × 34.9 cm)
    Courtesy of Mia I. Groszkowski

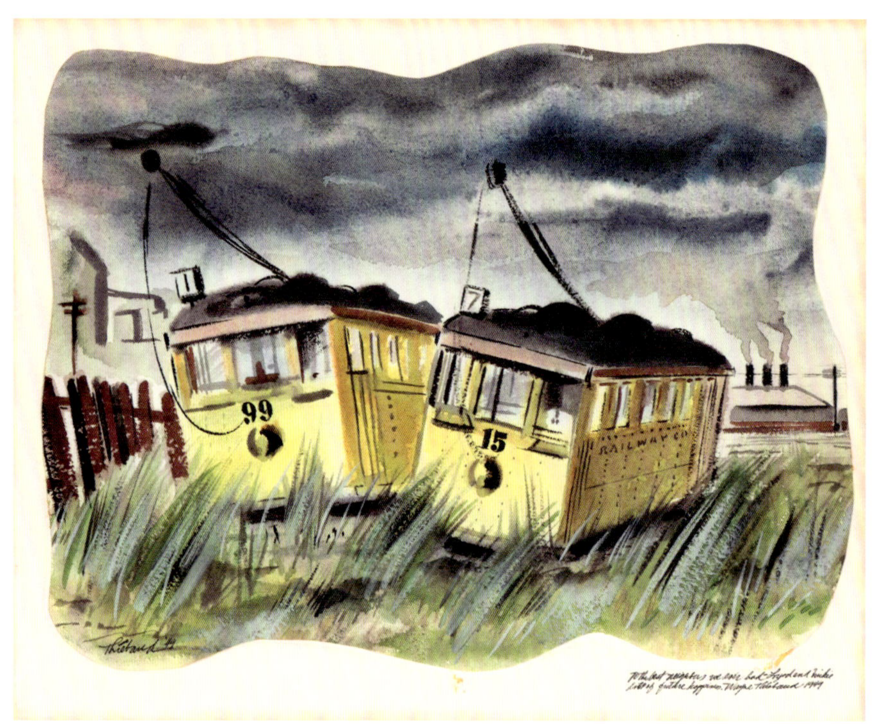

4. **MARKET IN MEXICO**, 1954
   Pen and ink
   24 × 30 inches (61 × 76.2 cm)
   From the artist's studio

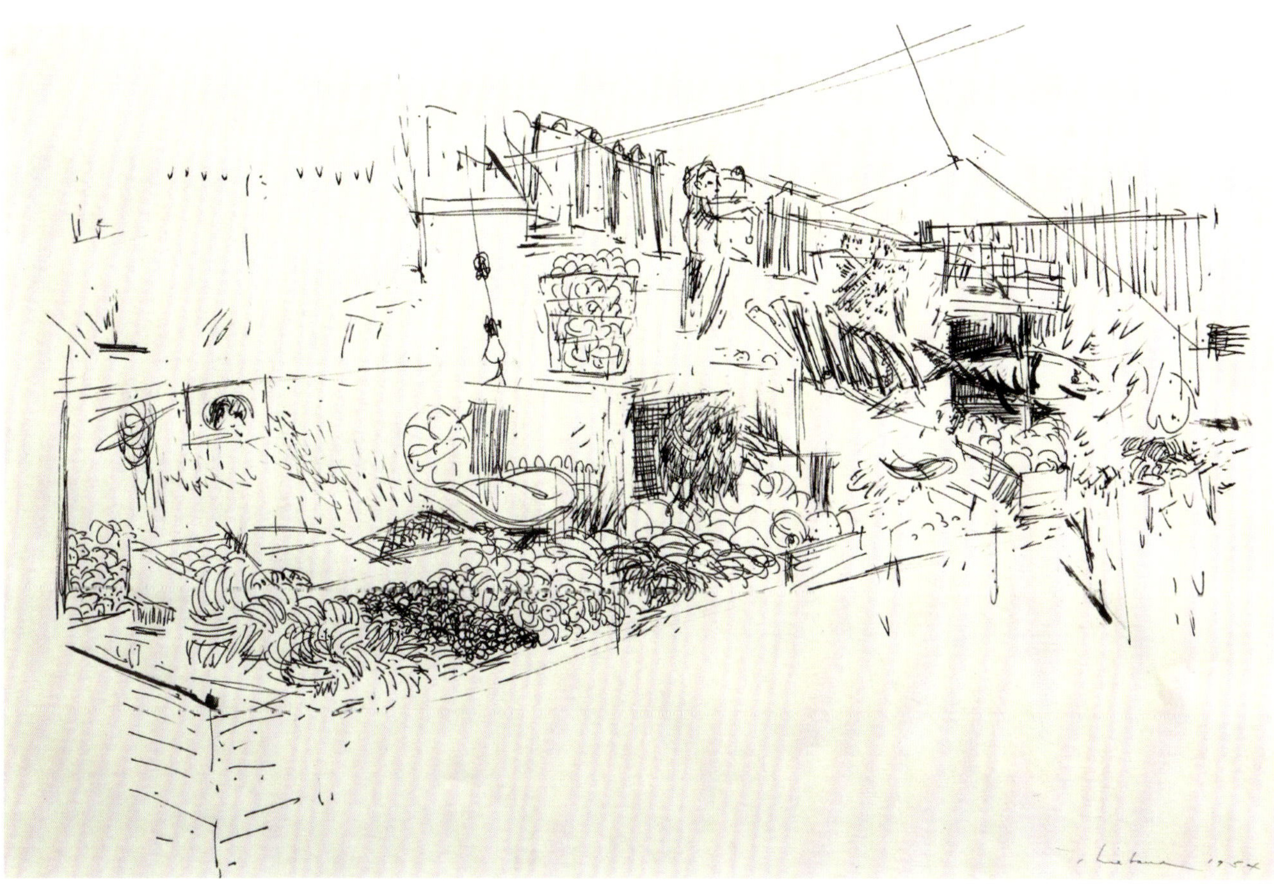

5. **FRANZ KLINE, NYC**, 1956
Graphite
18½ × 15½ inches (47 × 39.4 cm)
From the artist's studio

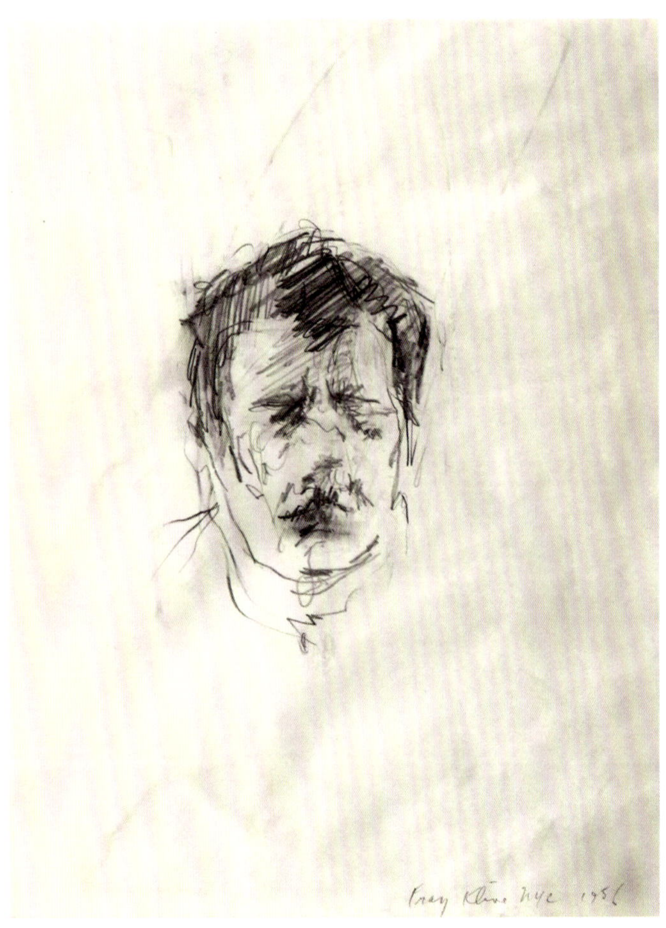

6. **NEW YORK CITY WINTER**, 1956
    Brush and ink and watercolor
    20 × 24 inches (50.8 × 61 cm)
    From the artist's studio

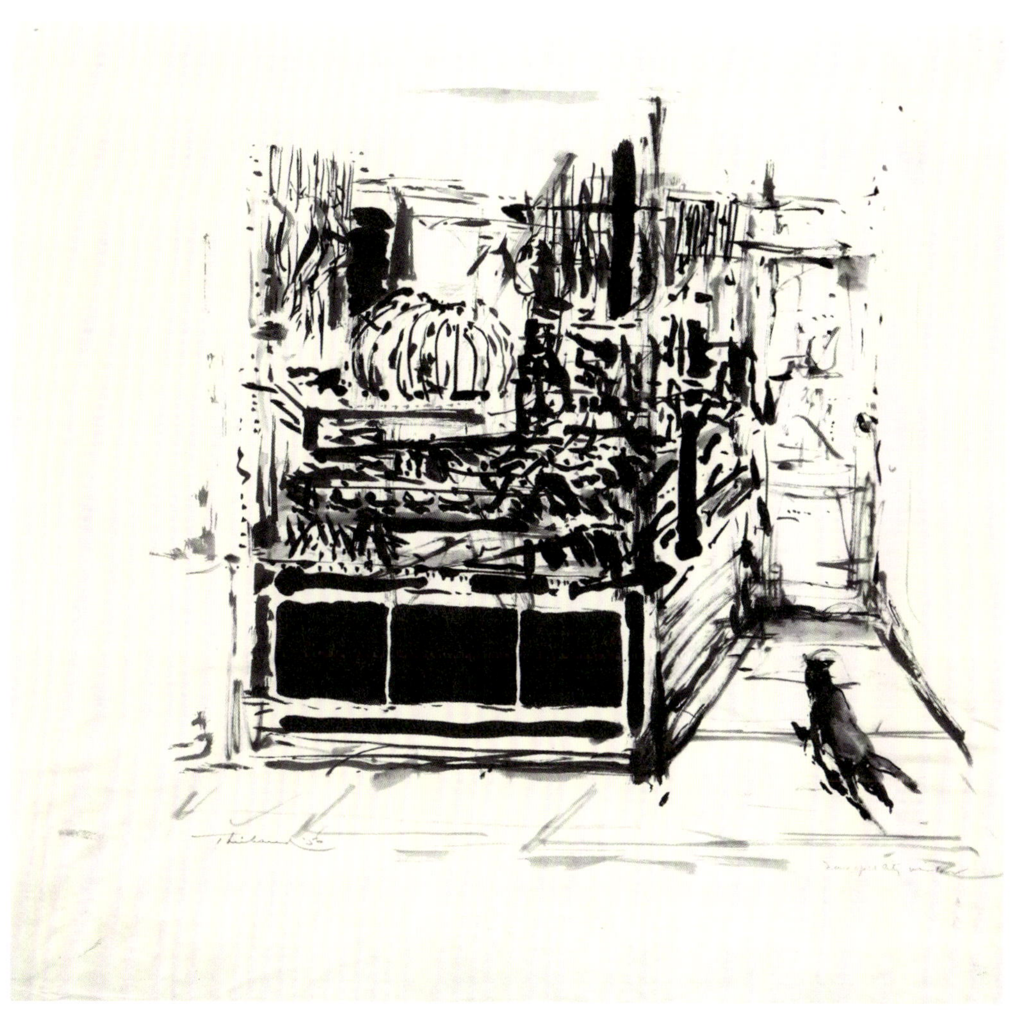

7. **SHELF OF PIES**, 1960
    Brush and ink, watercolor, and charcoal
    19 × 25 inches (48.3 × 63.5 cm)
    Private collection

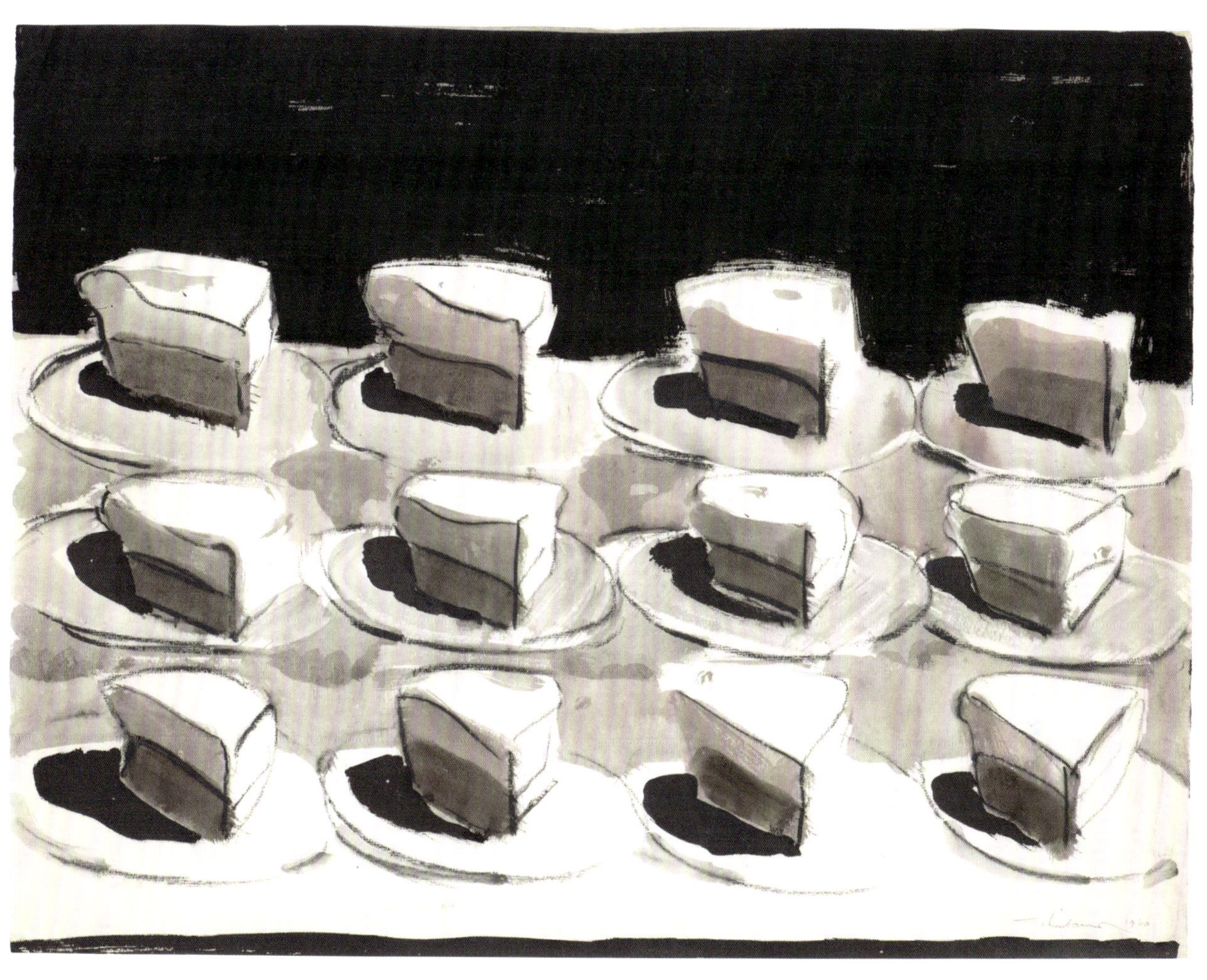

8. **DELICATESSEN COUNTER**, 1961
Ink, oil, watercolor, and graphite
16 × 26¼ inches (40.6 × 66.7 cm)
Collection of Christine and David Provost

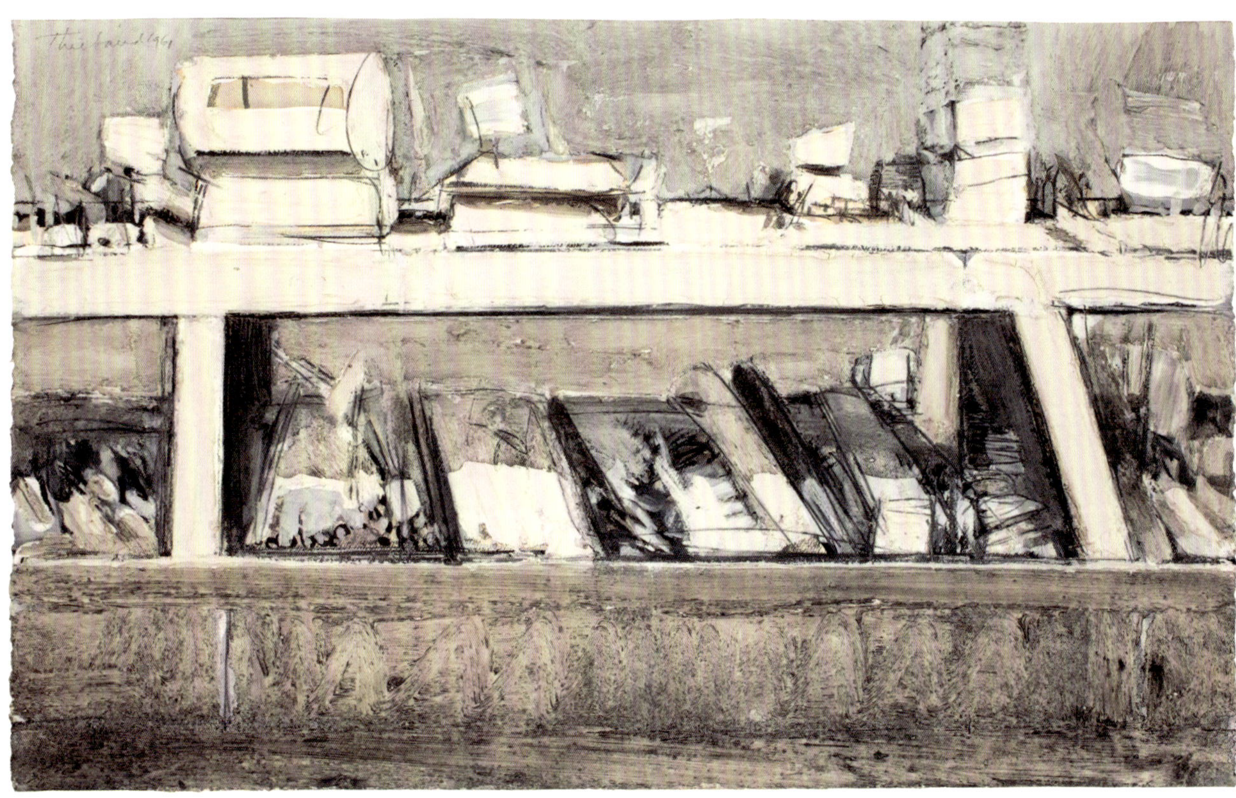

9. **TOY COUNTER**, 1962
   Graphite
   14½ × 15¾ inches (36.8 × 40 cm)
   From the artist's studio

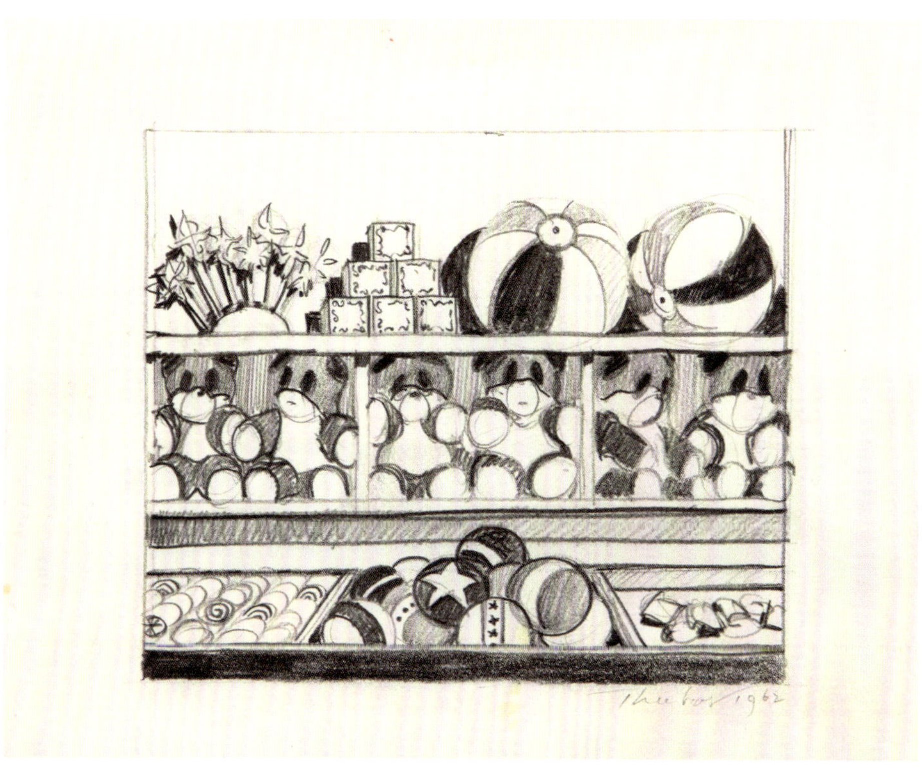

10. **LAYER CAKES**, 1964
    Brush and ink and graphite
    13¼ × 20¼ inches (33.7 × 51.4 cm)
    Collection of Karen and Brian Conway

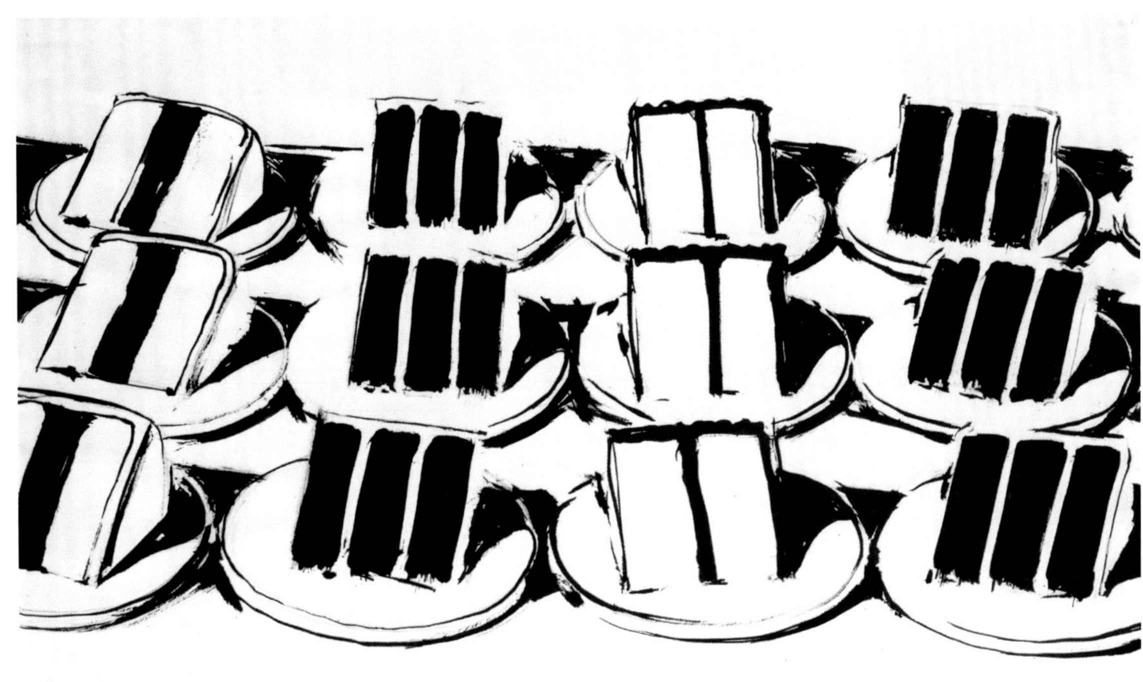

11. **HAMBURGERS**, 1964
Brush and ink
15½ × 20 inches (39.4 × 50.8 cm)
Allan Stone Collection, courtesy Allan Stone Projects, NY

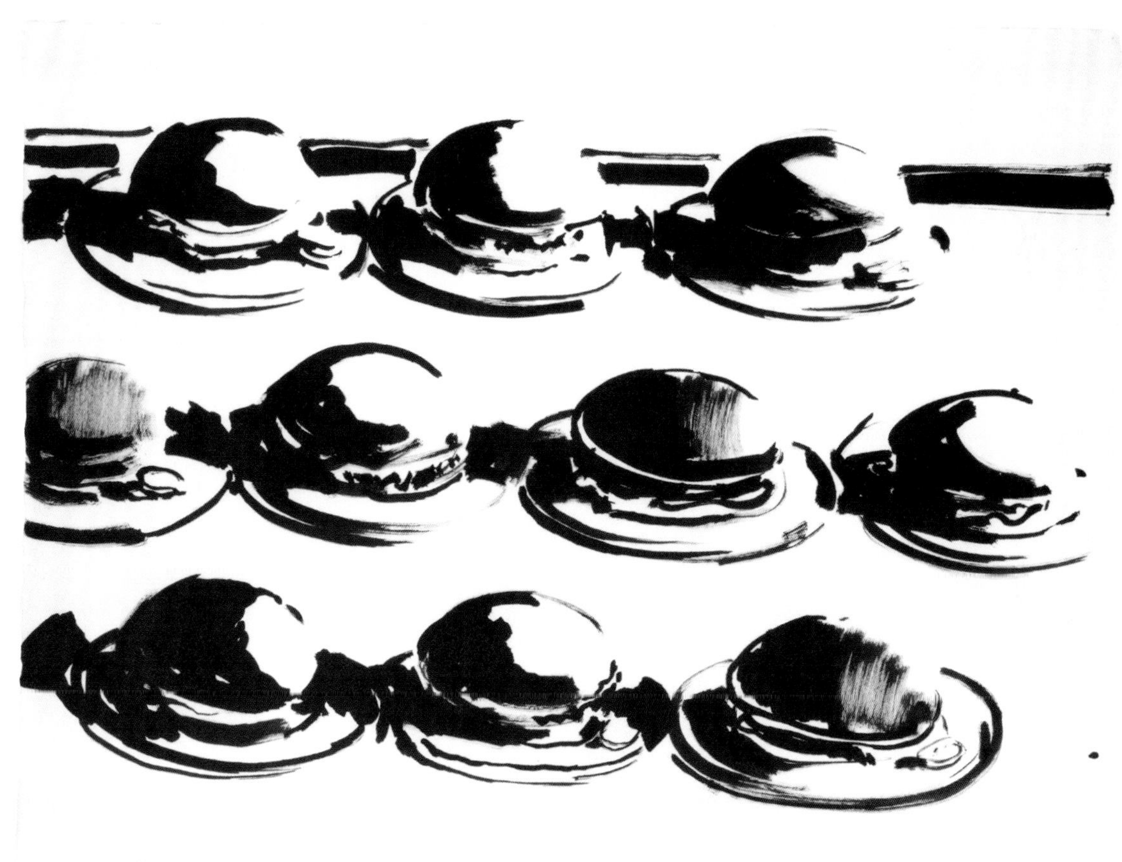

12. **FOOD COUNTER**, 1964
Brush and ink and oil
10½ × 17⅛ inches (26.7 × 43.5 cm)
Private collection

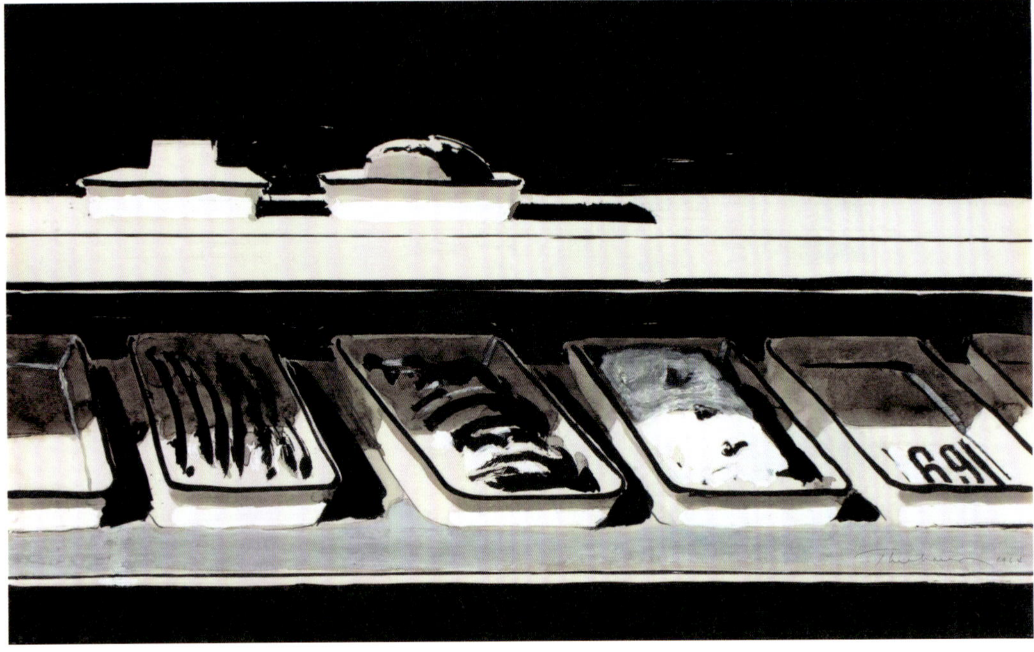

13. **DELICATESSEN**, 1964
Watercolor and graphite
12⅝ × 9¼ inches (32.1 × 23.5 cm)
Private collection, courtesy Acquavella Galleries

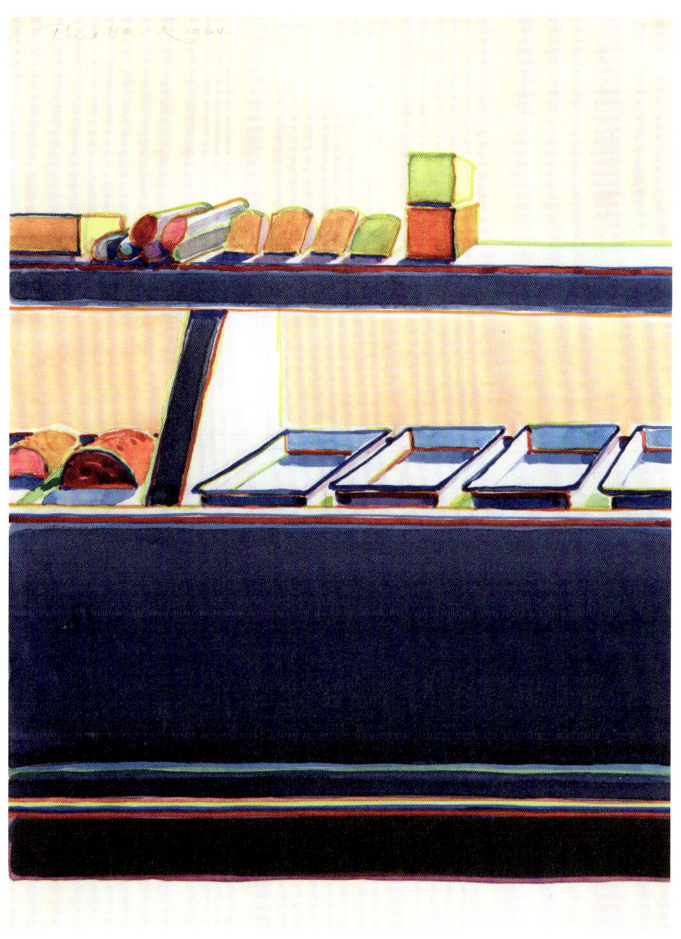

14. **CANDY STICKS**, 1964
Watercolor and graphite
11¼ × 15 inches (28.6 × 38.1 cm)
Yale University Art Gallery,
Bequest of Susan Morse Hilles

15. **PAGE OF SKETCHES
WITH CANDY STICKS**, 1960s
Graphite and ballpoint pen
7⅞ × 9⅞ inches (20 × 25.1 cm)
From the artist's studio

16. **PEPPERMINT STICKS**, 1964
Brush and ink
9 × 9½ inches (22.9 × 24.1 cm)
Allan Stone Collection,
courtesy Allan Stone Projects, NY

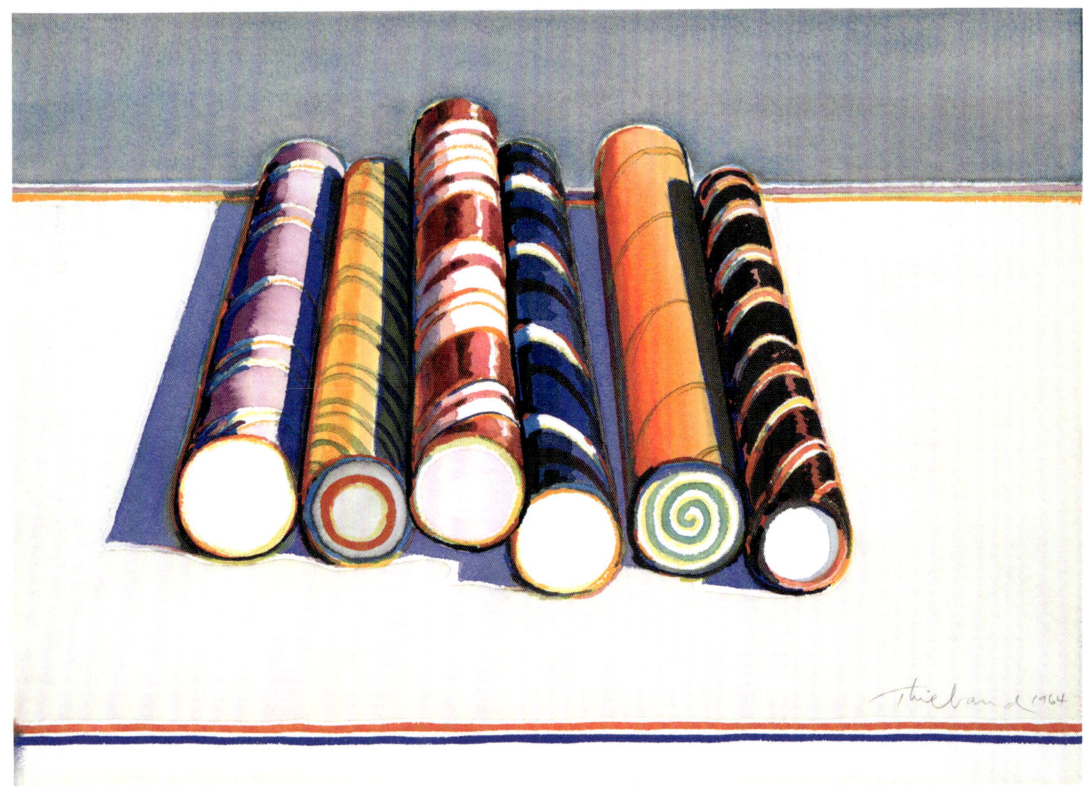

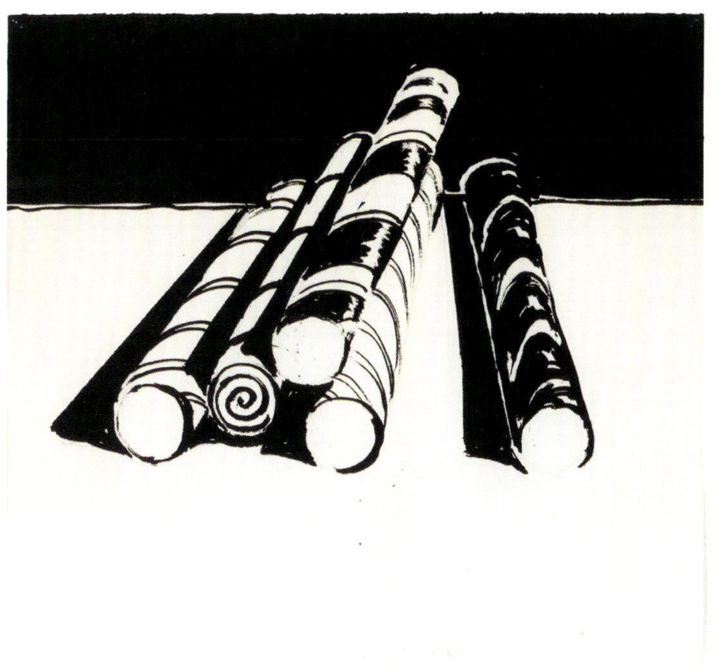

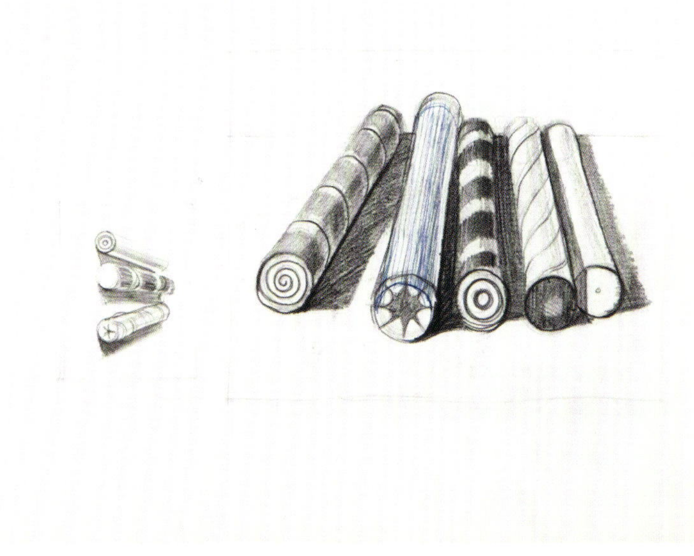

17. **THREE JELLY APPLES**, 1964
Graphite
12 × 13½ inches (30.5 × 34.3 cm)
Private collection, courtesy Acquavella Galleries

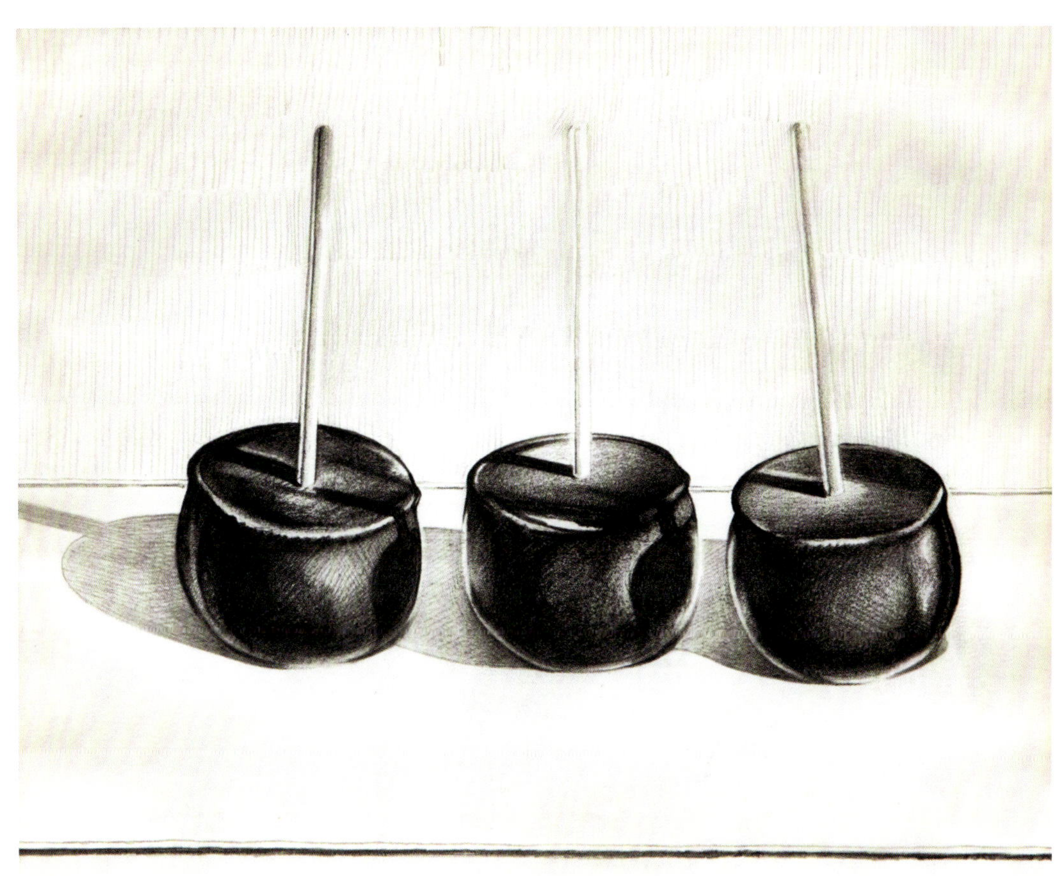

18. **NINE JELLY APPLES**, 1964
Watercolor and graphite
12 × 12 inches (30.5 × 30.5 cm)
Yale University Art Gallery,
Gift of George Hopper Fitch, B.A. 1932

19. **CANDIED APPLES**, 1964
Brush and ink
7 × 11⁷⁄₁₆ inches (17.8 × 29.1 cm)
Allan Stone Collection,
courtesy Allan Stone Projects, NY

20. **PAGE OF SKETCHES WITH
PORTRAIT OF CLEMENT GREENBERG
AND CANDIED APPLES**, 1986
Pen and ink and watercolor
11 × 8½ inches (27.9 × 21.6 cm)
From the artist's studio

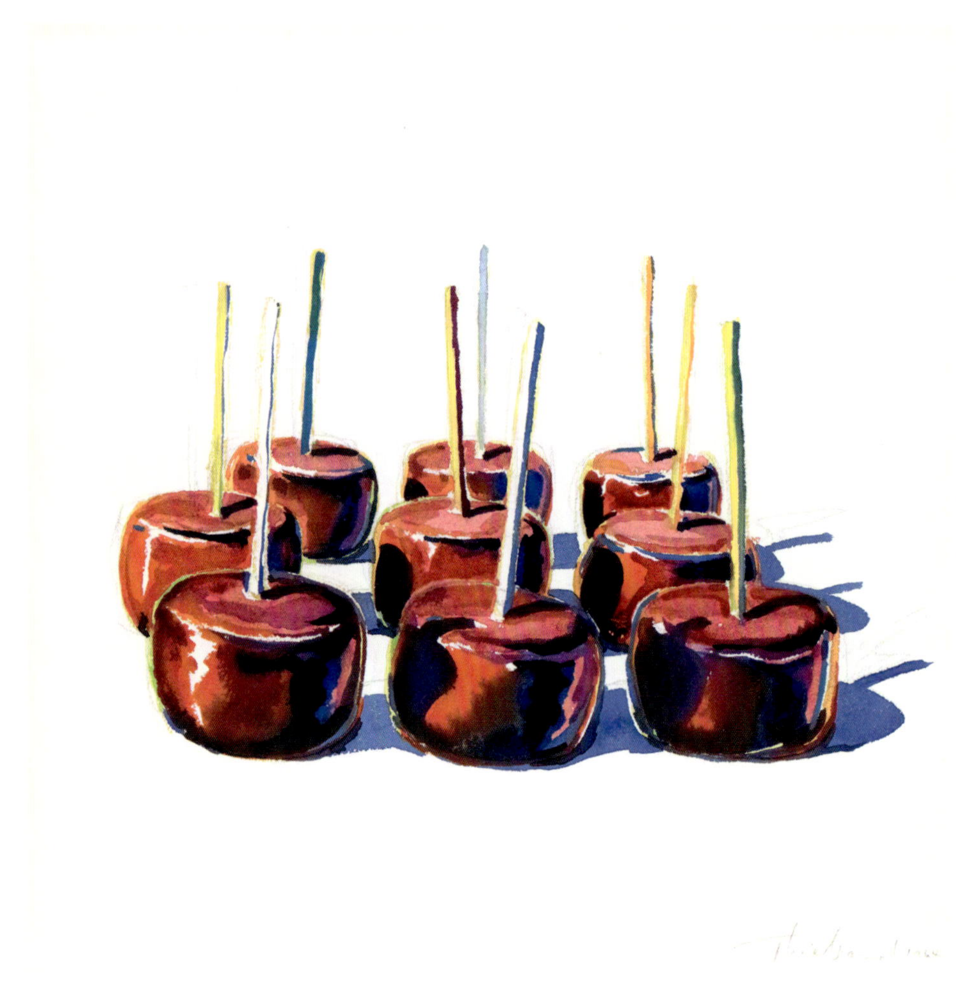

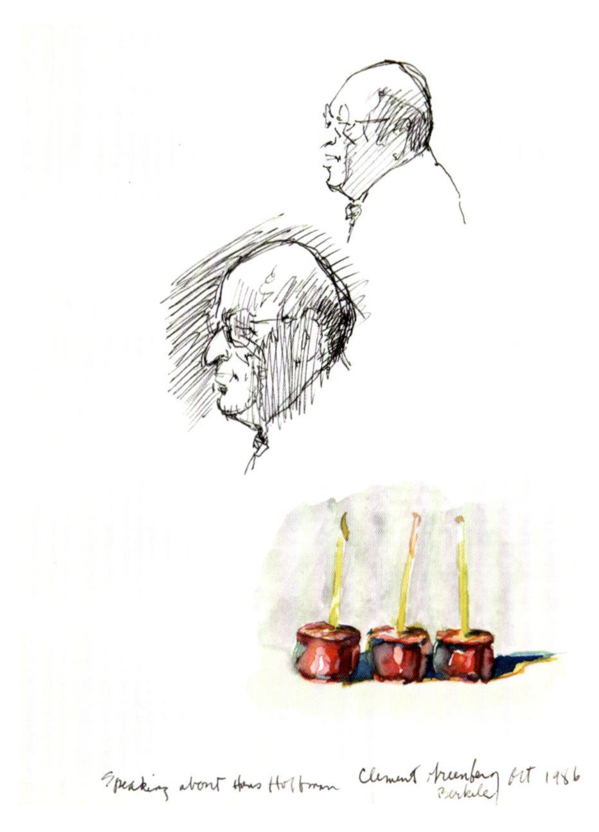

Speaking about Hans Hoffman   Clement Greenberg Oct 1986
                                                     Berkeley

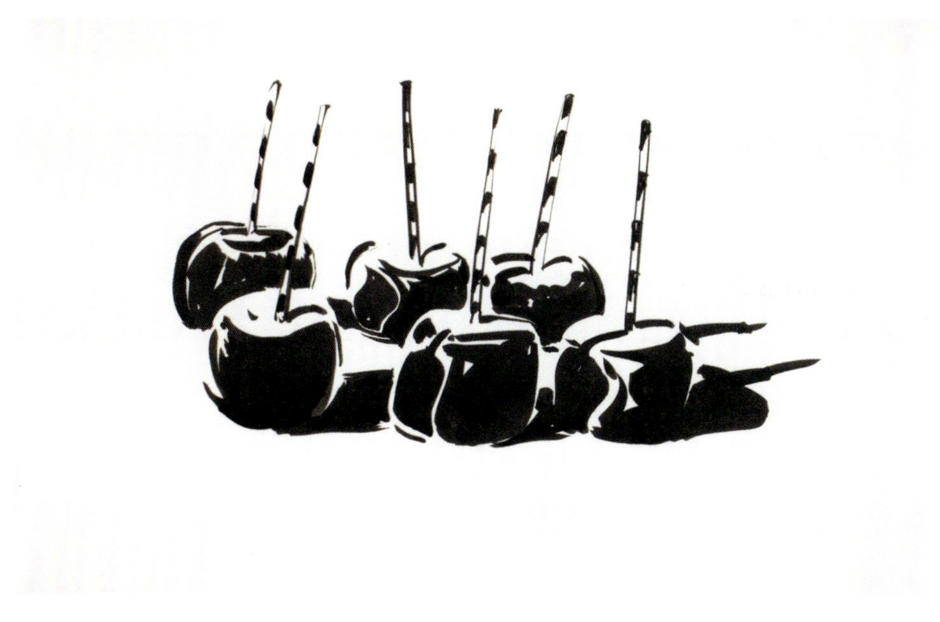

21. **ICE CREAM CONE**, 1964
Graphite
14 × 11 inches (35.6 × 27.9 cm)
Collection of Gretchen and John Berggruen,
San Francisco

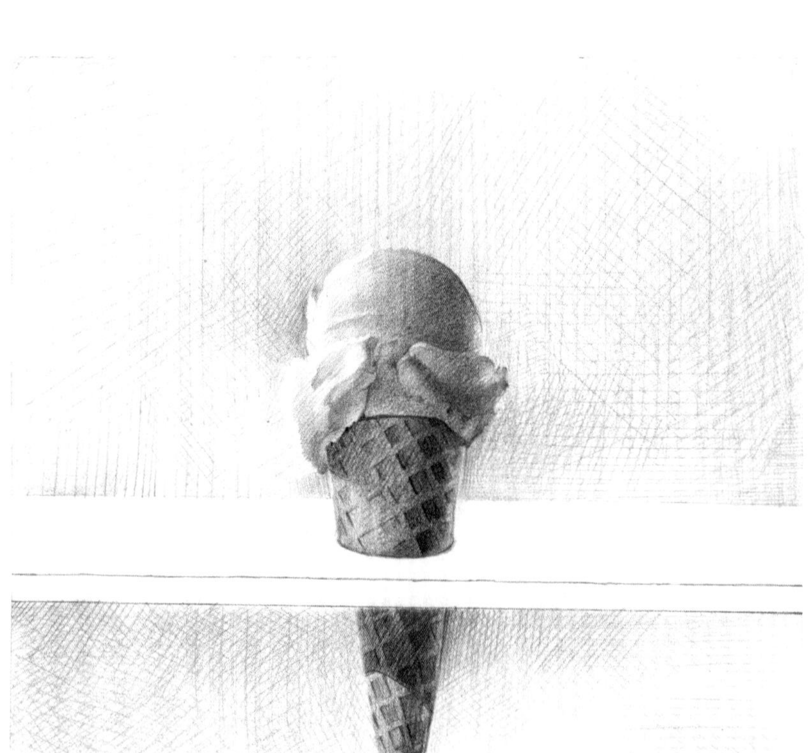

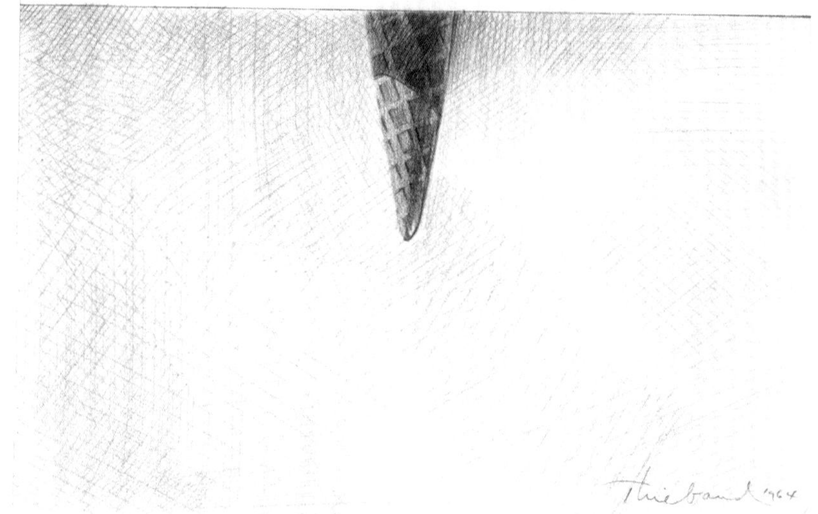

22. **UNTITLED (THREE ICE CREAMS)**, 1964
Pastel and graphite
9¼ × 12¼ inches (23.5 × 31.1 cm)
Private collection

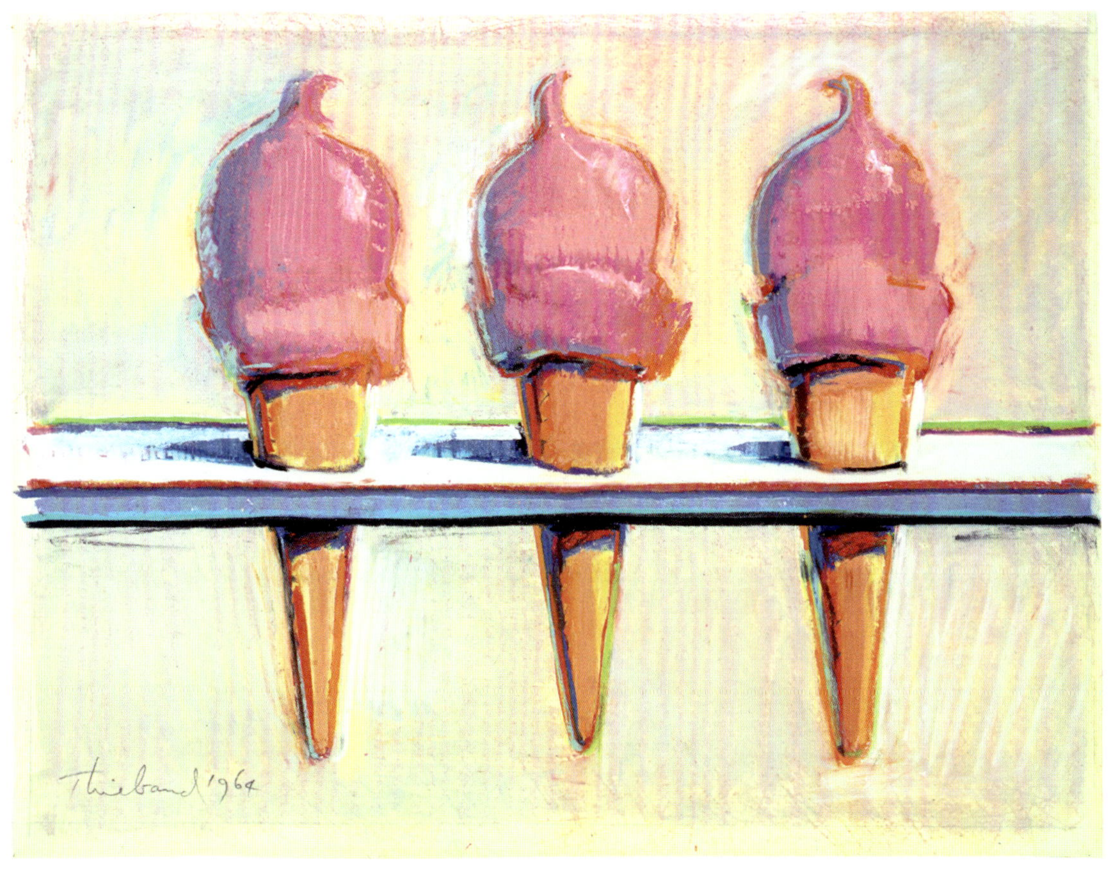

23. **DRINK SYRUPS**, 1964
Pastel
9¾ × 9¾ inches (24.8 × 24.8 cm)
Private collection

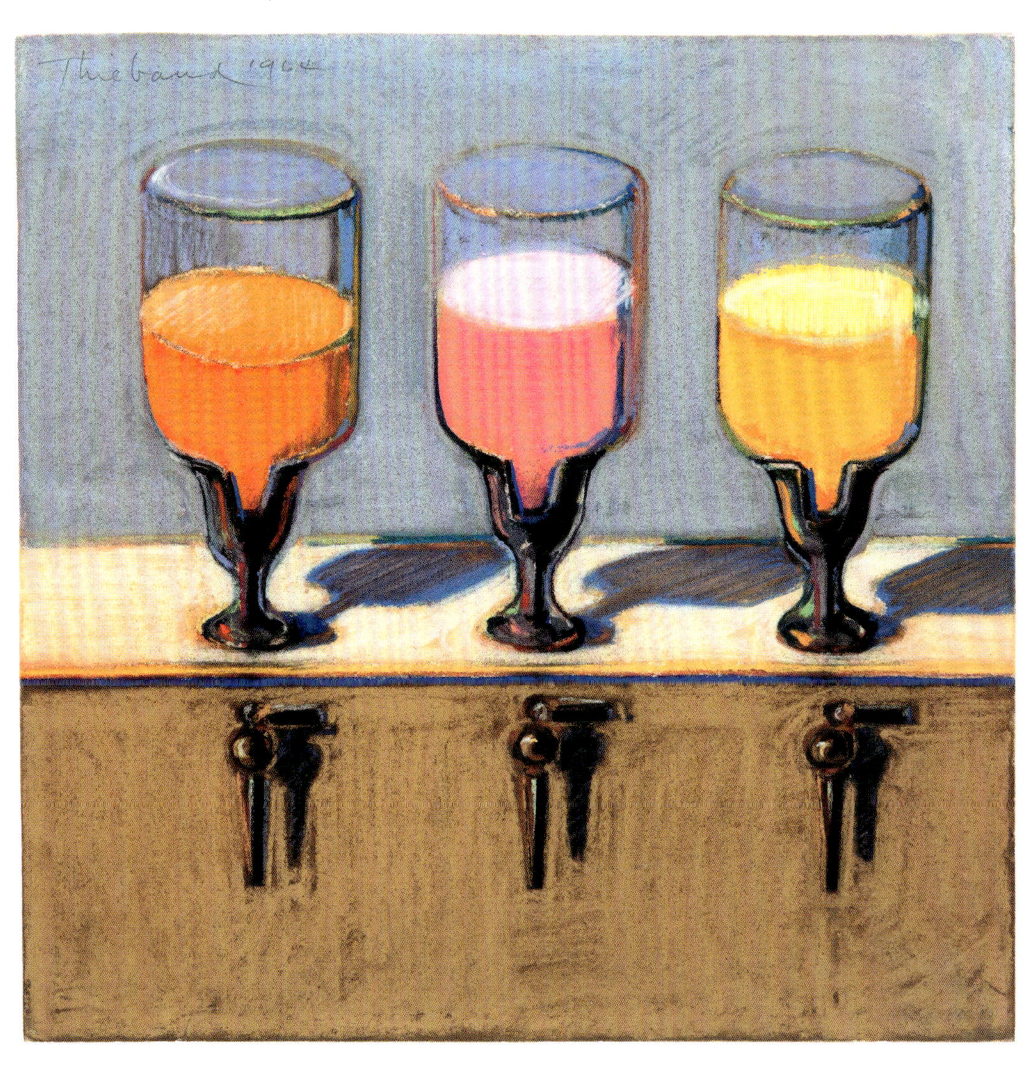

24. **LUNCH TABLE**, 1964
Watercolor and graphite
10 × 14⅛ inches (25.4 × 35.9 cm)
Collection of Alan and Ellen Meckler

25. **CAKES NO. 1**, 1967
Pastel and graphite
17 × 14 inches (43.2 × 35.6 cm)
Private collection, courtesy of Guggenheim,
Asher Associates

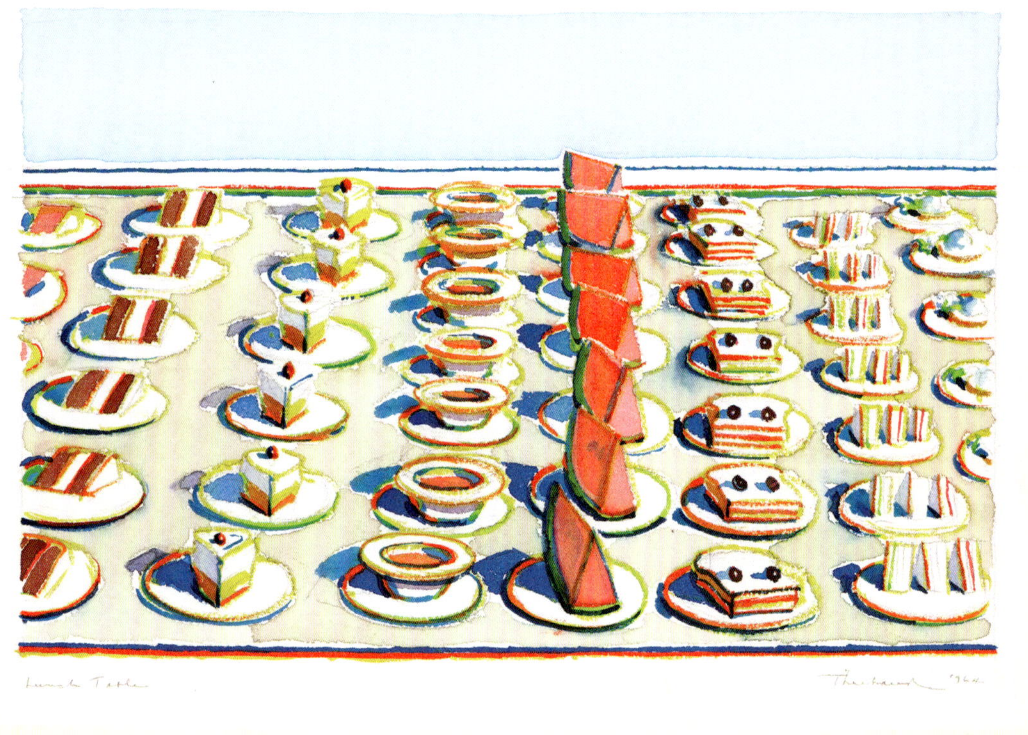

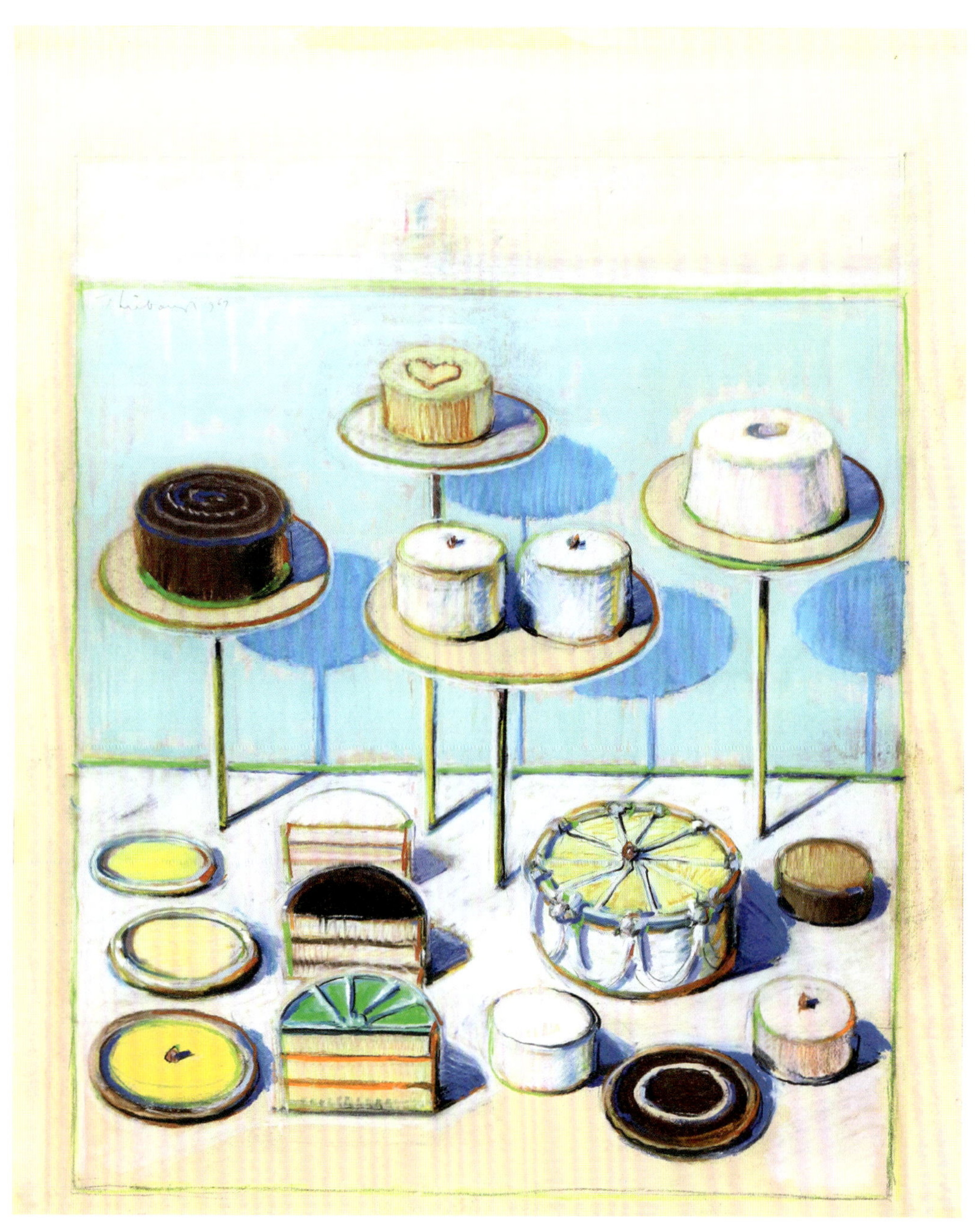

26. **PALM ROAD**, 1965
Brush and ink
10 ⅞ × 13 inches (27.6 × 33 cm)
Private collection,
courtesy Acquavella Galleries

27. **BALE ROWS**, 1966
Pastel on illustration board
6 ⅛ × 8 ¼ inches (15.6 × 21 cm)
Private collection

28. **COW RIDGE**, 1966
Pastel on illustration board
5 ⅝ × 7 ⅛ inches (14.3 × 18.1 cm)
Thiebaud Family Collection

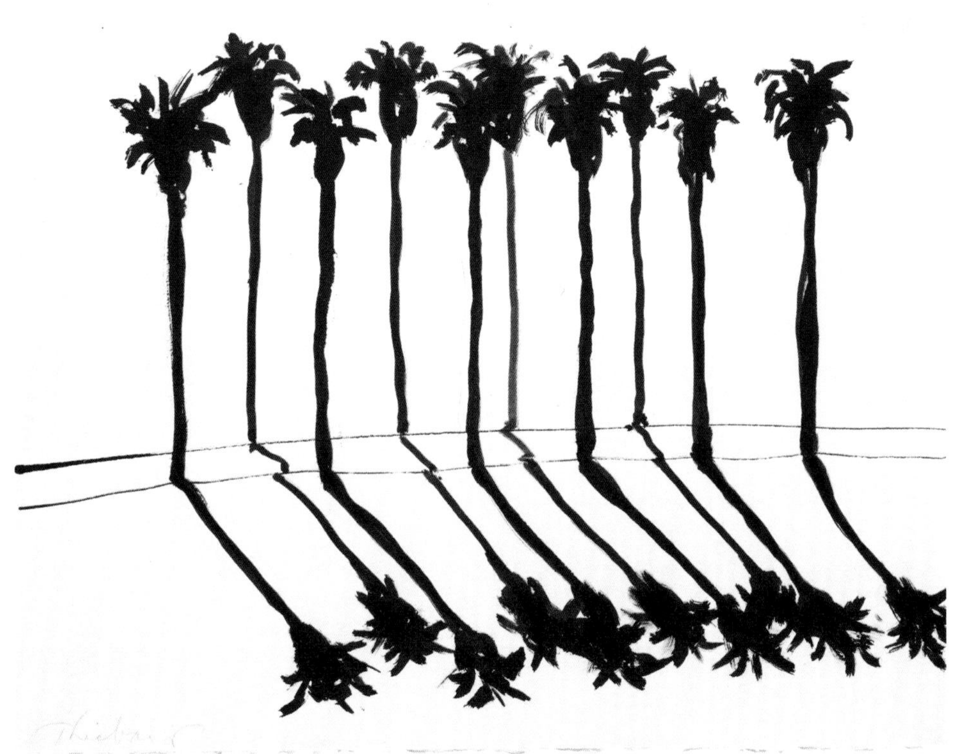

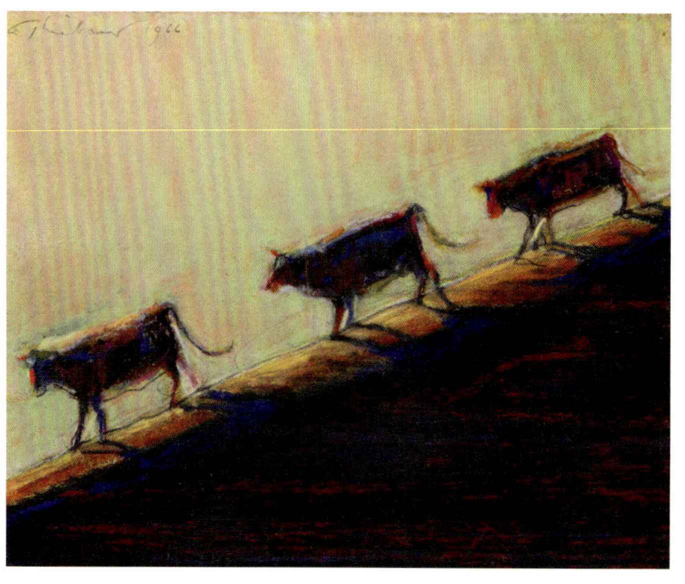

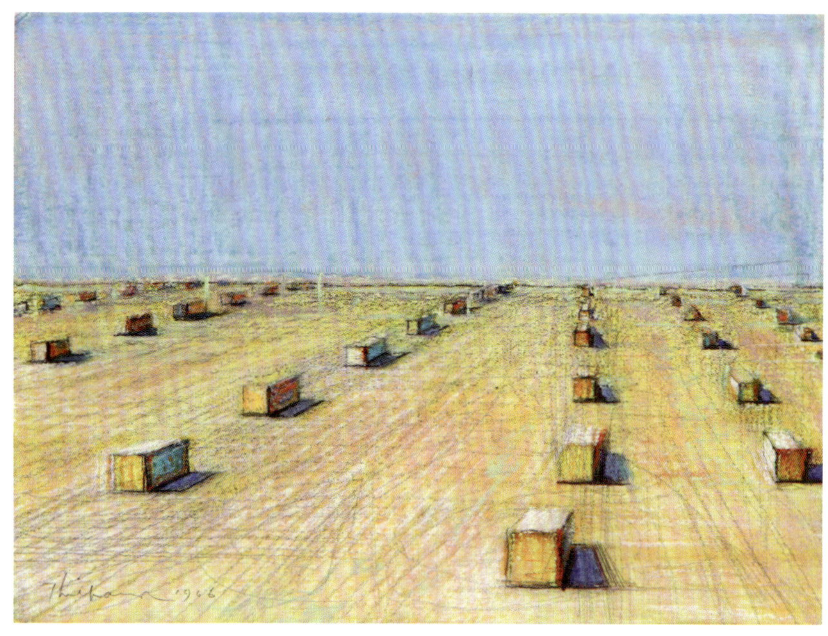

29. **FARM POND**, 1968
Pastel on illustration board
11¾ × 10⅞ inches (29.9 × 27.6 cm)
Private collection

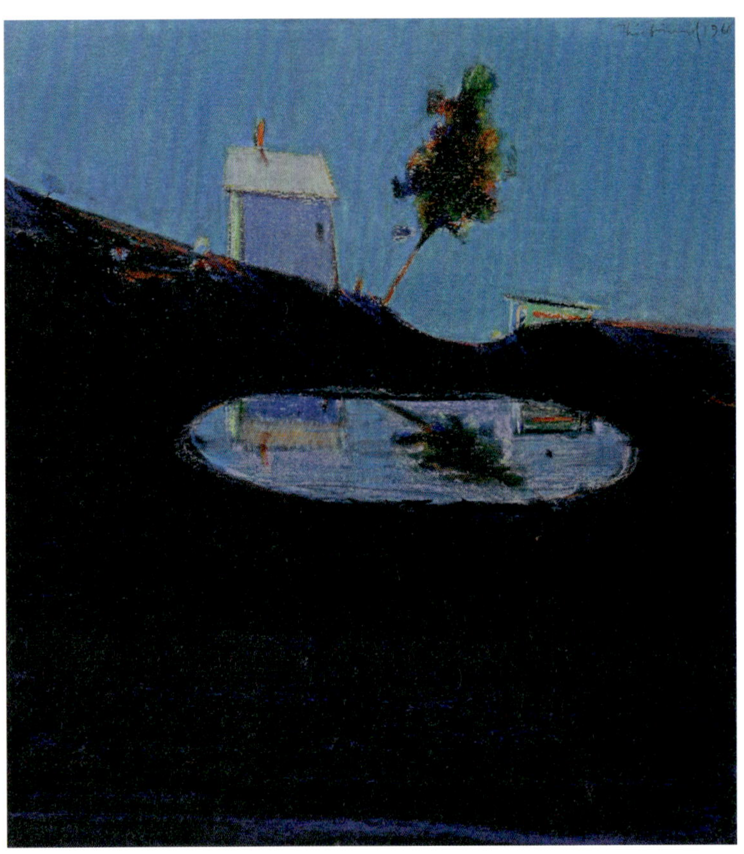

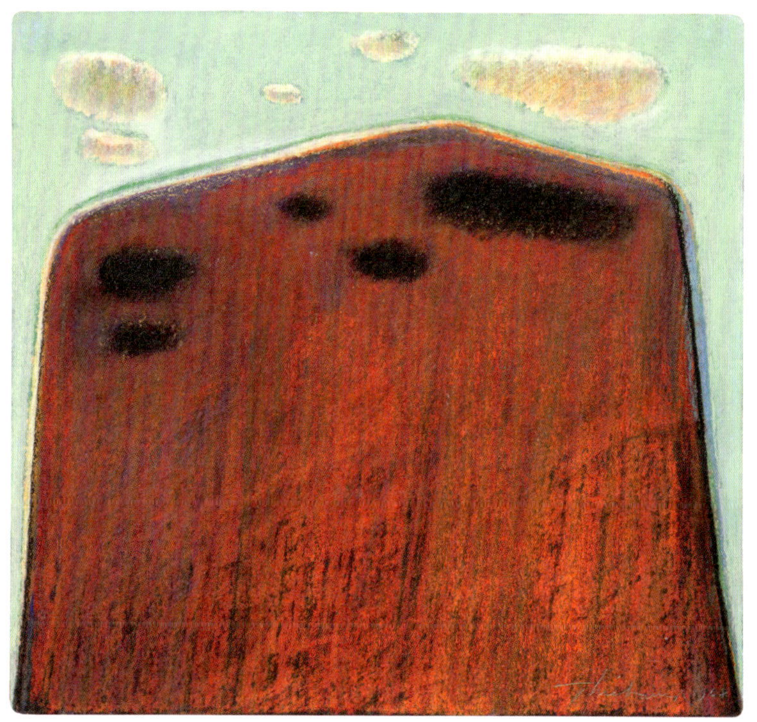

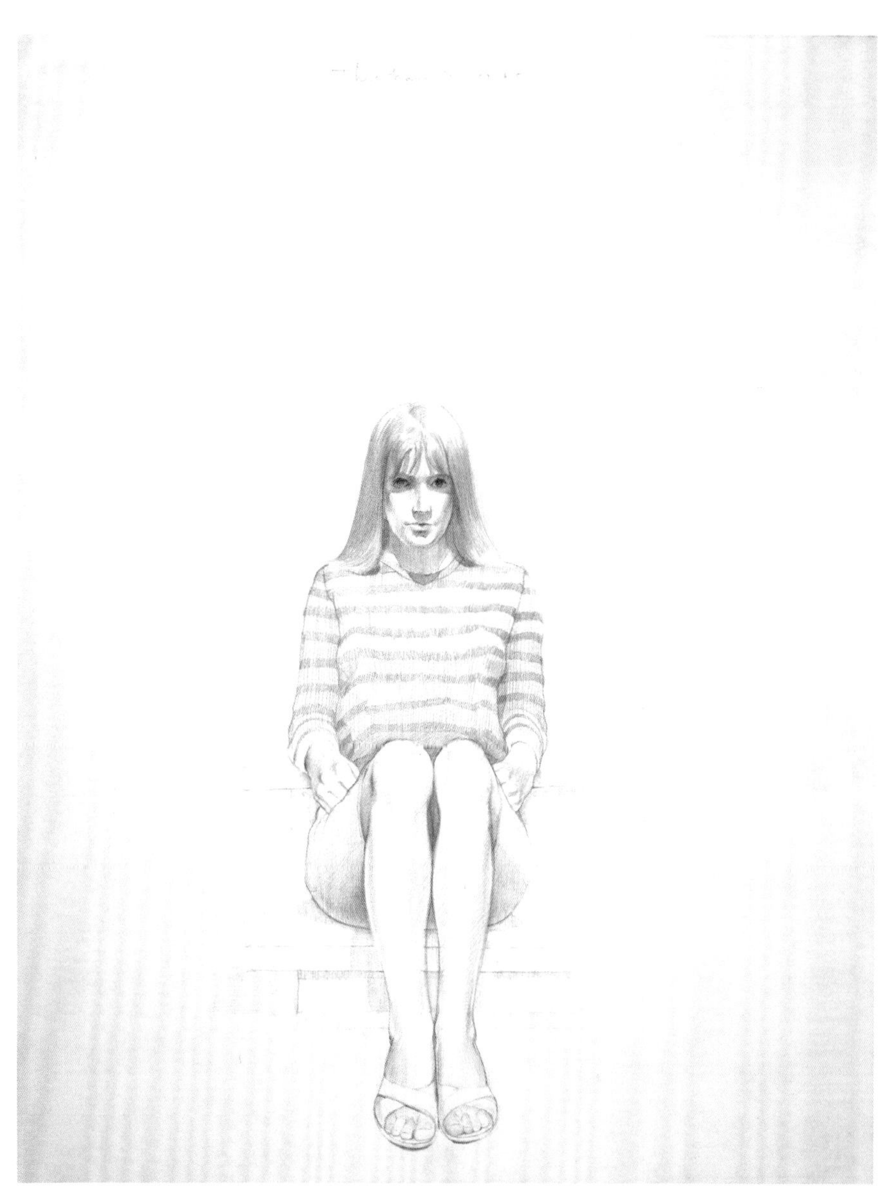

32. **MALLARY ANN**, 1966
Graphite
17 × 14 inches (43.2 × 35.6 cm)
Allan Stone Collection, courtesy Allan Stone Projects, NY

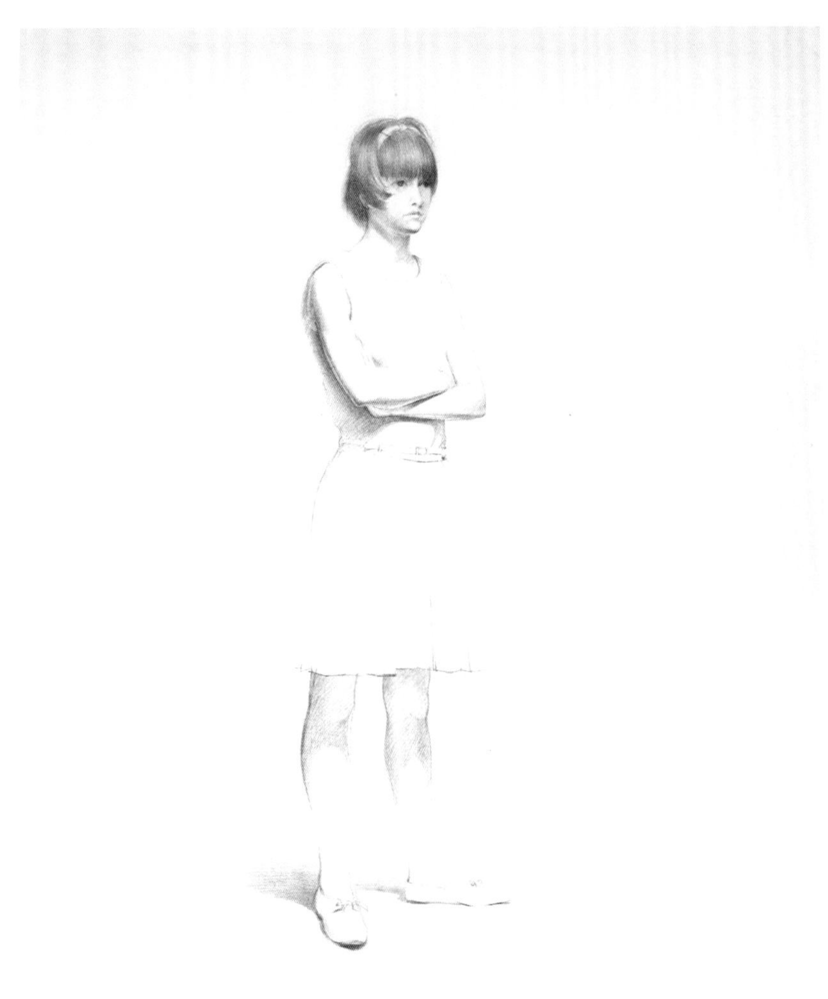

33. **TENNIS GIRL**, 1967
Graphite
9 × 7½ inches (22.9 × 19 cm)
Thiebaud Family Collection

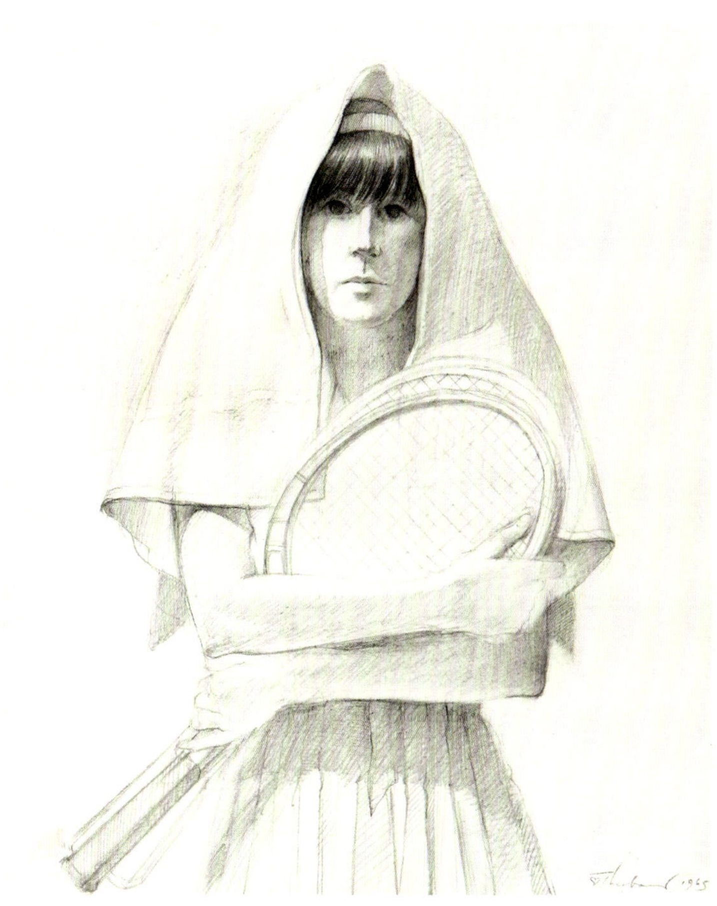

34. **DOG**, 1967
Graphite
9⅛ × 7⅛ inches (23.2 × 18.1 cm)
Private collection

35. **SPECTACLES AND BEE STILL LIFE**, 1971
Charcoal
30 × 22¼ inches (76.2 × 56.5 cm)
Collection of Alan and Ellen Meckler

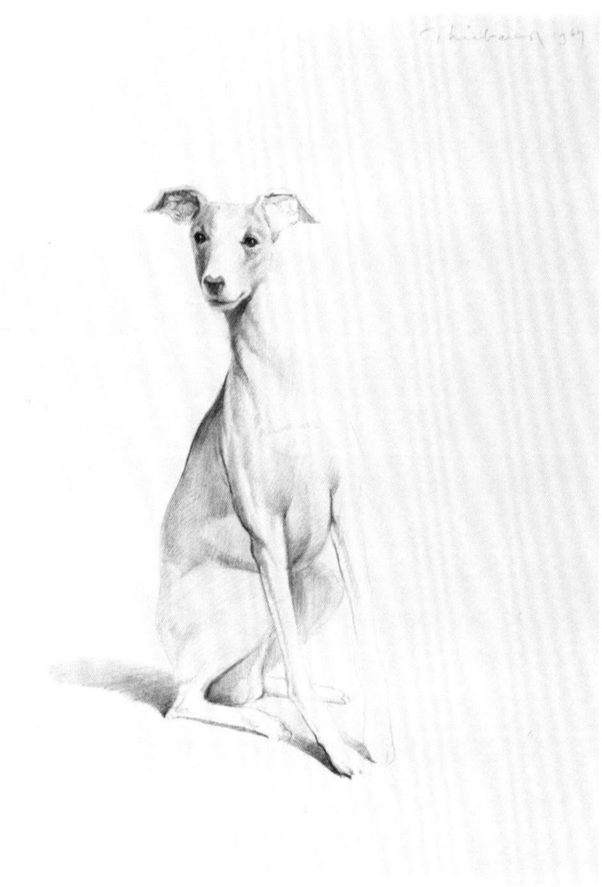

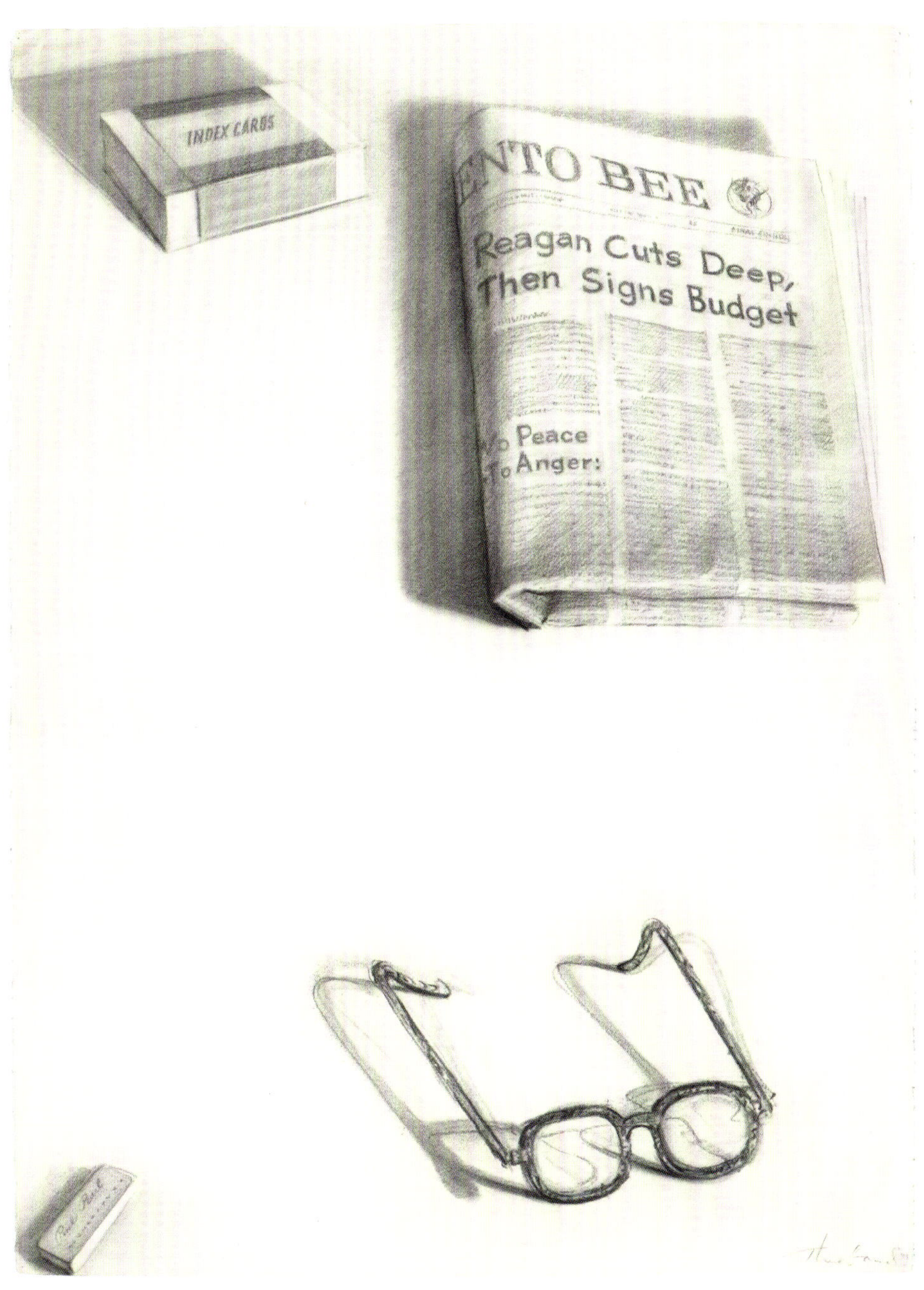

INDEX CARDS
ENTO BEE
Reagan Cuts Deep,
Then Signs Budget
Peace
To Anger:

36. **TOYS**, 1971
    Charcoal
    22¼ × 29¾ inches (56.5 × 75.6 cm)
    From the artist's studio

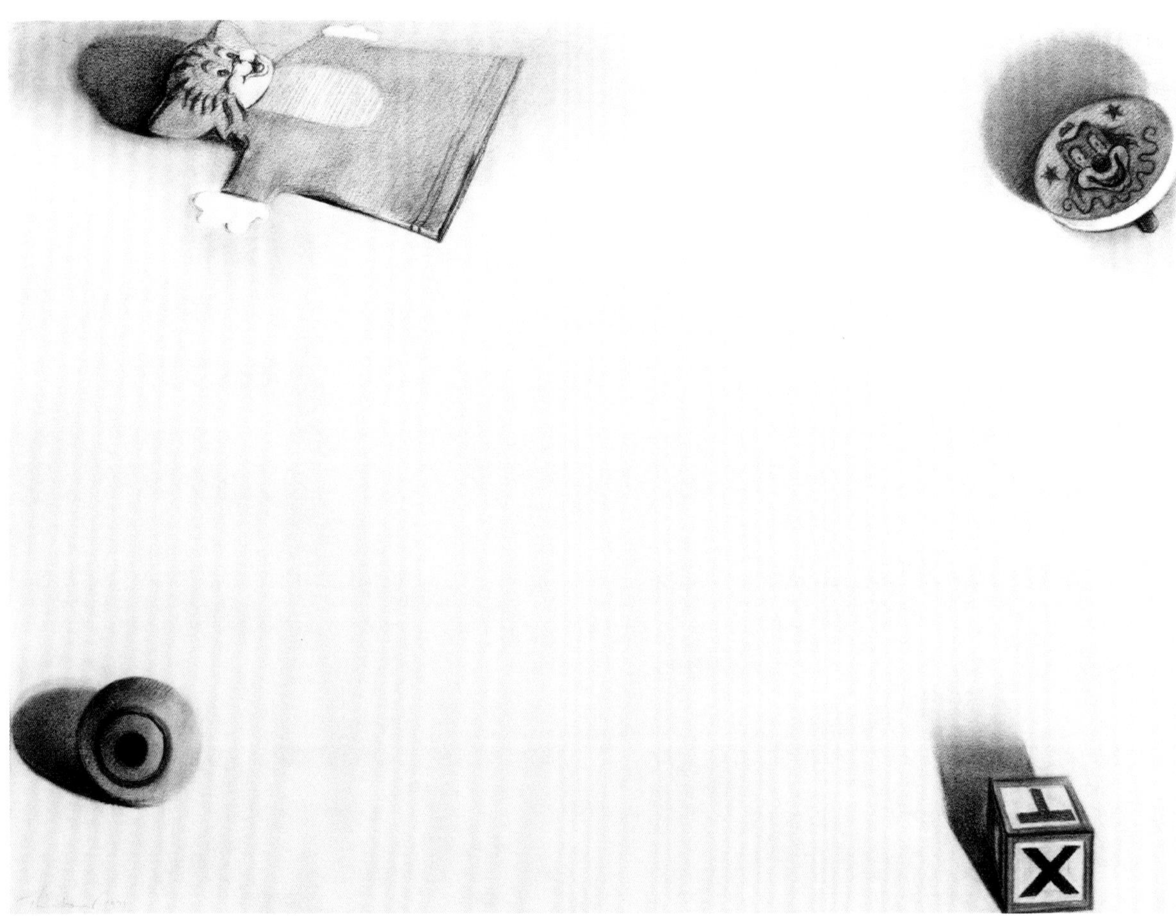

   WAYNE THIEBAUD DRAFTSMAN

 RADIO STILL LIFE, 1971–73
    Charcoal
    22 × 30 inches (55.9 × 76.2 cm)
    From the artist's studio

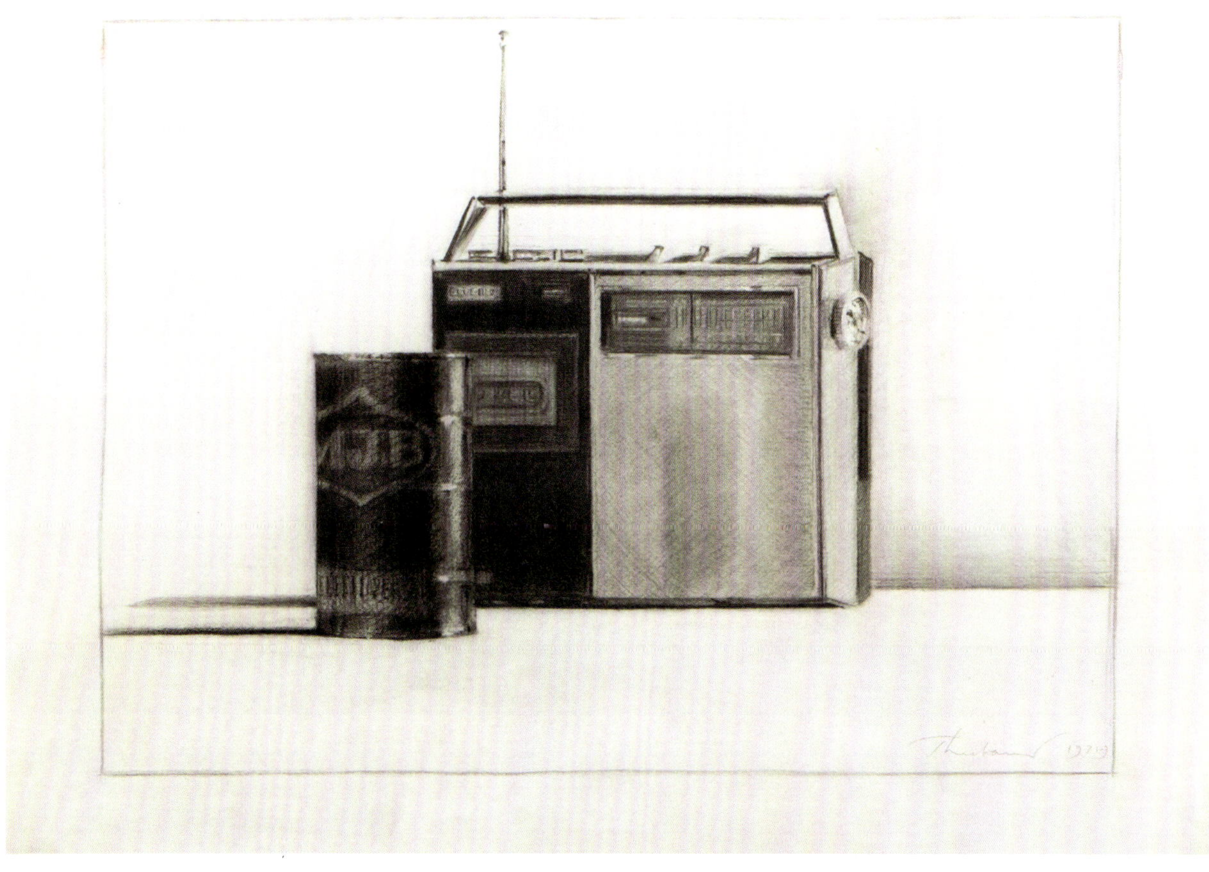

38. **CONDIMENTS**, 1972
Pastel
16 × 22¼ inches (40.6 × 56.5 cm)
Collection of Alan and Ellen Meckler

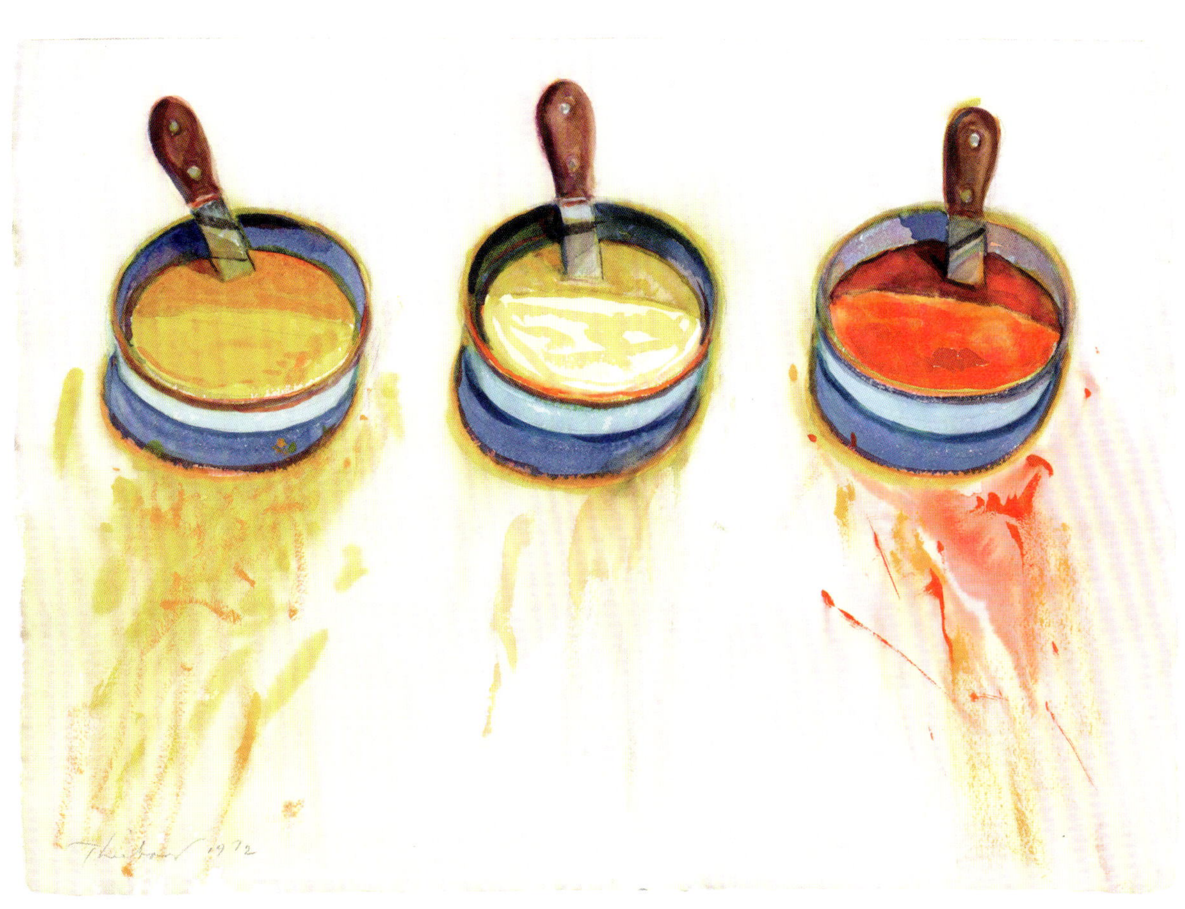

 SELF-PORTRAIT, ca. 1970
Graphite
9 × 11¼ inches (22.9 × 28.6 cm)
From the artist's studio

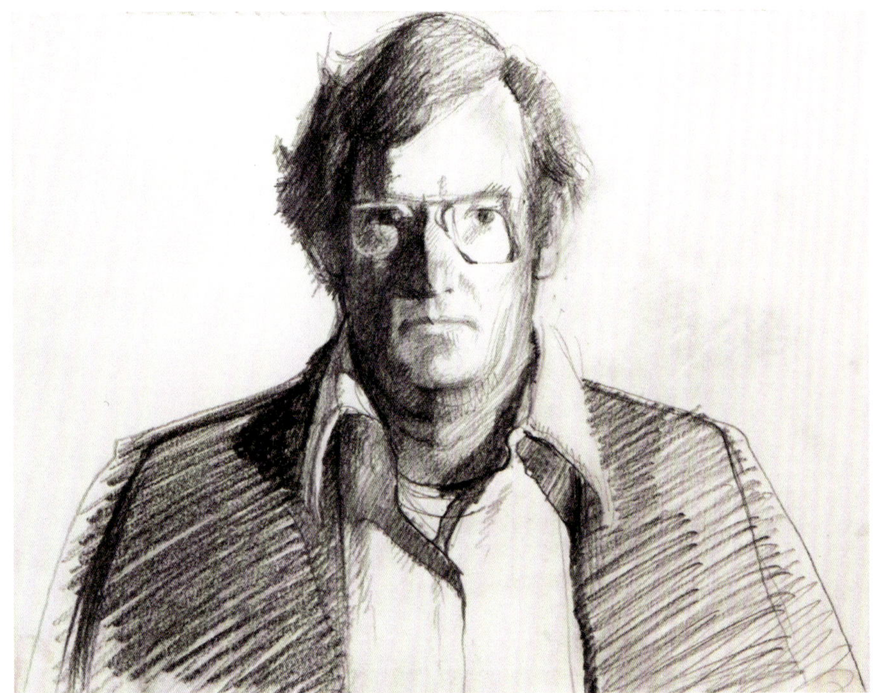

40. **PASTEL SCATTER**, 1972
Pastel
16 × 20⅛ inches (40.6 × 51.1 cm)
Thiebaud Family Collection

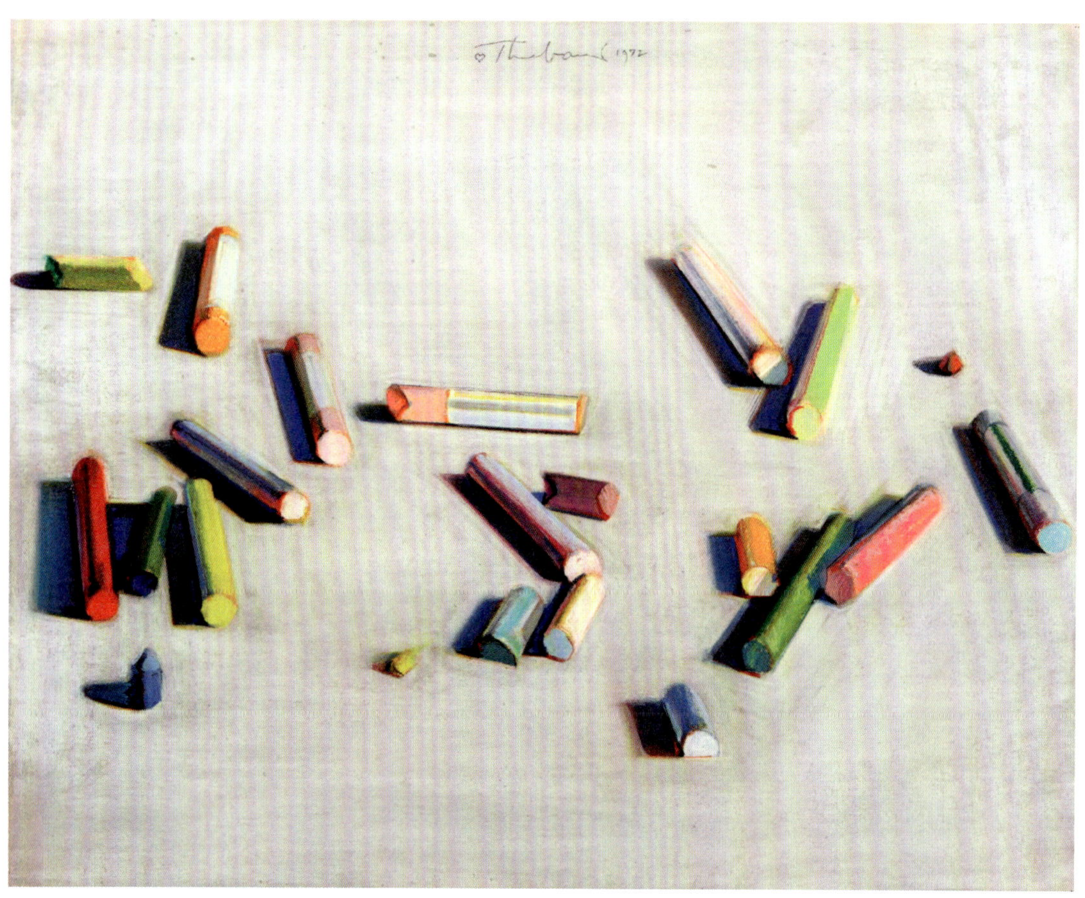

41. **ROCK RIDGE**, 1972
Pastel on illustration board
33 × 20 inches (83.8 × 50.8 cm)
Private collection

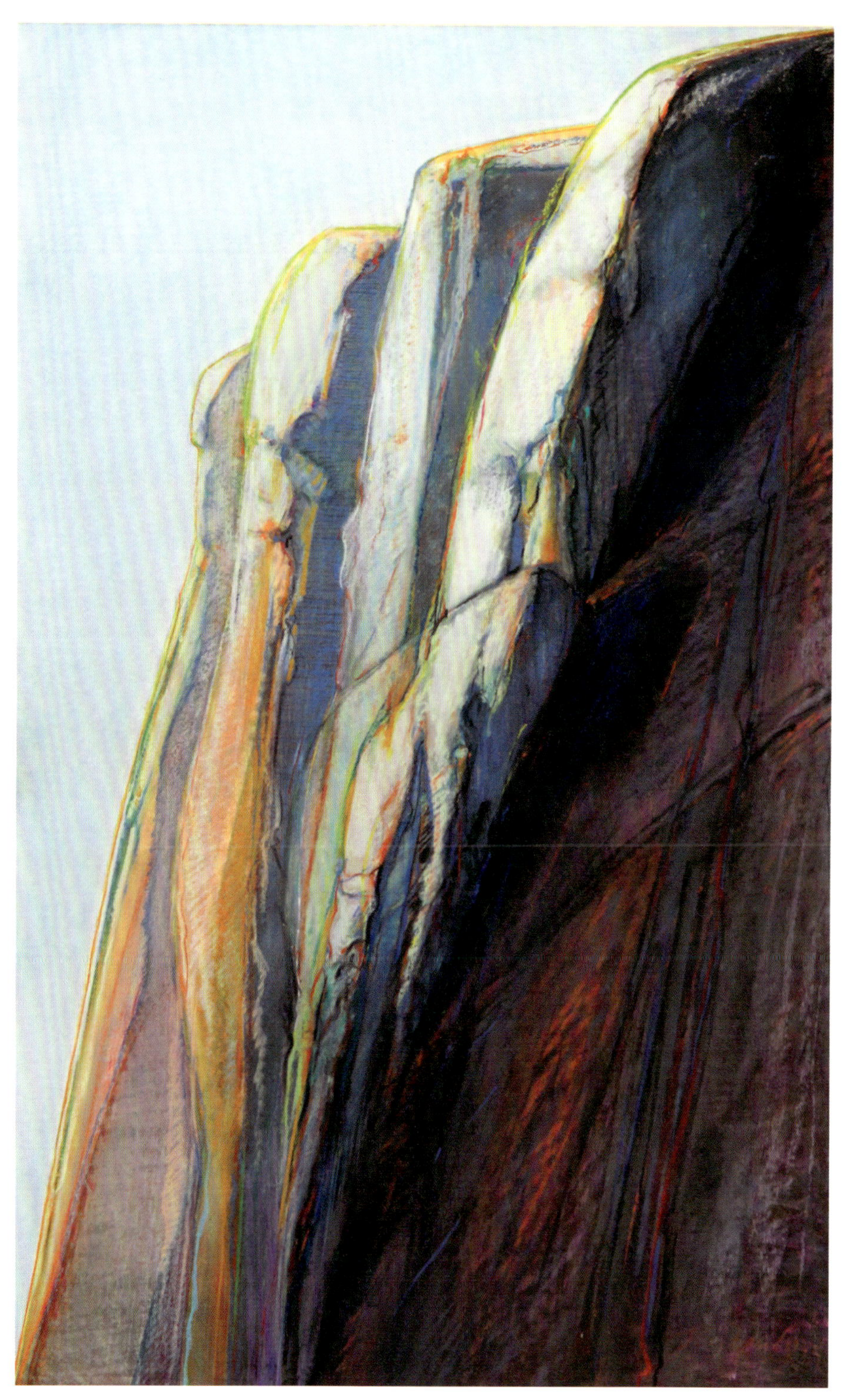

42. **CIRCLE OF FISH**, 1973
Pastel
8¾ × 14⅞ inches (22.2 × 37.8 cm)
The Putt-McCann Art Collection,
in memory of Charlie and Glenna Campbell

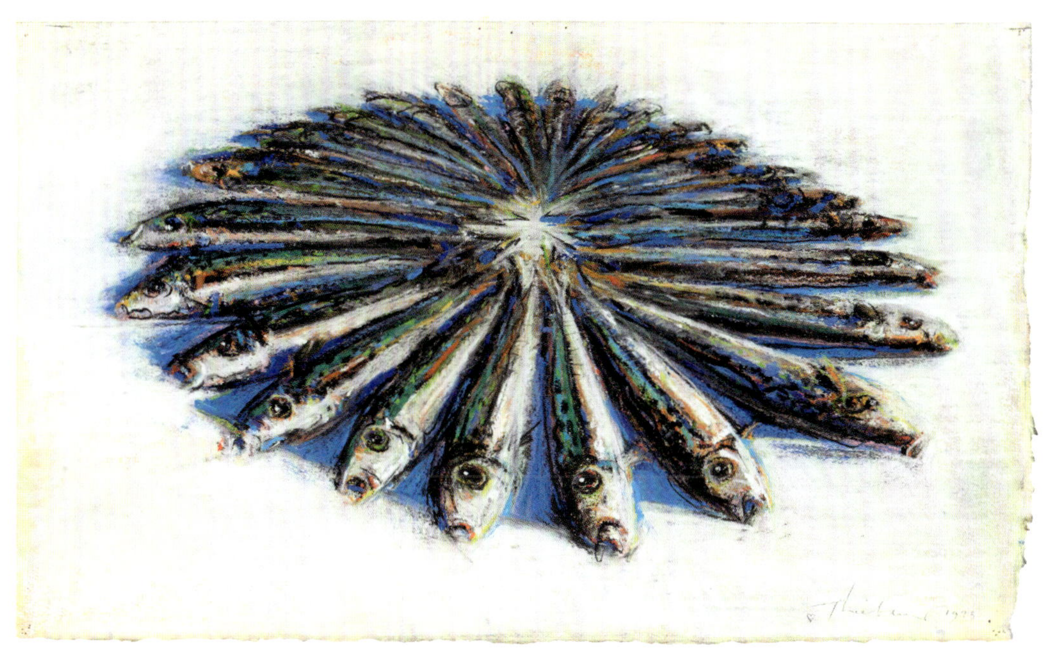

43. **UNTITLED (AFTER MORANDI)**, 1979
Graphite
11 × 8½ inches (27.9 × 21.6 cm)
From the artist's studio

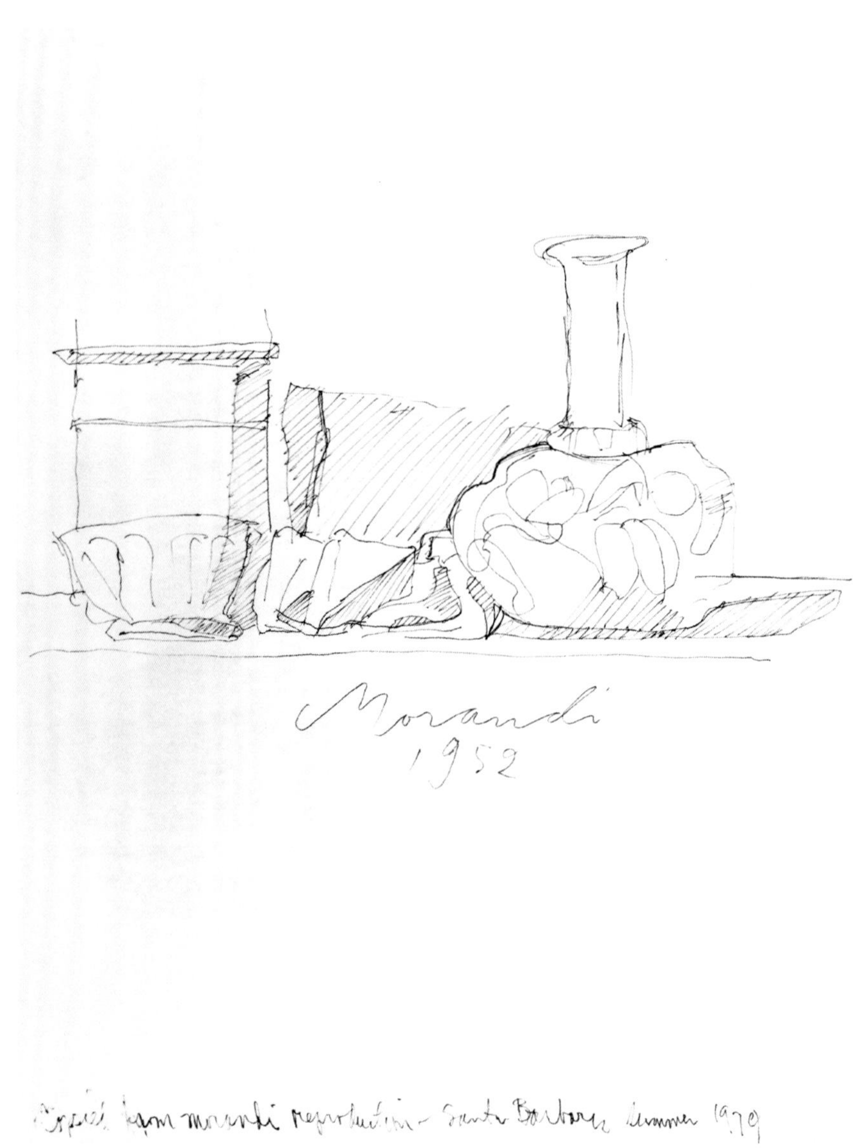

44. **UNTITLED (AFTER DAUMIER)**, 1975
Graphite
9 × 11 inches (22.9 × 27.9 cm)
From the artist's studio

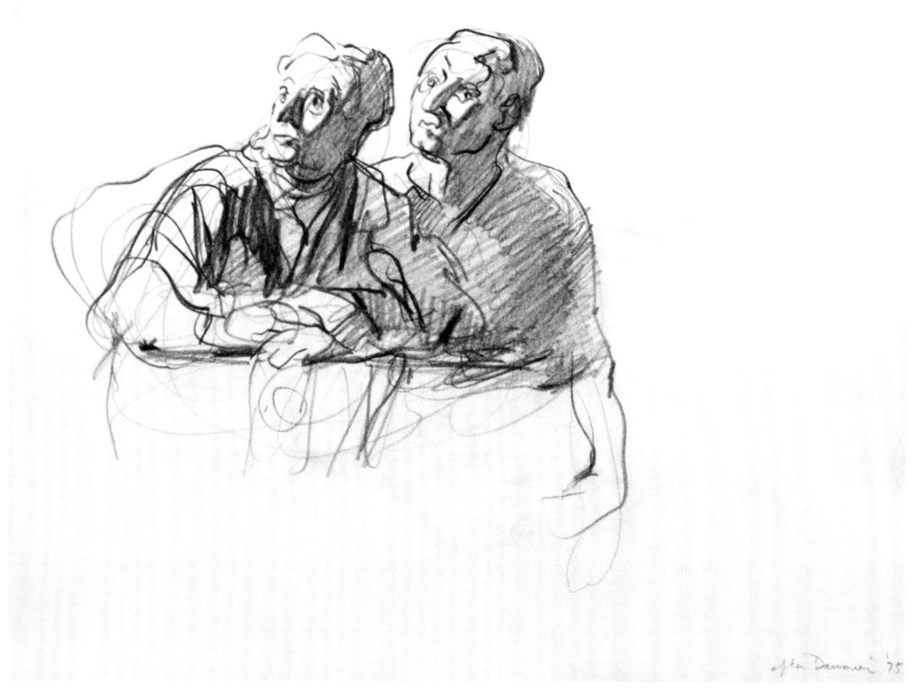

45. **PAGE OF SKETCHES
WITH STUDY FOR *CITYSCAPE***, 1970s
Graphite
11¼ × 8¾ inches (28.6 × 22.2 cm)
From the artist's studio

46. **CITYSCAPE**, 1970s
Graphite
15 × 11 inches (38.1 × 27.9 cm)
Private collection

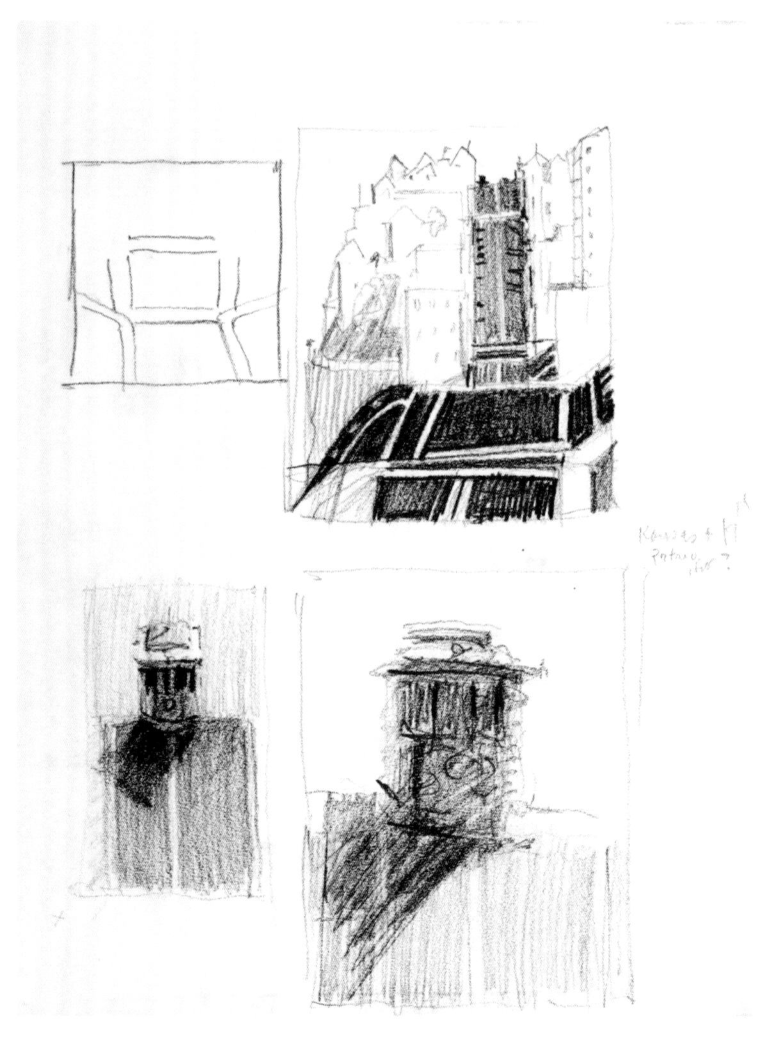

WAYNE THIEBAUD DRAFTSMAN

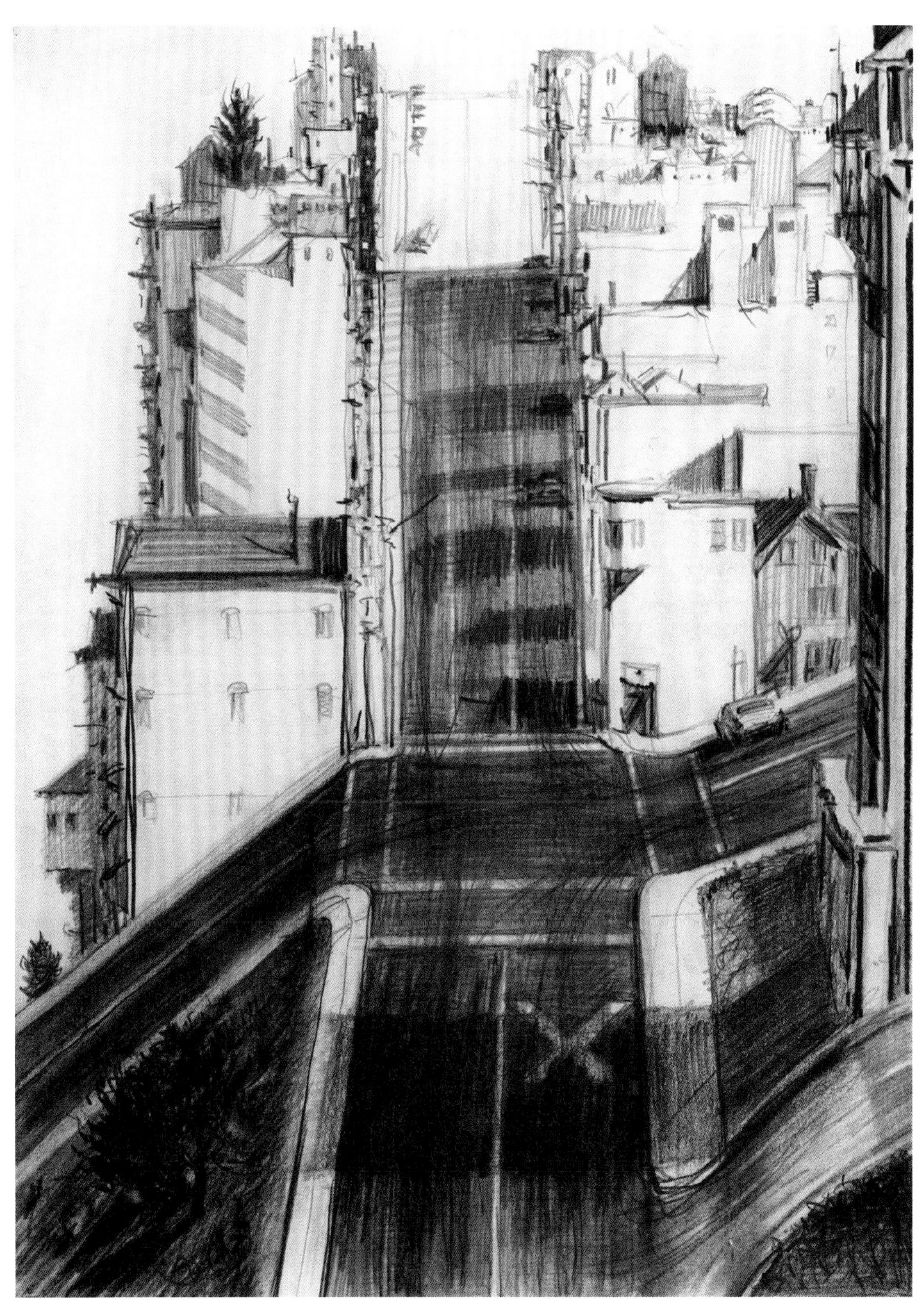

47. **UNTITLED (INTERSECTION)**, 1977–78
Graphite
16 × 20 inches (40.6 × 50.8 cm)
Allan Stone Collection, courtesy Allan Stone Projects, NY

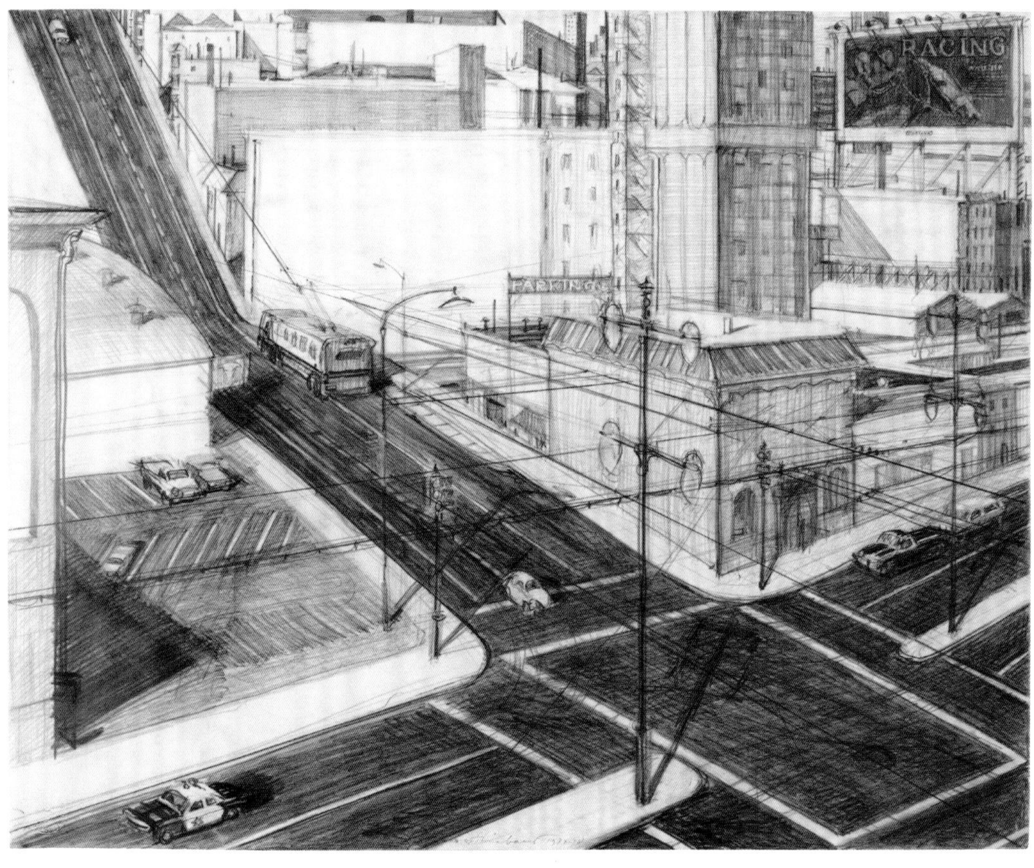

48. **DIAGONAL CITY**, 1978
   Graphite
   23¼ × 29⅛ inches (59.1 × 74 cm)
   Collection of Harry W. and Mary Margaret Anderson

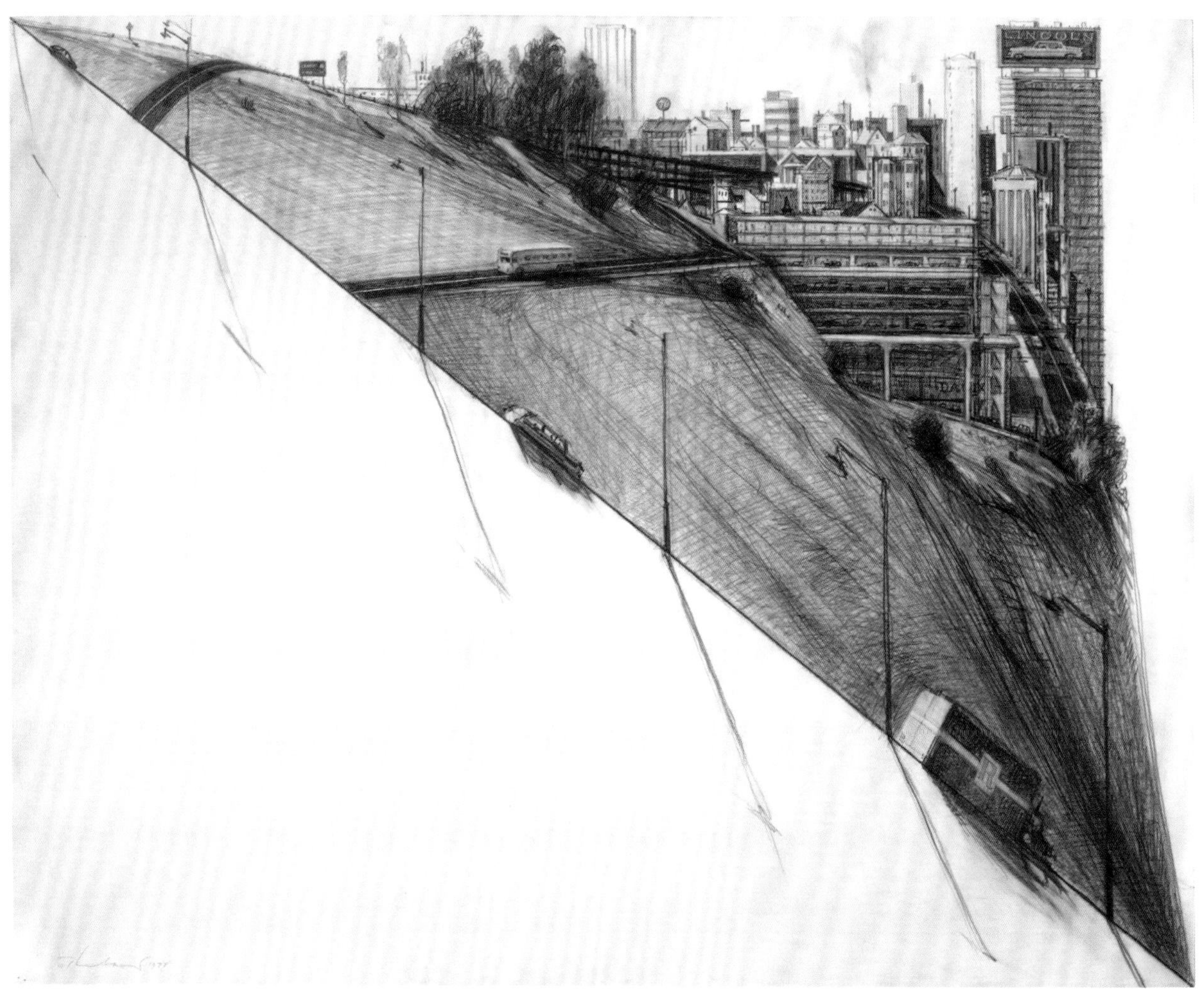

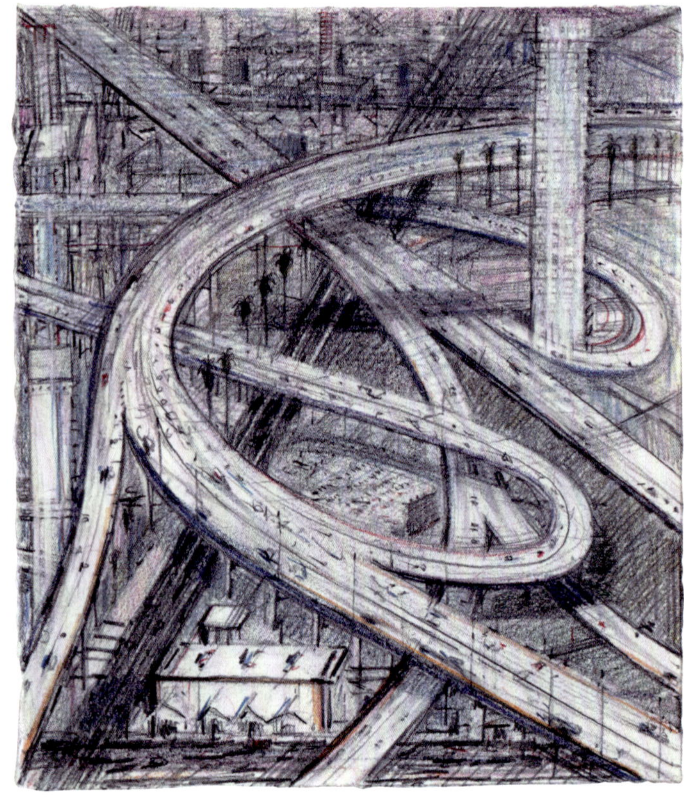

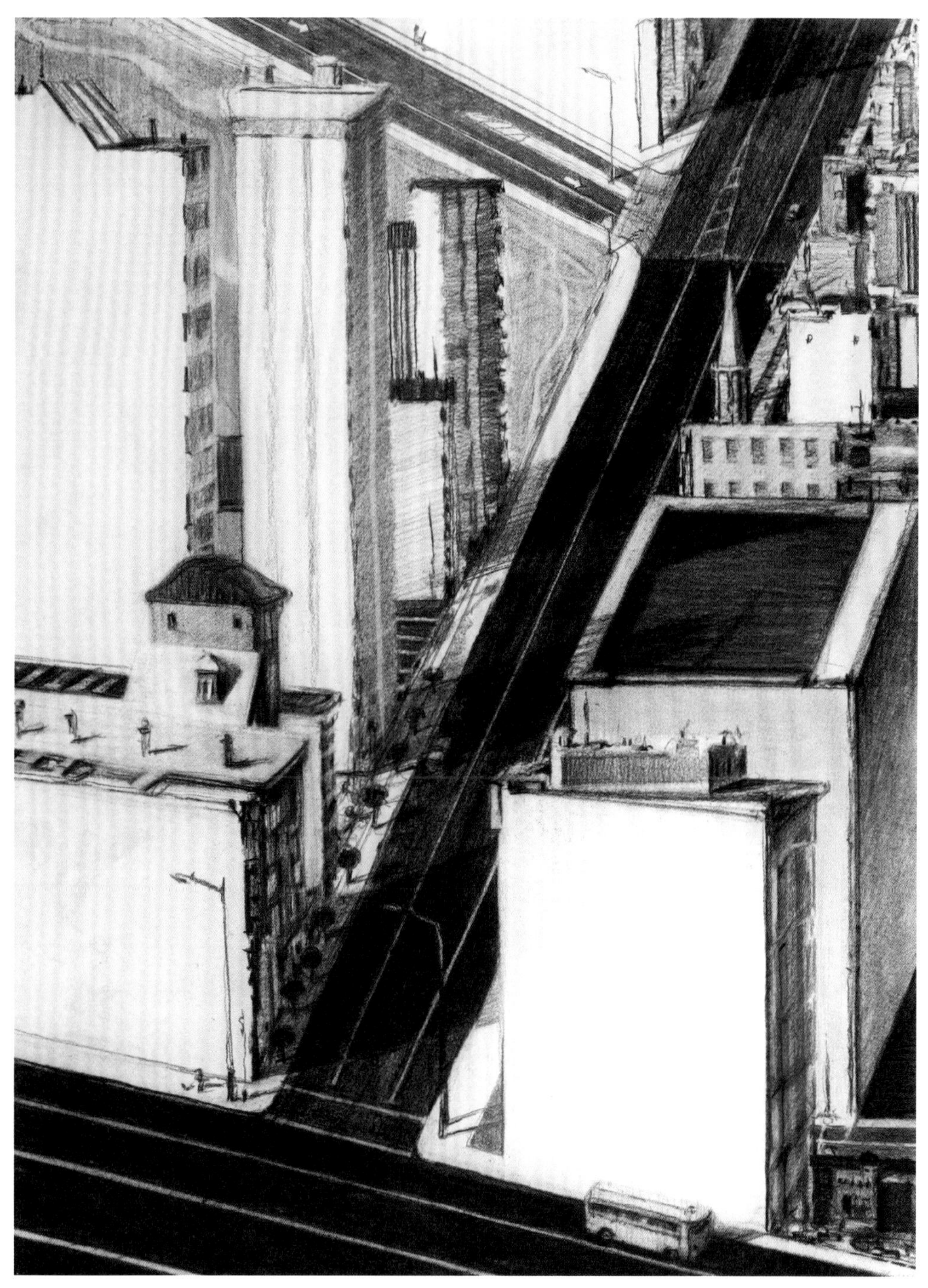

51. **PAGE OF SKETCHES WITH
CITYSCAPE AND FIGURES**, 1970s
Graphite
11¼ × 8½ inches (28.6 × 21.6 cm)
From the artist's studio

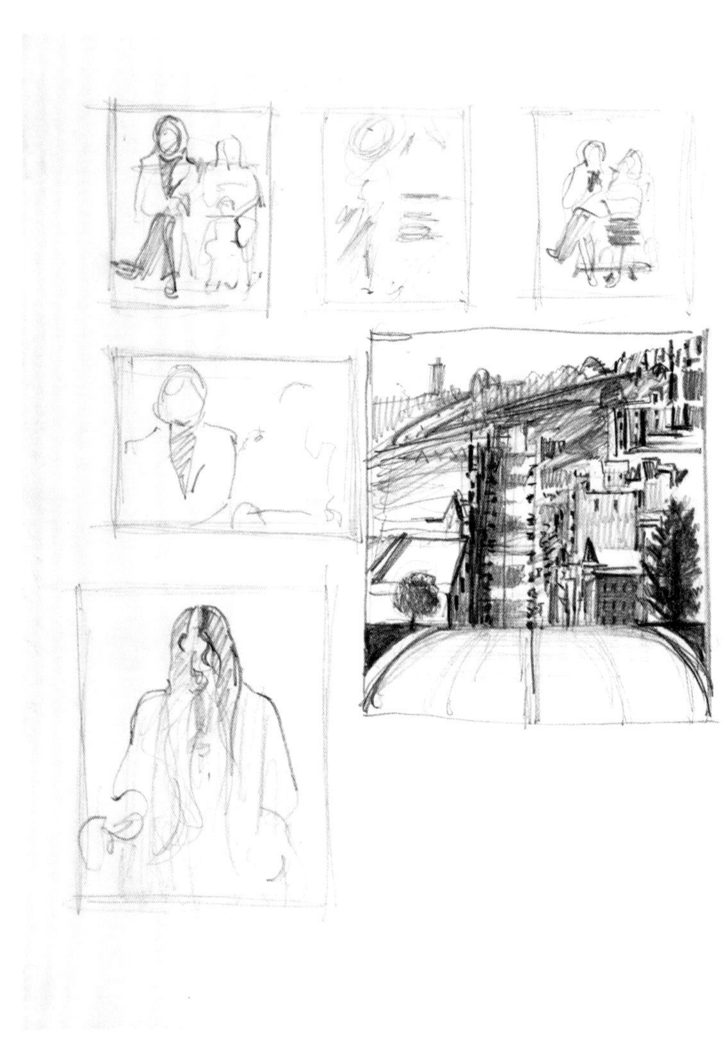

52. **LIGHTED CITY**, 1986
Watercolor
11½ × 9 inches (29.2 × 22.9 cm)
Private collection

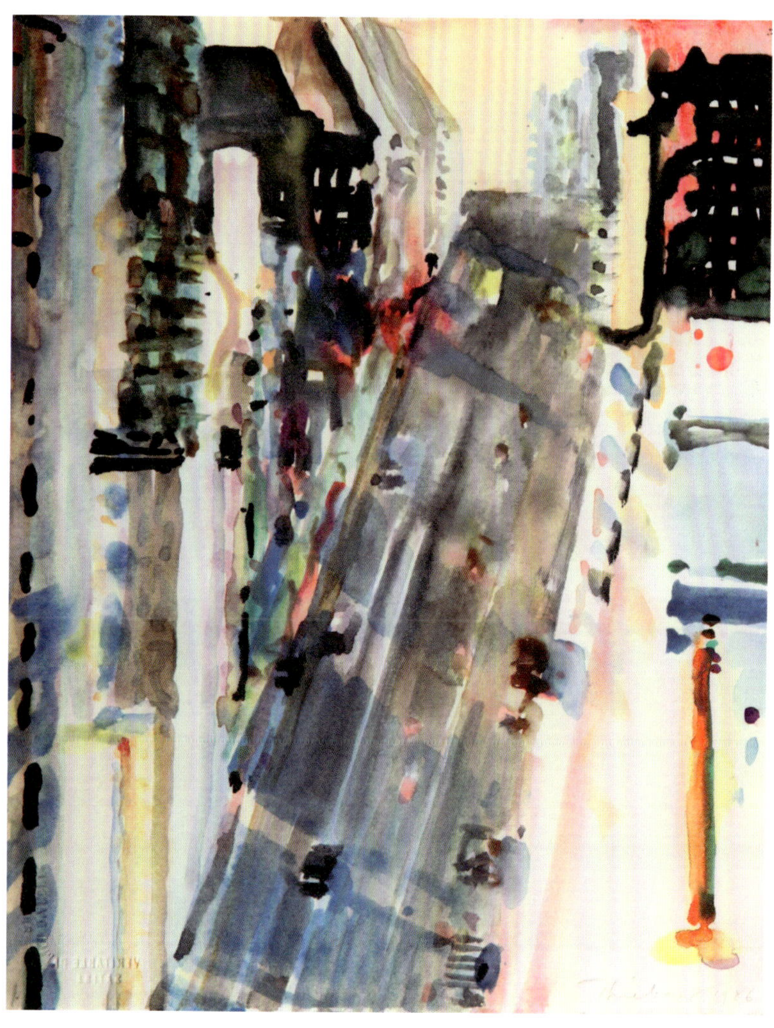

53. **STUDY FOR A CITYSCAPE**, 1970s–80s
Graphite
11⅛ × 8¾ inches (28.3 × 22.2 cm)
From the artist's studio

54. **WIDE DOWNSTREET**, 2001
Pastel
30 × 22½ inches (76.2 × 57.2 cm)
Private collection, courtesy Acquavella Galleries

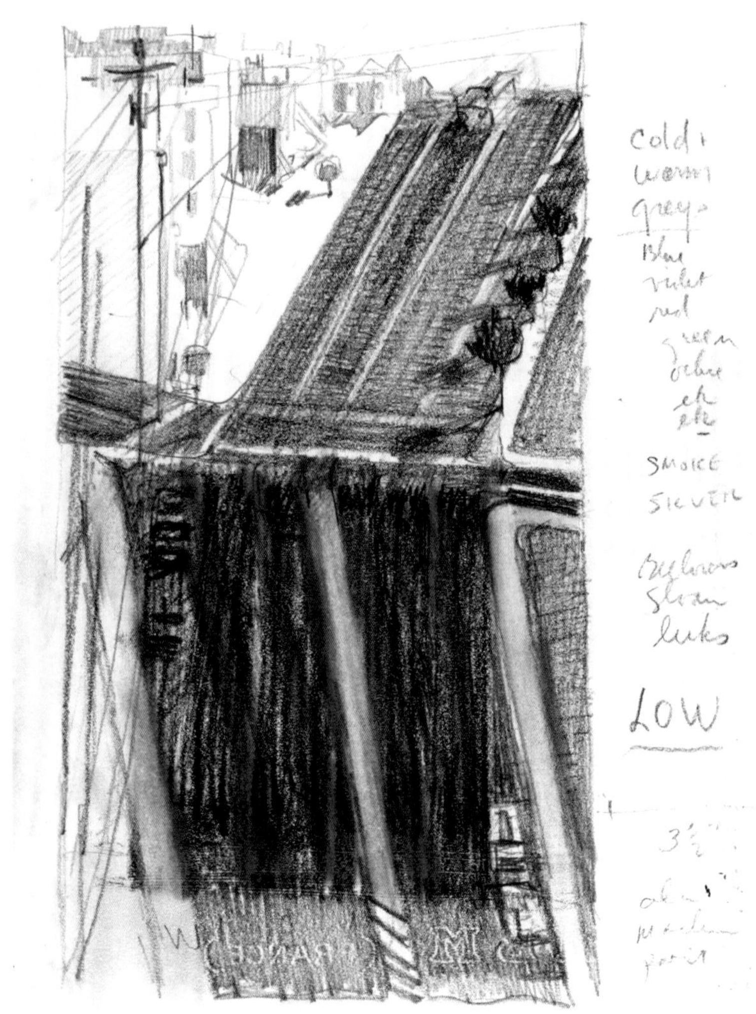

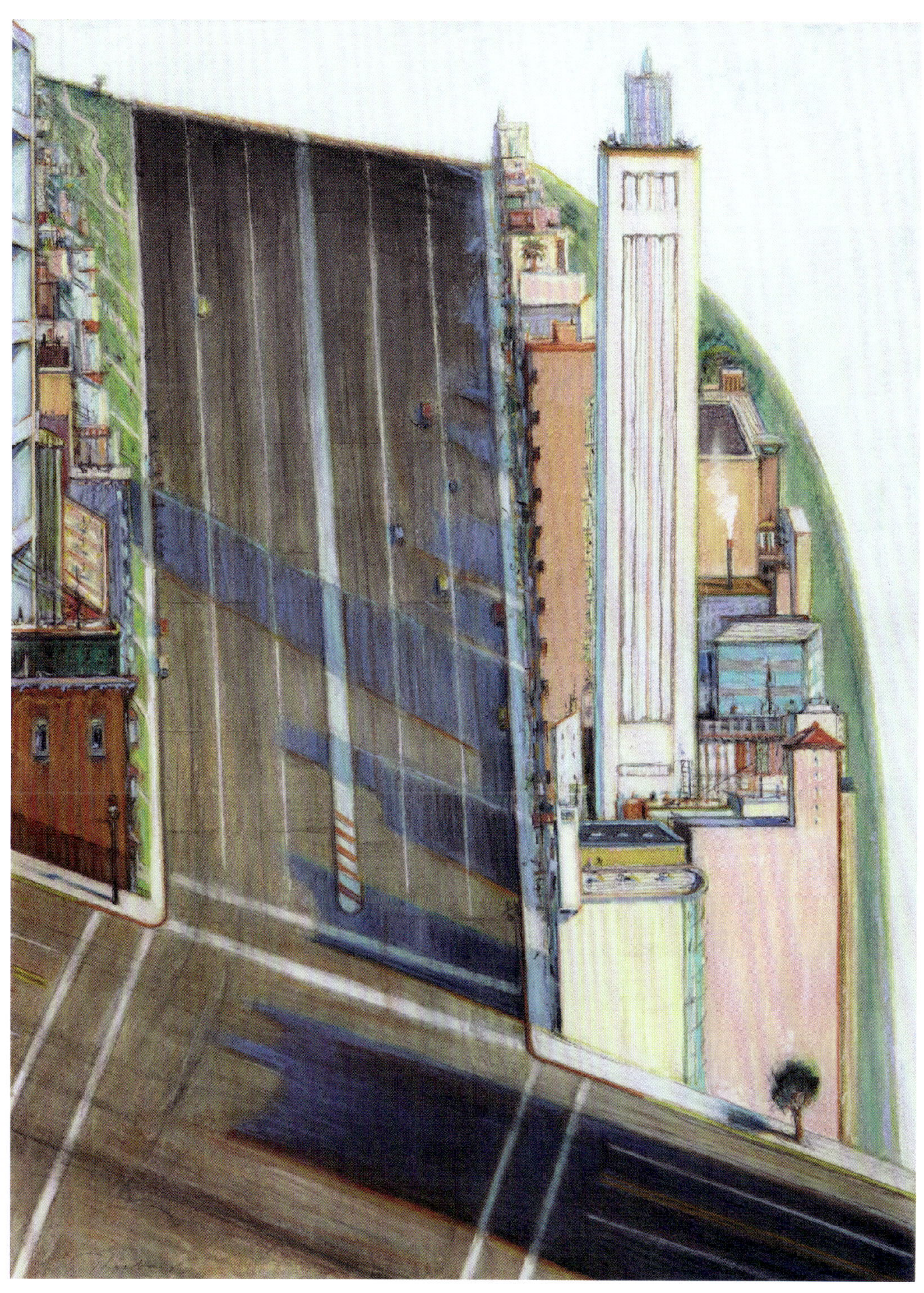

55. **CANDY BALL MACHINE**, 1977
Gouache and pastel
23¾ × 17¾ inches (60.3 × 45.1 cm)
Collection of Gretchen and John Berggruen,
San Francisco

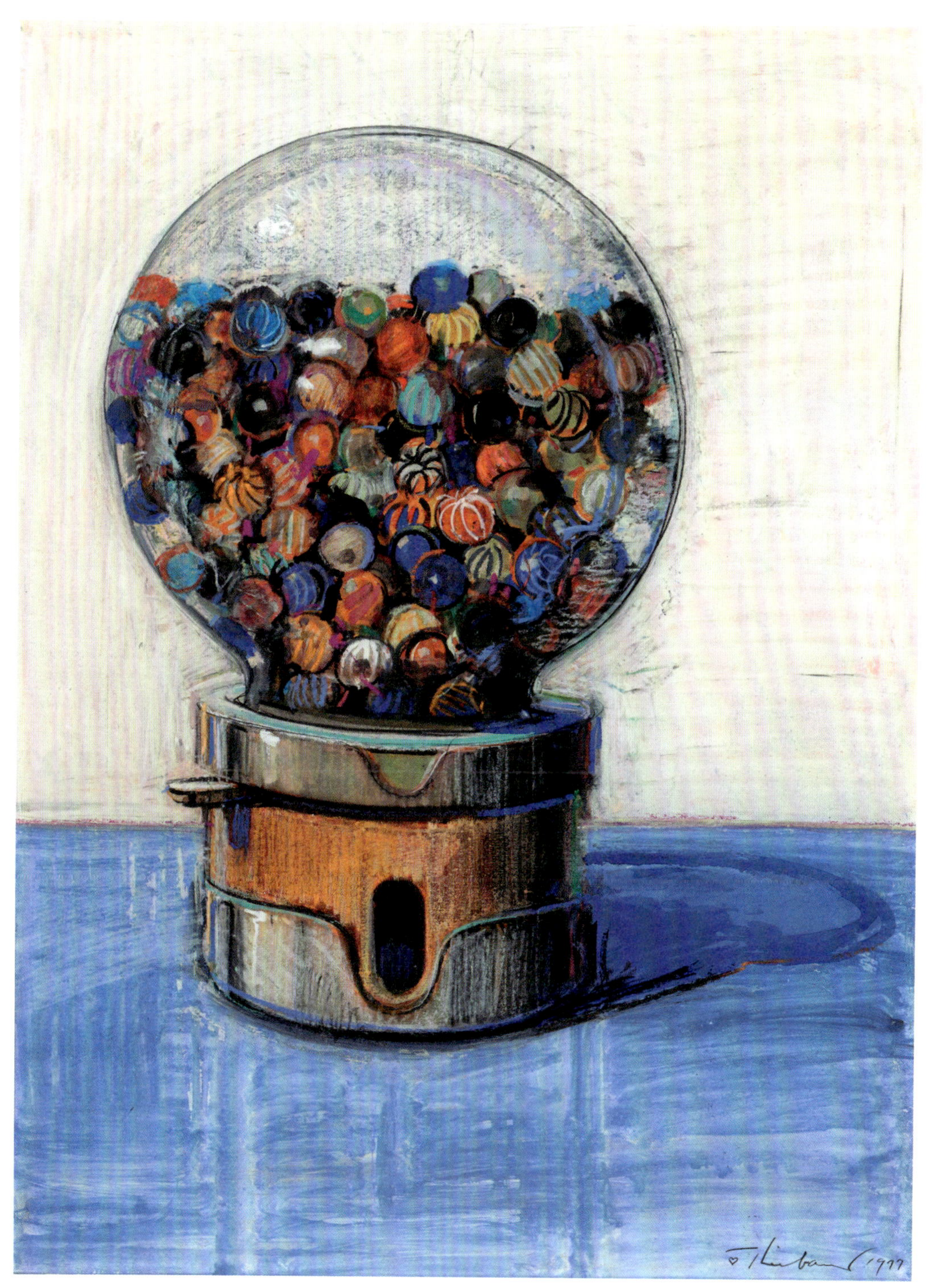

56. **FOUR CUPCAKES**, 1988
Watercolor and charcoal
8⅛ × 11½ inches (20.6 × 29.2 cm)
Thiebaud Family Collection

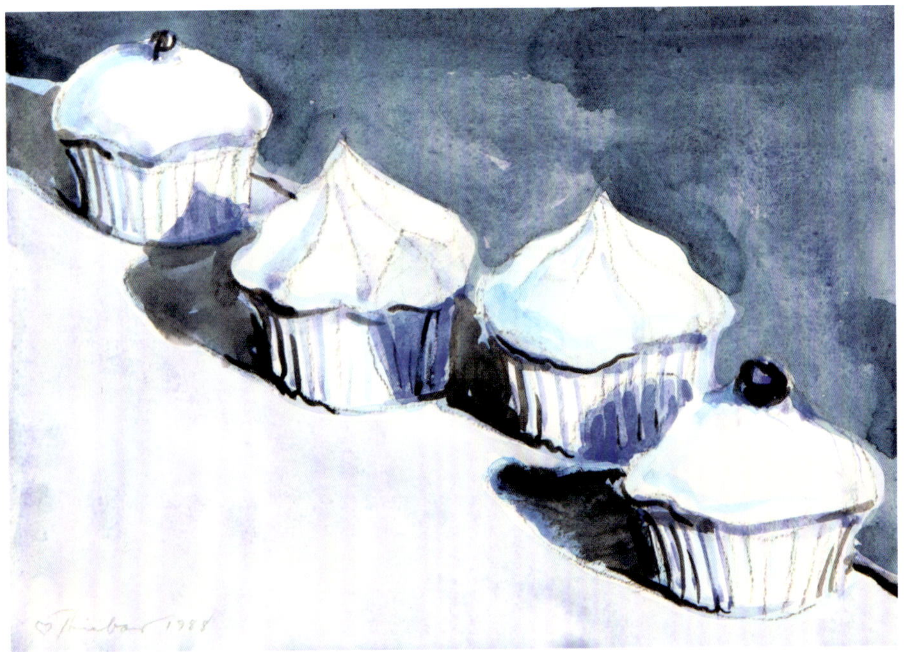

57. **SALT SHAKER**, 1979
   Watercolor and pastel
   7¾ × 7¾ inches (19.7 × 19.7 cm)
   Thiebaud Family Collection

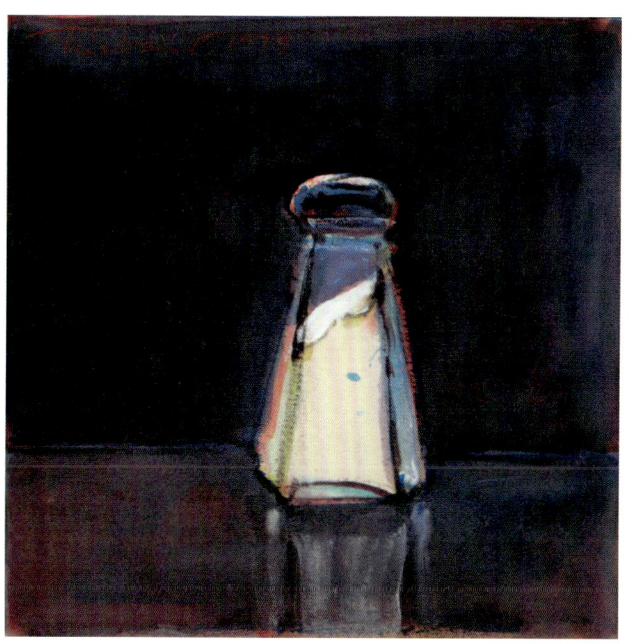

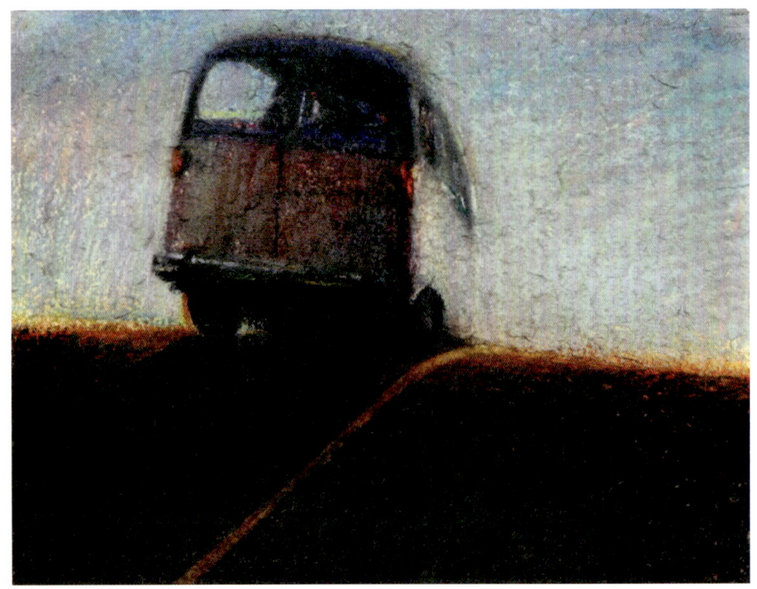

59. **UNTITLED (RECLINING NUDE)**, 1982
Pastel
30½ × 40 inches (77.5 × 101.6 cm)
From the artist's studio

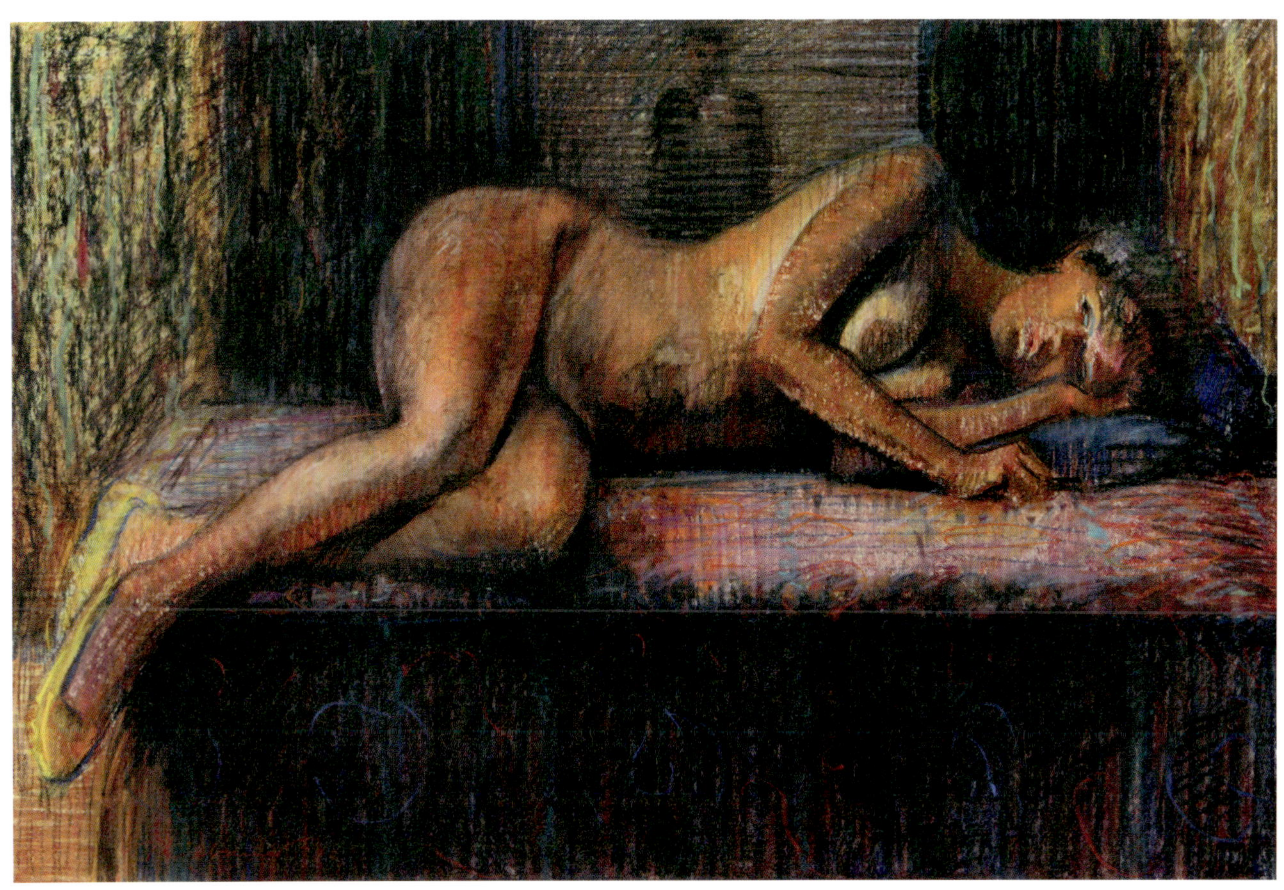

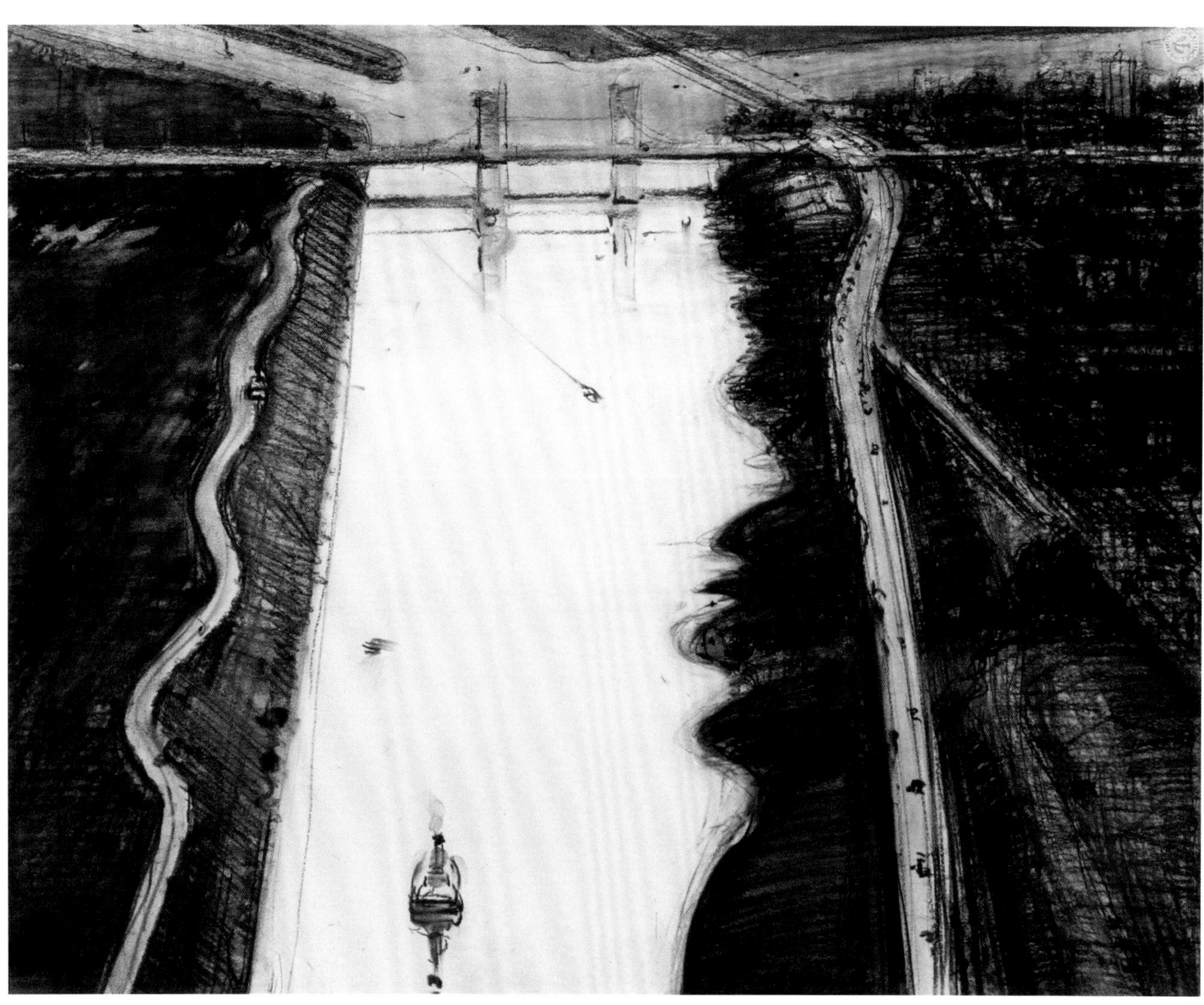

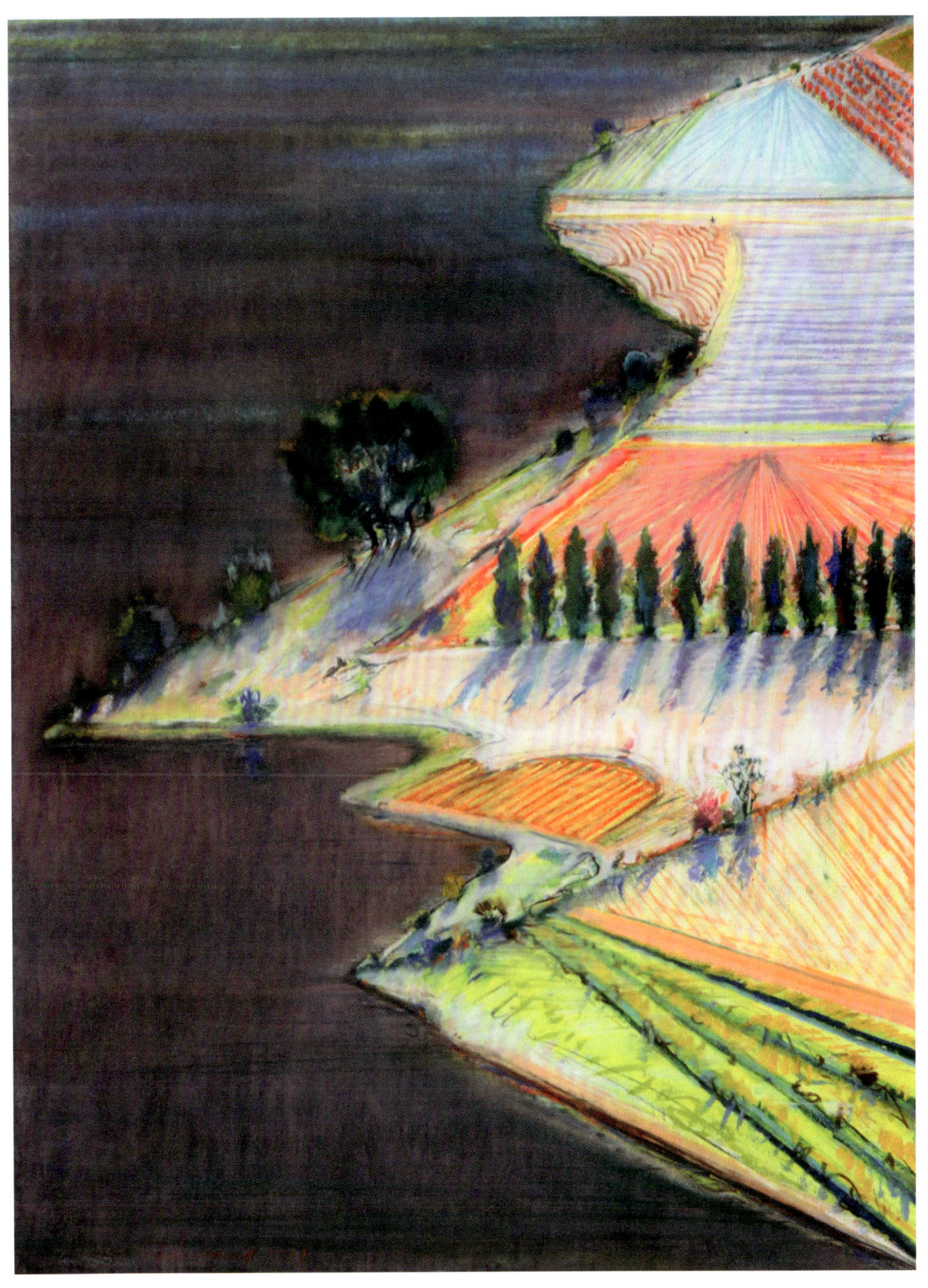

62. **PAGE OF SKETCHES WITH
RIVER SCENES AND UPSIDE-DOWN
ICE CREAM CONES**, ca. 2002
Pen and ink and pastel
11 × 14¼ inches (27.9 × 36.2 cm)
From the artist's studio

63. **STUDY FOR *BROWN RIVER***, 2002
Charcoal
23½ × 18 inches (59.7 × 45.7 cm)
From the artist's studio

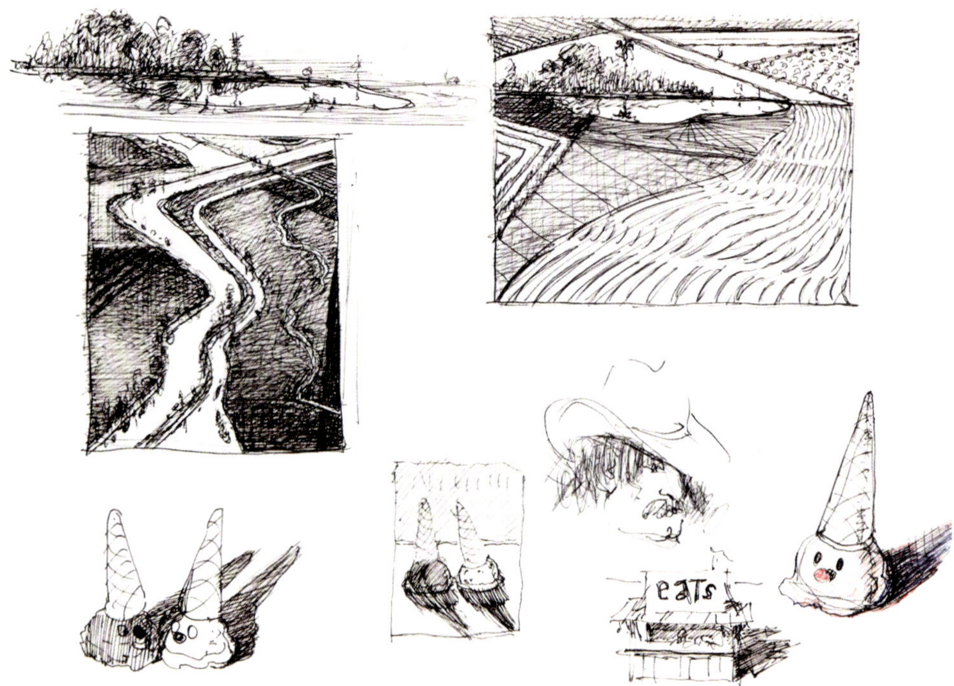

WAYNE THIEBAUD DRAFTSMAN

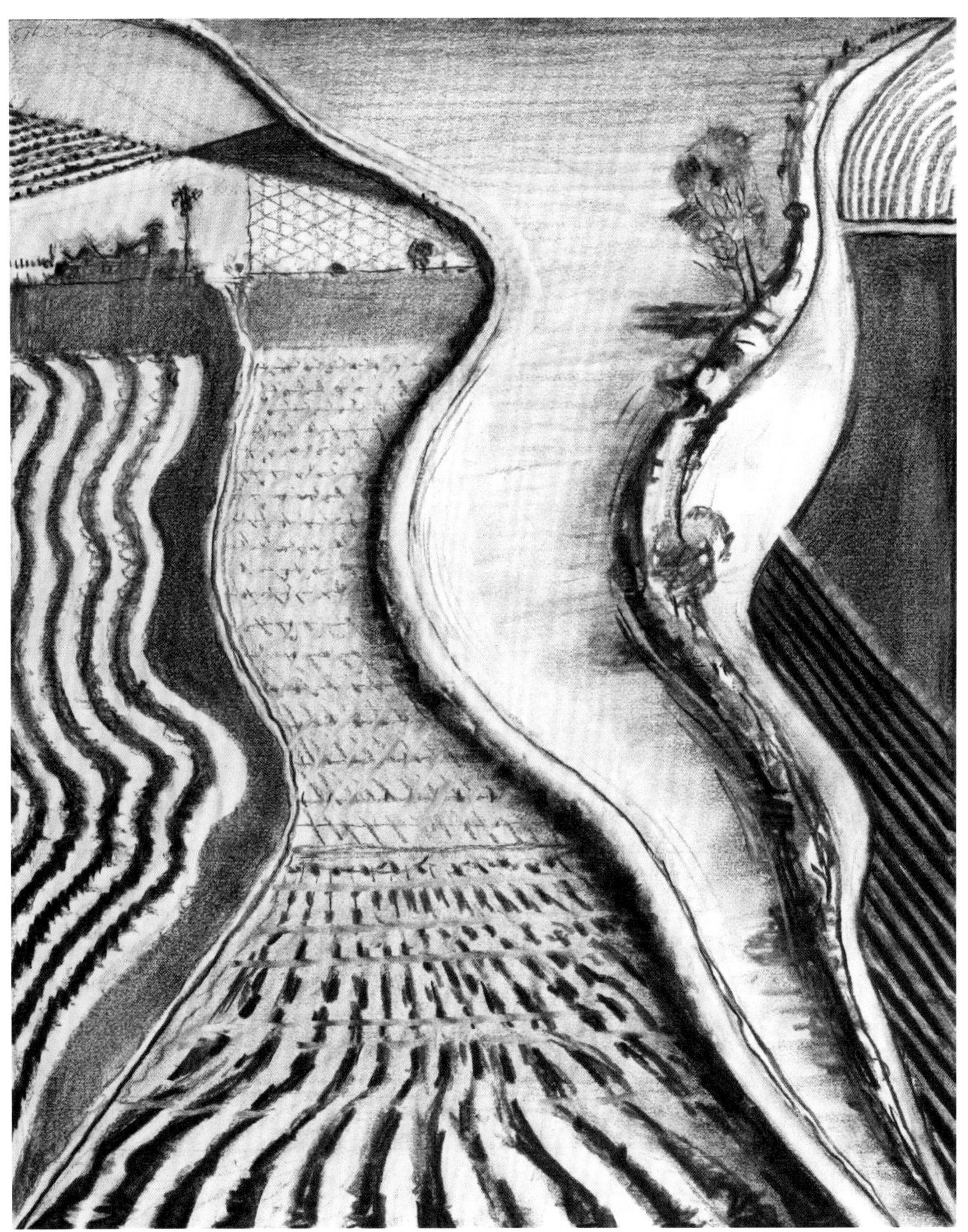

Thumbnails and Notations

Thiebaud's Sketches

"There is, in my view," Wayne Thiebaud declared, "a terrific difference in attitude between what are, in effect, called public drawings and private drawings." The difference, he explained, is primarily one of function. Private drawings are intended "to find out something, to make notations, or just to experiment. You want to feel . . . that these are things that will never be seen, as opposed to public drawings."[1] Such a distinction harks back to the practice of drawing widespread in artists' workshops from the sixteenth to the nineteenth centuries. Artists traditionally separated preparatory sketches, which they kept for themselves, from finished drawings, which they exhibited and sold to collectors and patrons. Although the categories have largely lost their relevance in the twentieth century, when the cult of spontaneity and raw expression, together with changes in studio practices, have blunted the distinction, Thiebaud is faithful to tradition. His sketches form a body of work separate from his other drawings. Whether done as part of a daily exercise— like a pianist practicing scales—or to jot down ideas for paintings, they represent an essential aspect of his activity as a draftsman and highlight the importance of drawing in his process.

Most of Thiebaud's sketches are done on loose sheets gathered in a leather spring-back binder or fastened to a clipboard (Fig. 1). The method allows him to use different kinds of paper depending on the medium—often pen and ink, but also pencil, pastel, watercolor, and even oil. The sheets measure on average 8½ × 11 or 11 × 14 inches and usually contain a multiplicity of small sketches, lined up in rows. Some are devoted to a single theme—ties on a rack, for instance, or cityscapes (Nos. 66 and 76)—but in many cases, studies of different subjects are drawn side by side. Thus a cake display can be found between a hat shop window and a hilly landscape (No. 73). Unsuspected echoes—both formal and iconographic—spring from such juxtapositions, contributing to the charm and attraction of these sheets.

Thiebaud makes sketches primarily to generate ideas for paintings and try
out compositional schemes. "You decide what the parameters are going to
be and then you try a series of shapes and patterns; then you try another
one. You might make ten or fifteen of these, thinking, 'Well, I'll make the
trees bigger here, something smaller here, change the patterns here.'
So you're in a sense sort of probing and thinking, doing research on what
might prove to be useful."[2] Following a classification proposed by art
historian Lizzie Boubli for Italian drawings, one can distinguish among
Thiebaud's sketches "variants of disposition," when a sheet includes different
compositions on a theme—an assortment of paint cans, or a figure standing
in front of a shop window (Nos. 78 and 73)—from "progressive variants,"
when the artist focuses on a single composition, experimenting with slight
modifications and adjustments, as in studies for two rows of pastries or a
cloud over a bluff (Nos. 64 and 71).[3]

Compositional sketches belong to an established genre in the history of
drawing. Sheets of studies, on which artists juxtapose several variants of the
same motif, abound among old-master drawings. Occasionally a framing line
isolates them. Most often, however, the artist uses the space of the sheet
with great freedom, scattering a flurry of figures of various scale in multiple
groupings. In these studies, the sheet becomes a conceptual field in which
figures float freely, jotted down with a total disregard for spatial logic.
Renaissance and Baroque Italian art offer many examples. Paolo Veronese,
for instance, produced a large number of compositional sketches in which
he developed his vision of a scene in an almost cinematographic manner,
multiplying the variants of the same subject or motif. The juxtaposition of
many figures on the same sheet could play a role in the process of inspiration
itself by suggesting potential groupings.[4] One of his drawings in the Morgan
collection presents three possible compositions for a painting of the *Finding
of Moses* together with a detail of drapery at center and a quick architectural
sketch in the upper corner (Fig. 2). Variations in the pose, gestures, and
interactions among the figures animate the sheet, in which the scenes are
unified by an effect of chiaroscuro. Another drawing, by the seventeenth-
century Florentine artist Baldassare Franceschini, contains eight studies of a
female martyr (Fig. 3). Here too, the variety of poses, with the head turned
either to the left or to the right, impart a sense of rhythm to the whole page.
A progression from one draft to another is marked by differences in the
degree of finish of each study, the occasional addition of brown ink on top of
the red chalk, and the presence or absence of a framing line. Although each
study is meant to be independent from the others, their juxtaposition on
the same sheet creates a dynamic composition in which they appear to be
responding to each other.

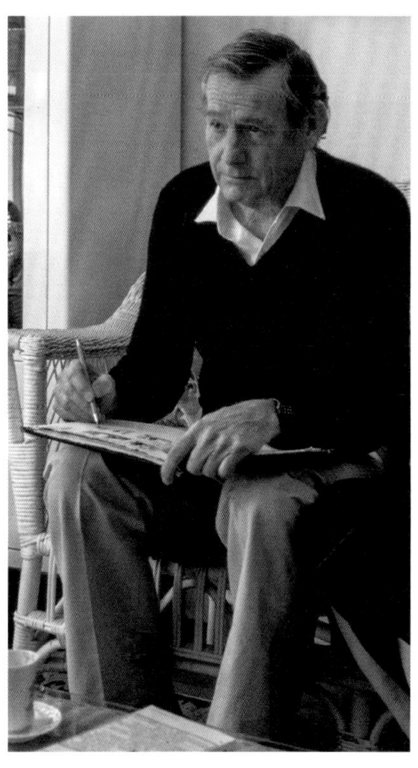

FIG. 1.
Thiebaud sketching, ca. 1982.
Photograph by Mary E. Nichols.

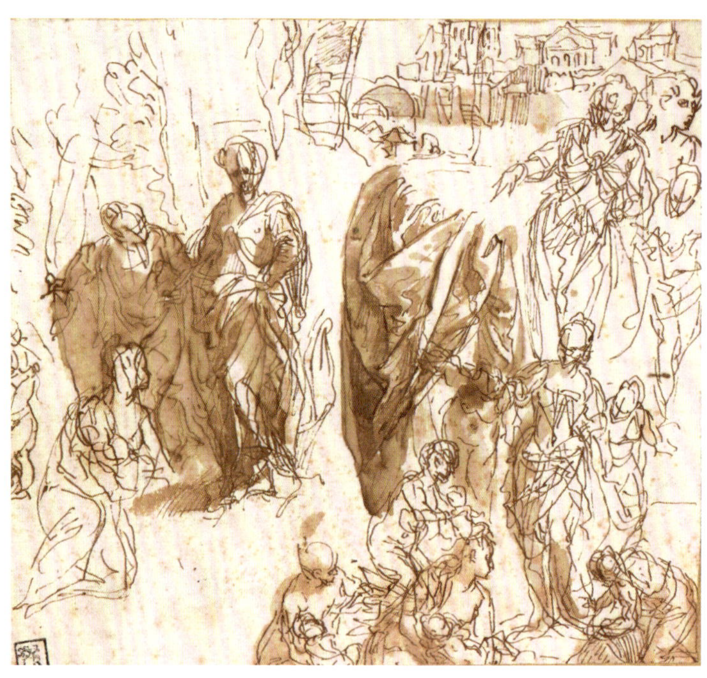

The same effect can be observed in Thiebaud's sketches, although in his case the correspondences are more deliberate. In spite of the multiplicity of seemingly unrelated studies, an overall sense of composition prevails throughout the page. Studies of paper cups, for instance, or of a group of jelly apples and watermelons are arranged according to the classic model of an inverted pyramid (Nos. 65 and 70). The eye is attracted to the single element at bottom center and makes its way up the sheet through the other elements distributed in a particular order. One can feel the experienced art director at work planning a layout. In many sheets, a strict compartmentalization of the different vignettes, each isolated by a framing line, calls to mind the organization of a storyboard or the panels of a comic book (Nos. 77–78 and 80). The origin of the framing line may also be traced to Thiebaud's work in publicity. Instruction manuals for creating advertising layout recommend first drawing a rectangle when making roughs, before trying out different combinations and permutations.[5] Thiebaud connected his sketch practice to his experience in the field: "This was one of the things I got out of the old art directors who always had you make lots of tiny little compositions before you made a large one."[6] The device of the rectangular frame, which defines the space of the study by isolating it from the rest of the page, signals a focus on composition issues—scale, proportions, spatial relationships—rather than on the rendering of details.

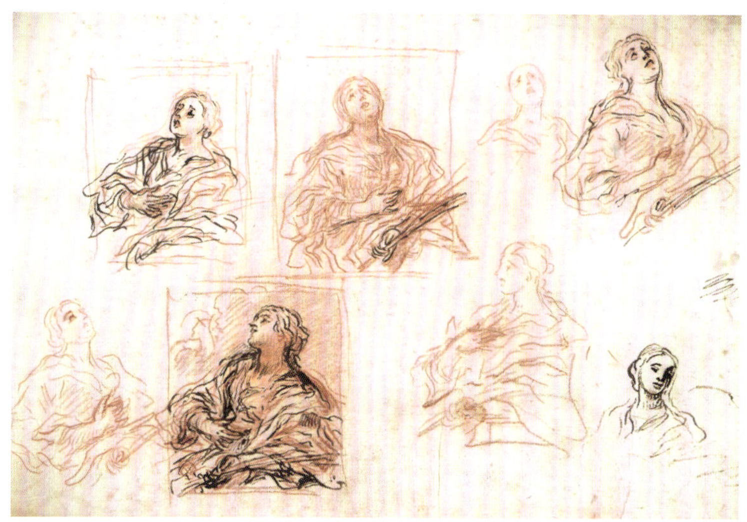

Interspersed among the compositional studies are drawings made from
observation, in the tradition of the artist busy sketching everywhere he goes.
"I actually can't think of anyplace I haven't taken a sketchbook—hospitals,
churches, ships, airplanes, even to the tennis courts," Thiebaud recalled.
"I make sketches while visiting different countries, walking in museums,
viewing athletic events, riding in the car, listening to concerts, watching
television, and attending lectures."[7] The artist seizes any opportunity to
make quick portraits, such as the two profiles of Clement Greenberg drawn
while the critic was giving a lecture on Hans Hofmann at Berkeley in
October 1986—a circumstance Thiebaud dutifully noted at the bottom of
the sheet (No. 20). Perhaps the reference to Hofmann inspired the small
watercolor on the same sheet: three candied apples in red and yellow, a bold
Hofmann-like combination of colors with the same degree of warmth. On
another sheet from the same year, next to landscape studies with trees
and clouds, Thiebaud captured pianist Vladimir Horowitz during a recital in
Moscow on 20 April 1986 (No. 72). The historical event, marking the
pianist's first return to the Soviet Union after sixty-one years, was televised
internationally—hence this sketch made from California.

Thiebaud's sketches include many self-portraits, a subject that allows him to
experiment freely. "It has to do with a willingness to take more liberties with
myself than I would with anybody else. I would feel self-conscious about asking

FIG. 3.
Baldassare Franceschini, *Eight Studies
of a Female Martyr*, second half of the
seventeenth century, pen and brown
ink over red chalk on paper. The
Morgan Library & Museum, New York,
gift of Janos Scholz; 1993.215.

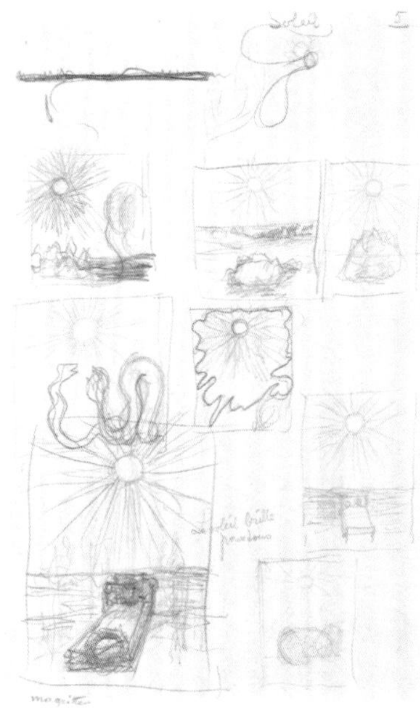

FIG. 4.
René Magritte, *Studies for* L'Au-delà,
1938, graphite on paper.
Private collection.

people to look the way I might look in a picture."[8] Three small self-portraits on one sheet show him trying out different lighting of his face (No. 68). The investigation was part of a broader inquiry into light effects, as can be deducted from the presence of two moonlight landscape studies on the same page.

Tracing relationships among various sketches on the same sheet highlights Thiebaud's preoccupations with particular formal issues. Experiments with different lighting or different vantage points, for example, are frequent unifying concepts. Thiebaud also carries compositional schemes over from one subject to another. Thus a suite of five cakes to the left of one sheet is echoed in a row of five heads forming a similar curve along the bottom edge (No. 73). Many sheets include at least one composition with cakes, as if the familiar motif was a kind of touchstone for all other subjects. The fluidity with which Thiebaud moves from one motif to another leads him to find inspiration for one subject in an entirely different one. In a sheet inscribed *Double Doubles*, two double hamburgers at top left appear to be the source for the motif of a cloud and its shadow on a hill developed on the rest of the page—the cloud and shadow mimicking the shape of the buns (No. 71). Similar formal echoes can be observed in the juxtaposition of a Sacramento River landscape with upside-down ice cream cones, or clown cones. Both present a wide shape at the bottom progressively narrowing toward the top, with the tilled field even providing a counterpart to the cones' wafer pattern (No. 62).

The practice of making several small, framed sketches on the same sheet is notable in the work of another twentieth-century artist who, like Thiebaud, had a background in advertising. Not only did René Magritte begin his career as a commercial draftsman, designing wallpapers, posters, fashion plates, and book illustrations, he remained involved in this type of production throughout most of his career—an experience that informed many aspects of his paintings. Like Thiebaud, he drew such sketches to explore different ideas for compositions or to try out variants of a single image as in his eight studies for the painting *L'Au-delà* (Fig. 4). For both artists, the process appears to have derived from the practice of advertising layout.

But the modern artist whose sketches Thiebaud admired particularly was Piet Mondrian, who also relied on thumbnail drawings to work out his paintings— "hundreds of marvelous little compositional plans that indicate his visual thinking."[9] Some of them were jotted down on the most unassuming supports, such as cigarette packages or milk tablet wrappers. In them Mondrian experimented with compositional variants, changing the proportions of his rectangles, moving ever so slightly an internal division, or adjusting the width of a line (Fig. 5). Mondrian scholar Robert Welsh has described them as "a storehouse of alternative compositional types."[10] Overestimating, in his enthusiasm, their actual number, Thiebaud described them at length: "Sometimes he could make as many as a hundred little three inch by two inch, or four inch by five inch drawings of placements for a particular piece. Where the lines would intersect, how much space in one area as opposed to another. . . . This testing out different set ups is one of the very basic needs of any serious artist." Thiebaud shared Mondrian's obsessive search for the "right" composition through endless alterations and adjustments— "a pretty neurotic activity," he conceded.[11]

For Thiebaud, the sketch is not the "unthinking scribbling" associated with the romantic notion of the artist caught in the fire of creation, rapidly throwing on paper confused lines from which he will make sense later.[12] On the contrary, he refers to his sketches as "thinking drawings," comparing them to "scientific research papers."[13] Beyond the charm of their immediacy and humor of their subjects, they are a place of inquiry and investigation—part of the methodology of research that characterizes Thiebaud's highly intellectual and analytical approach to making art.

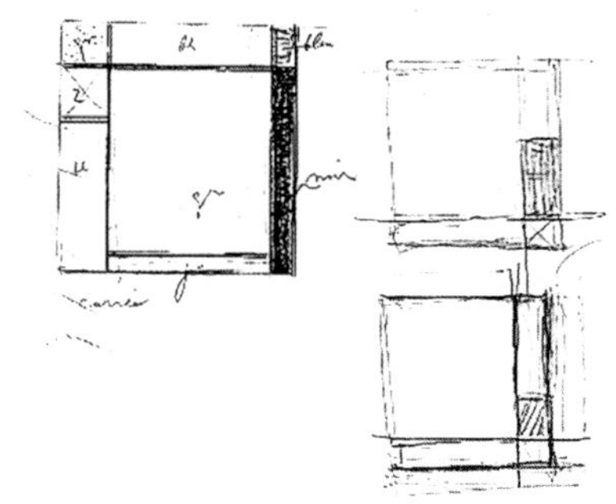

FIG. 5.
Piet Mondrian, *Sketchbook 1925 Sheet A: Three Square Compositions*, 1925, charcoal on paper. Private collection.

Notes

1. Quoted in Constance W. Glenn, *Wayne Thiebaud: Private Drawings, the Artist's Sketchbook*, New York, 1987, p. 2.

2. Stephen C. McGough, "An Interview with Wayne Thiebaud," in *Thiebaud Selects Thiebaud: A Forty-Year Survey from Private Collections*, exhibition catalogue, Crocker Art Museum, Sacramento, 1996, p. 12.

3. Lizzie Boubli, *Savoir-faire. La variante dans le dessin italien au XVIe siècle*, exhibition catalogue, Musée du Louvre, Paris, 2003, pp. 74 and 84.

4. Deanna Petherbridge, *The Primacy of Drawing: Histories and Theories of Practice*, New Haven and London, 2010, p. 29, and Lizzie Boubli, *L'Atelier du dessin italien à la Renaissance: Variante et variation*, Paris 2003, pp. 93–95.

5. Charles L. Whittier, *Creative Advertising*, New York, 1955, pp. 258–59.

6. Alessia Masi, "Interview to Wayne Thiebaud," *Wayne Thiebaud at Museo Morandi*, Museo Morandi, Bologna, 2011, p. 47.

7. Quoted in Laurie S. Hurwitz, "Wayne Thiebaud's Studied Sensuality," *American Artist* 57, no. 615 (October 1993), pp. 29–30.

8. "Thiebaud on the Figure: An Interview by Bill Berkson," in *Wayne Thiebaud: Figurative Works, 1959–1994*, exhibition catalogue, The Wiegand Gallery, College of Notre-Dame, Belmont, CA, 1994, n.p.

9. Constance Lewallen, "Interview with Wayne Thiebaud," *View* (Point Publications, San Francisco) 6, no. 6 (Winter 1990), p. 9.

10. Robert Welsh, "Mondrian as Draftsman," in *Mondrian Zeichnungen, Aquarelle, New Yorker Bilder*, exhibition catalogue, Staatsgalerie, Stuttgart, 1980, p. 54.

11. Masi, p. 47.

12. On the sketch and the metaphor of fire, see Petherbridge, pp. 39–45.

13. Constance W. Glenn, "A Conversation with Wayne Thiebaud," *Architectural Digest* 39, no. 9 (September 1982), p. 68, and *Wayne Thiebaud: Figure Drawings*, exhibition catalogue, Campbell-Thiebaud Gallery, San Francisco, 1993, n.p.

Sketches

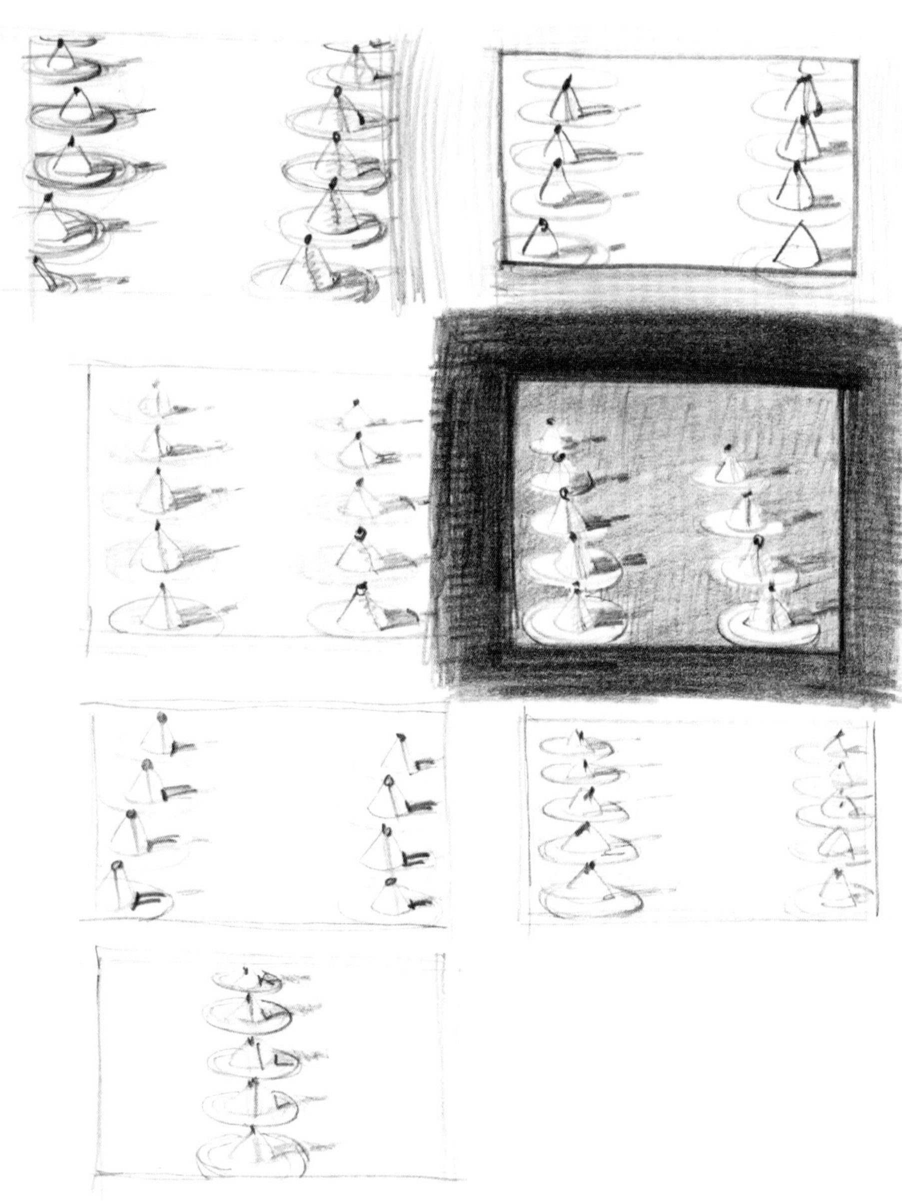

65. **PAGE OF SKETCHES WITH PAPER CUPS**, 1960s
Graphite
10⅞ × 8½ inches (27.6 × 21.6 cm)
From the artist's studio

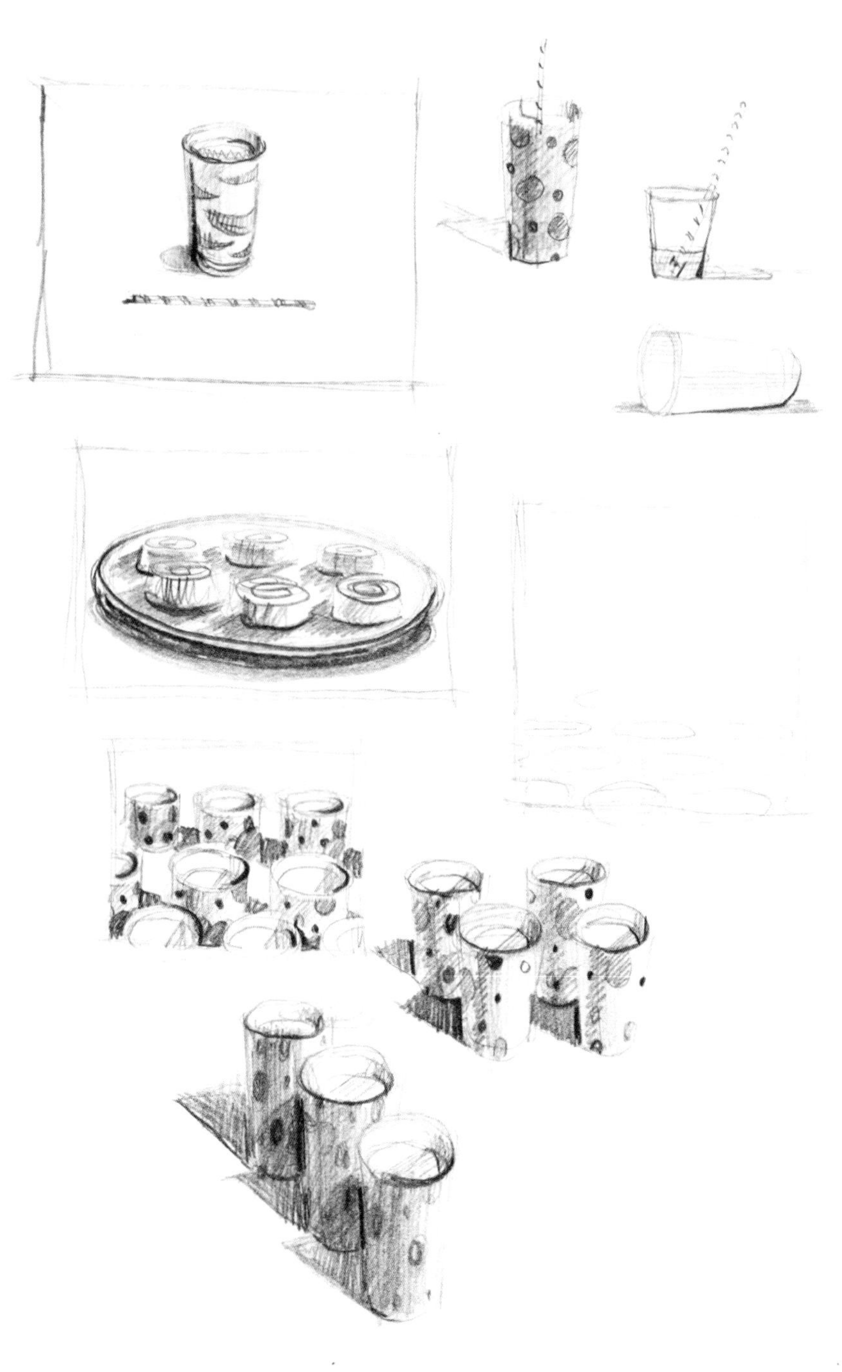

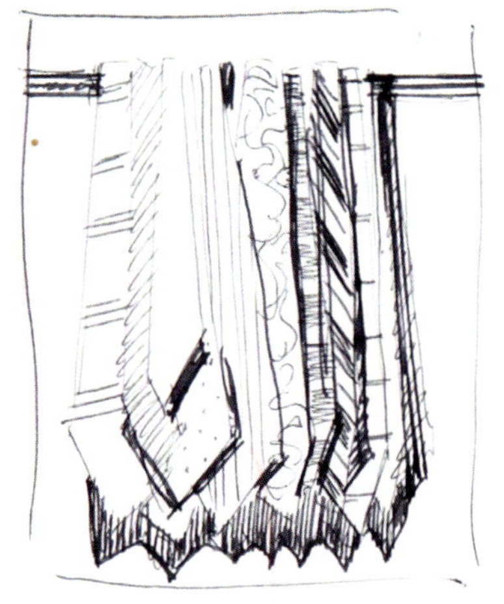

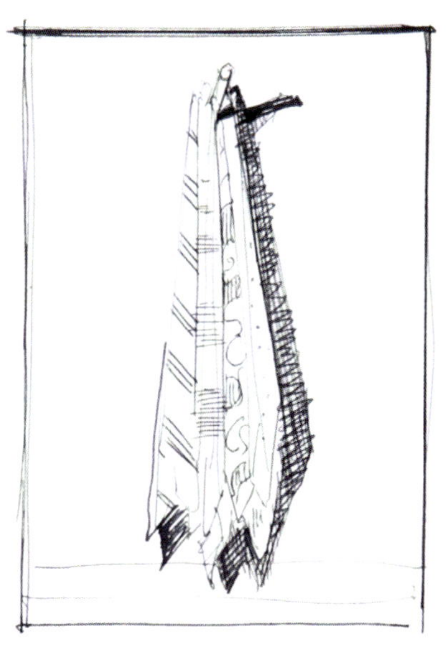

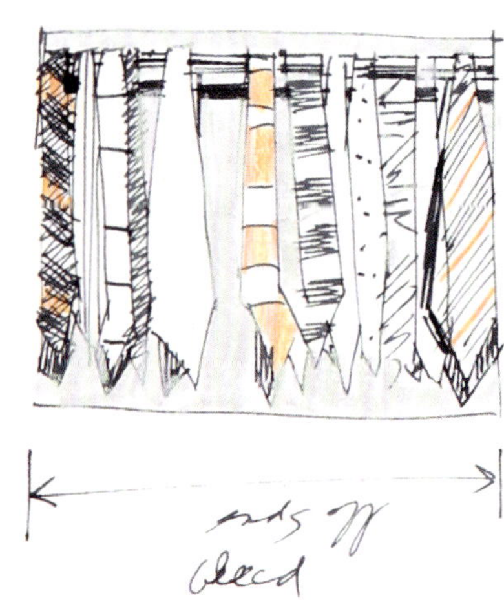

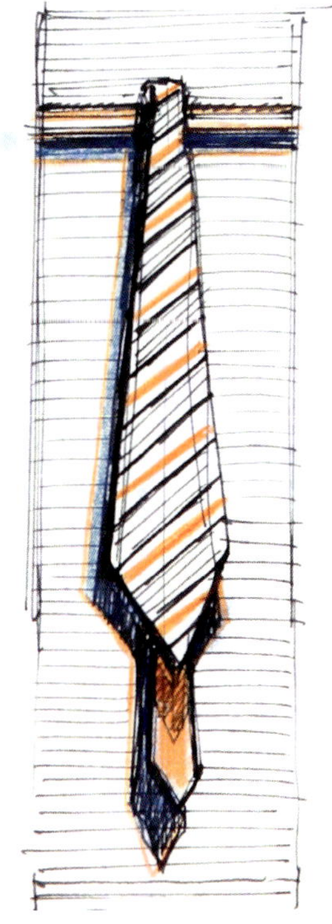

 PAGE OF SKETCHES WITH TRUCKS AND CARS, 1970s
Graphite
11⅛ × 8¾ inches (28.3 × 22.2 cm)
From the artist's studio

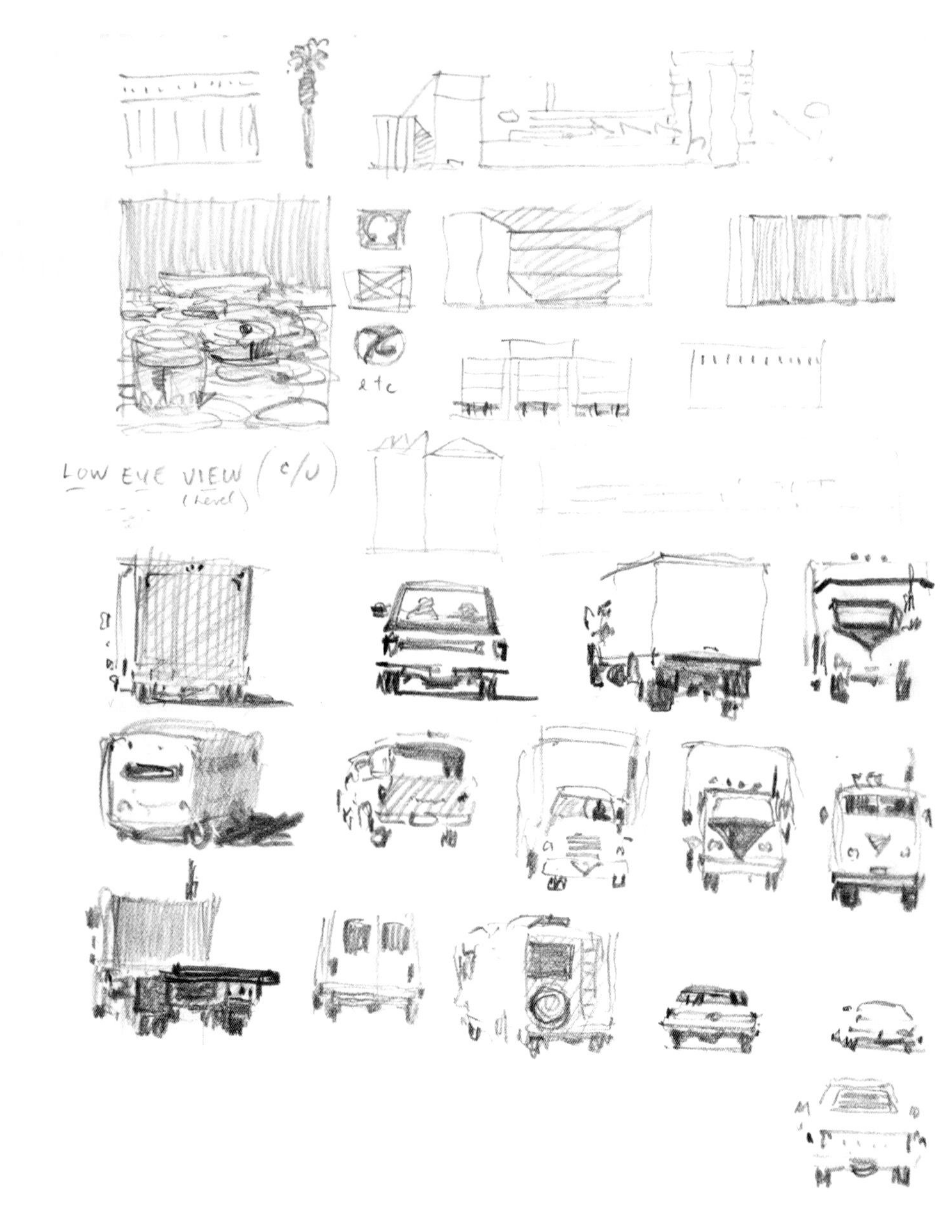

68. **PAGE OF SKETCHES WITH SELF-PORTRAITS**, 1970s
Ballpoint pen
11 × 8⅞ inches (27.9 × 22.5 cm)
From the artist's studio

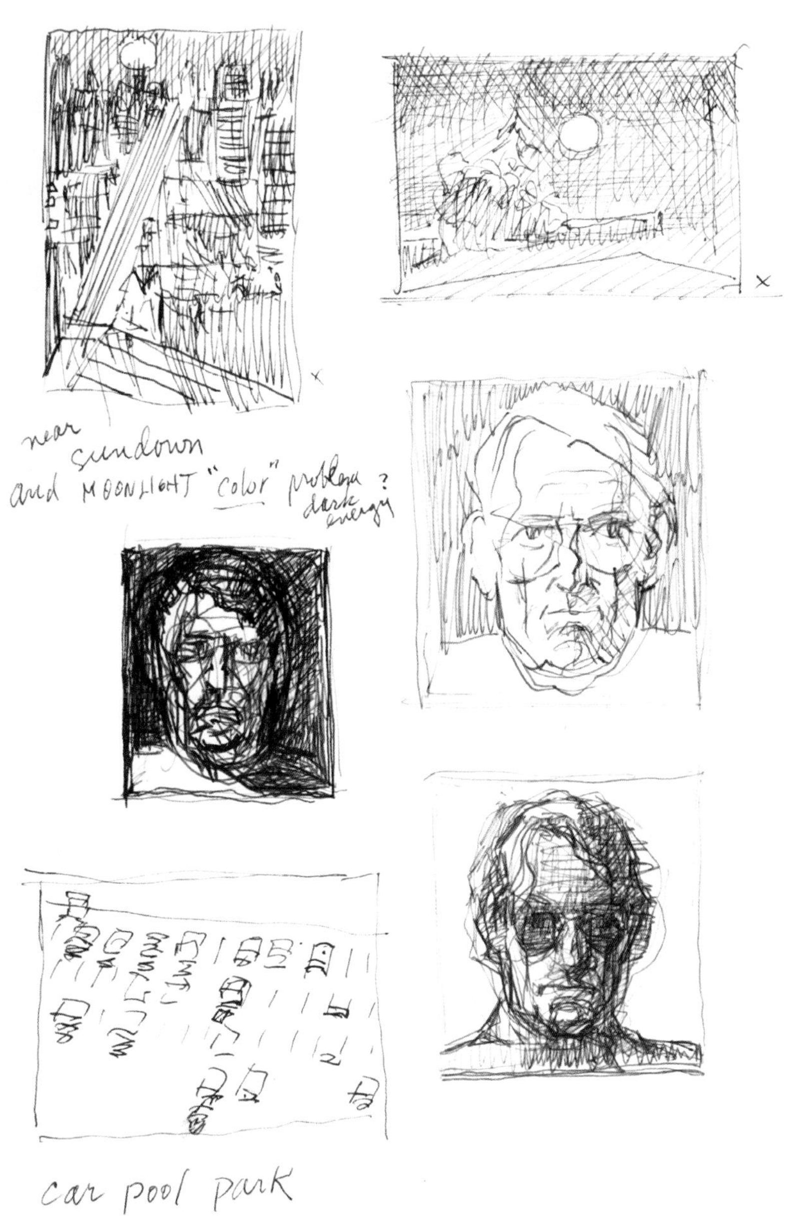

69. **PAGE OF SKETCHES WITH NOTES ON
MORGAN LIBRARY DRAWING EXHIBIT**, 1981
Graphite
11½ × 8⅜ inches (29.2 × 21.3 cm)
From the artist's studio

70. **PAGE OF SKETCHES WITH
CANDIED APPLES AND WATERMELON SLICES**, 1980s
Graphite
8½ × 11¼ inches (21.6 × 28.6 cm)
From the artist's studio

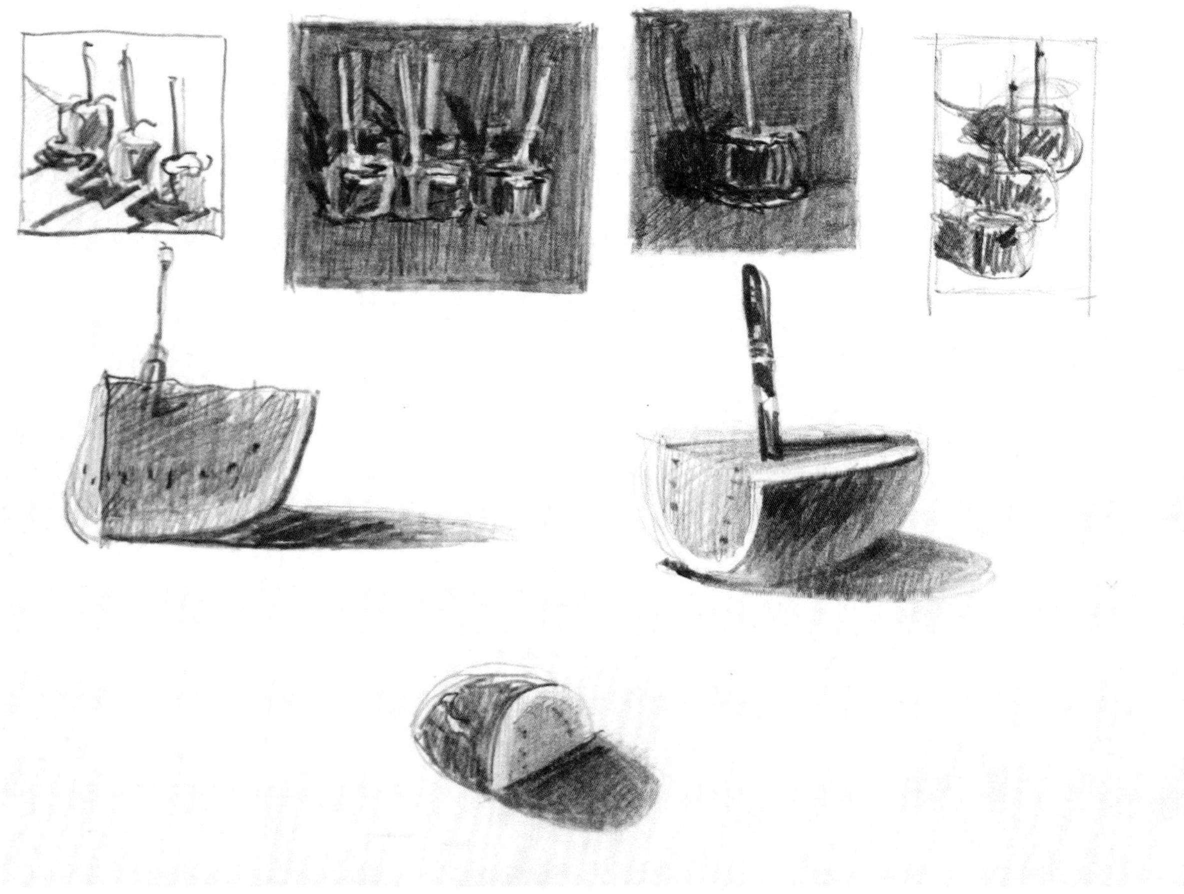

 PAGE OF SKETCHES "DOUBLE DOUBLES," 1980s–90s
Pen and ink
10⅜ × 13¾ inches (26.3 × 34.9 cm)
From the artist's studio

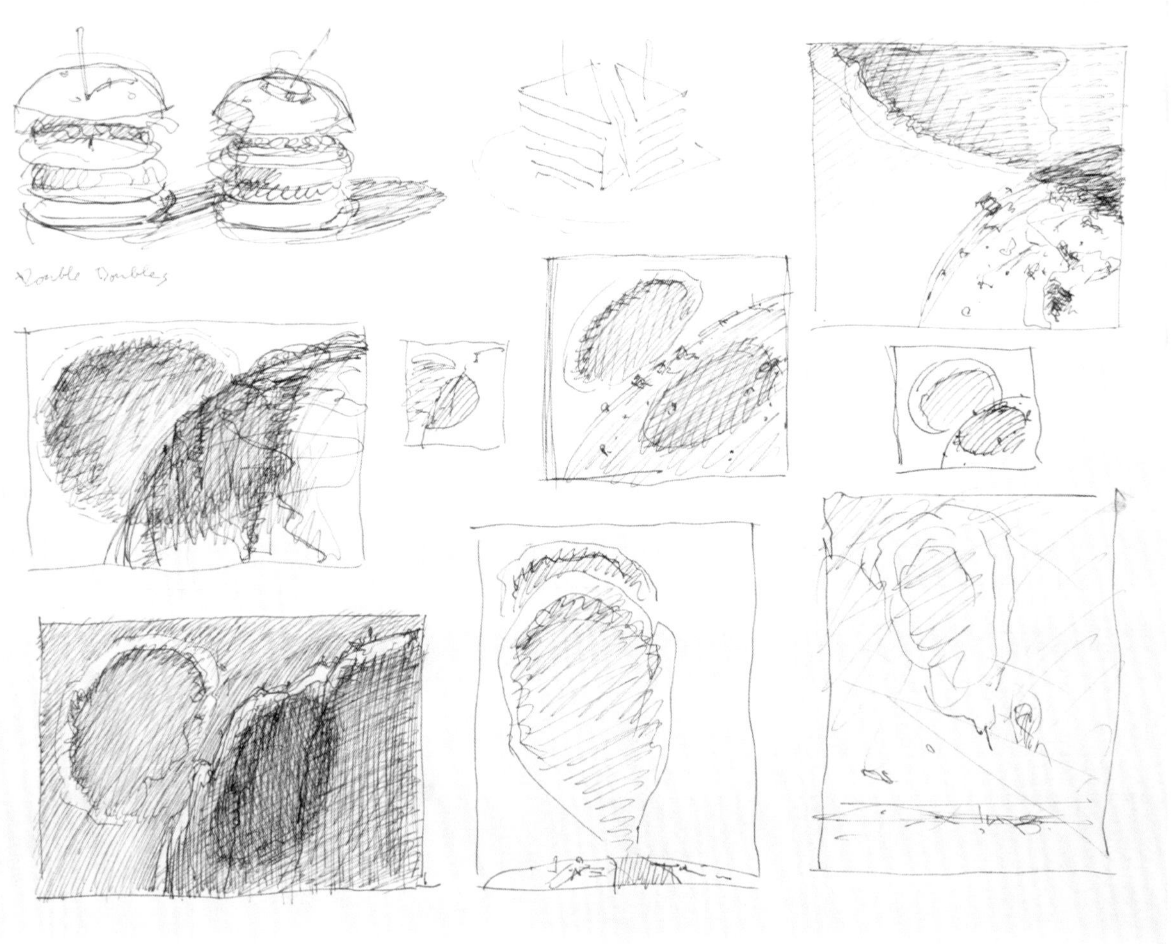

72. **PAGE OF SKETCHES WITH CLOUDS AND PORTRAIT OF HOROWITZ**, 1986
Pen and ink and graphite
11 × 14¼ inches (27.9 × 36.2 cm)
From the artist's studio

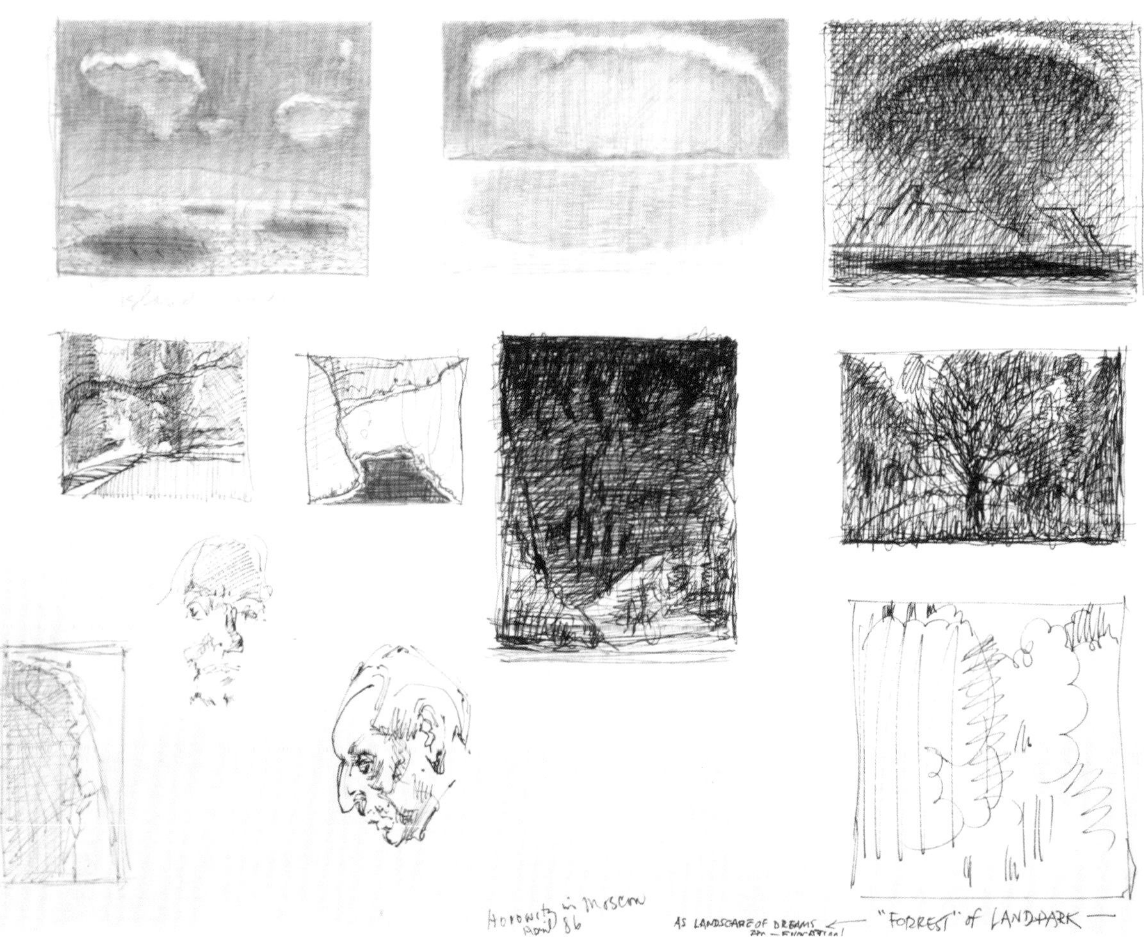

73. **PAGE OF SKETCHES "AROUND YOUNTVILLE,"** ca. 1990s
Pen and ink
10¼ × 14⅛ inches (26 × 35.9 cm)
From the artist's studio

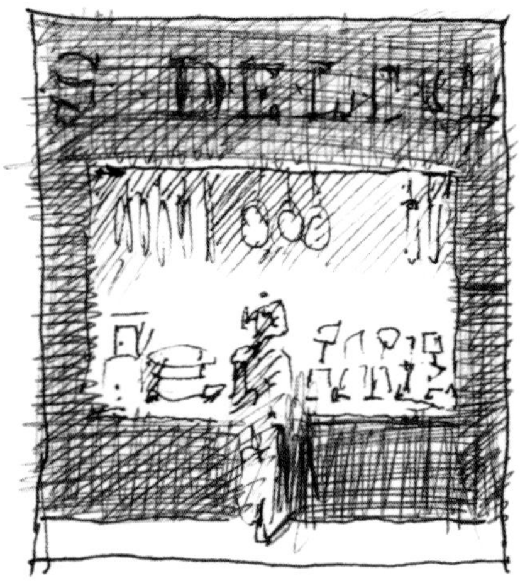

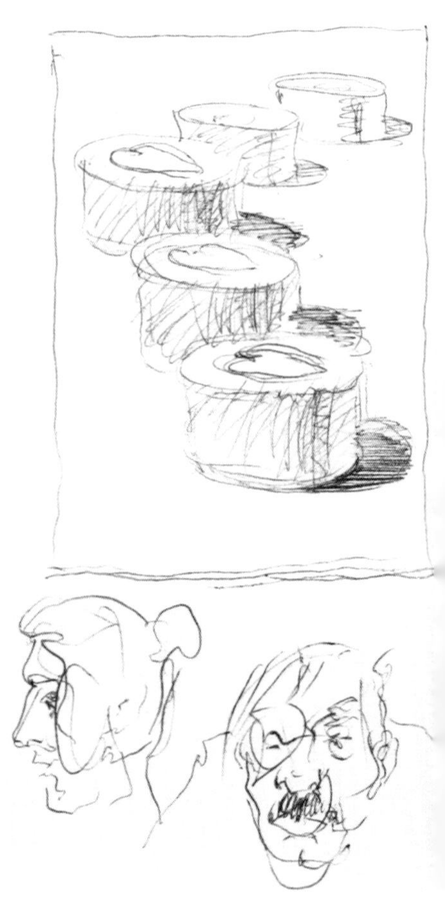

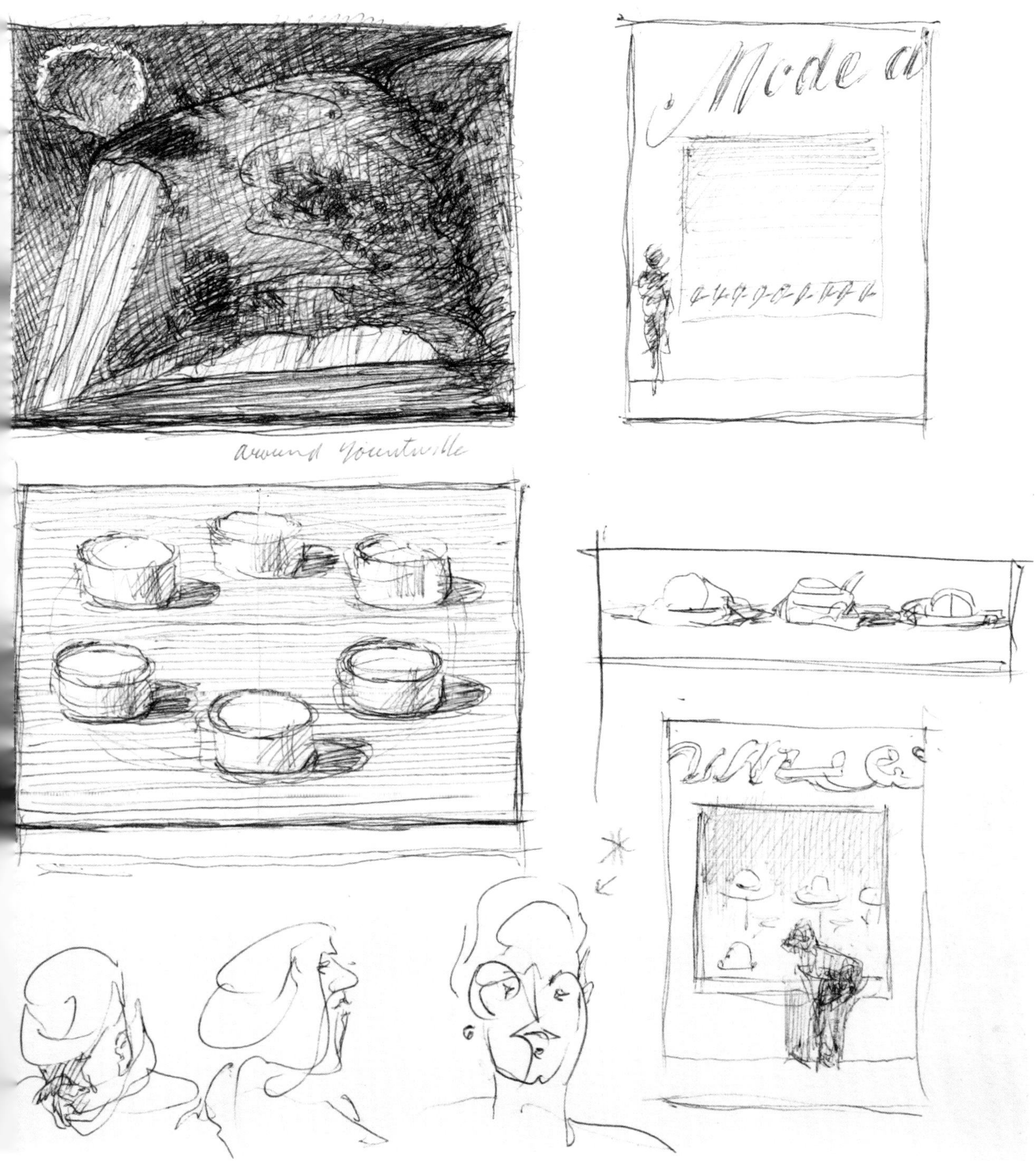

around Yountville

74. **PAGE OF SKETCHES WITH
MAN STANDING BEHIND PODIUM**, 1990s
Pen and black, red, and blue ink
11 × 14¾ inches (27.9 × 37.5 cm)
From the artist's studio

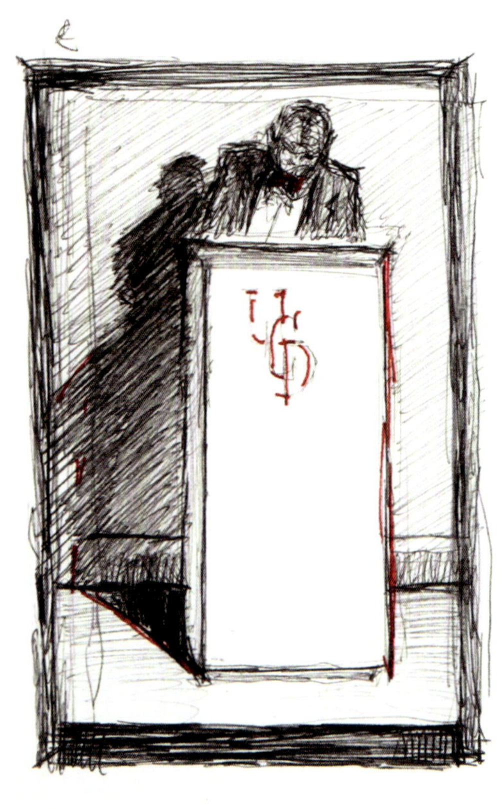

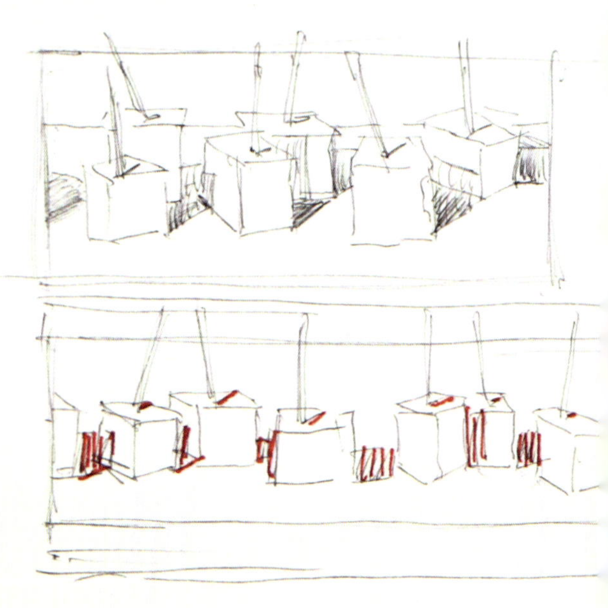

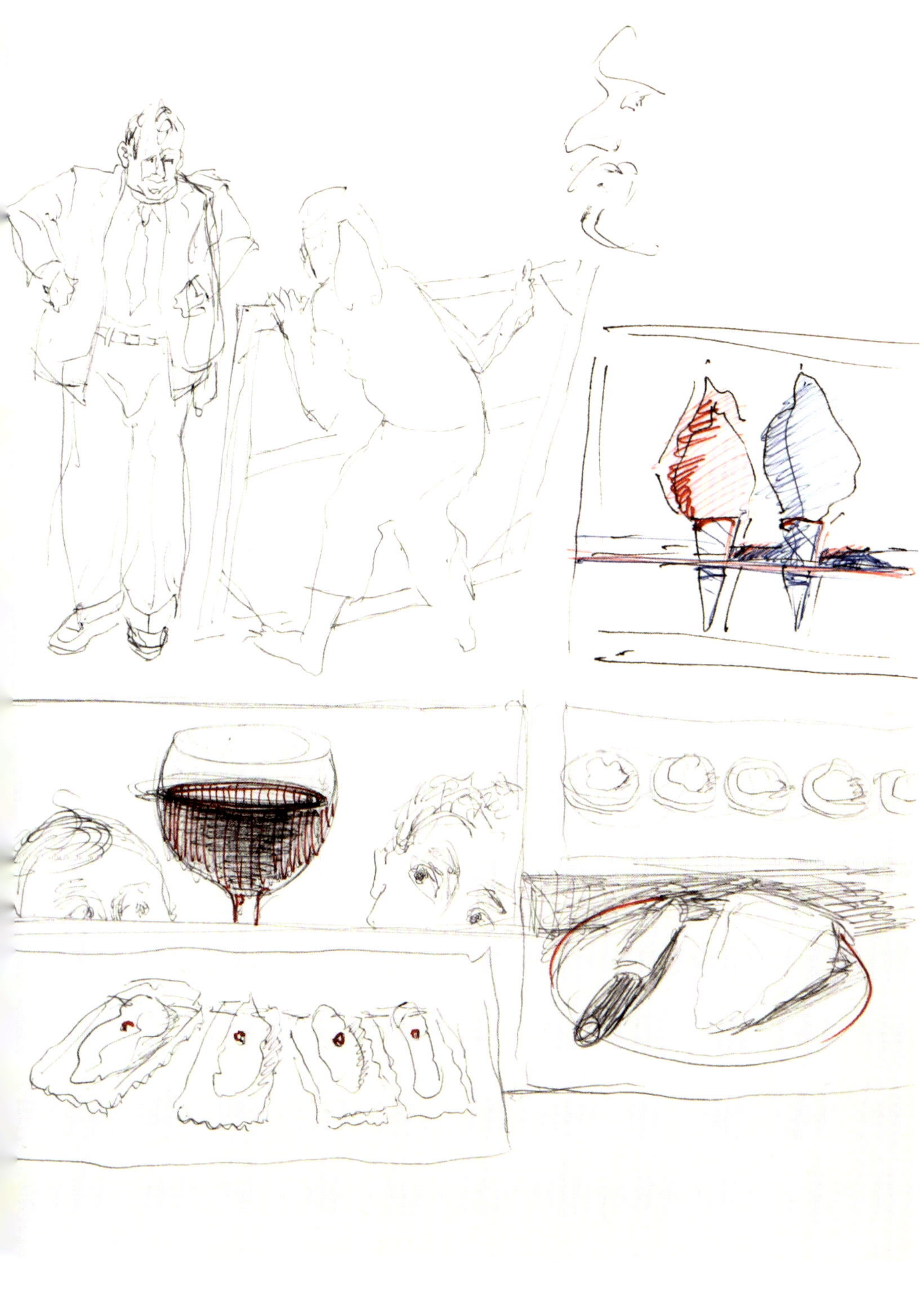

 PAGE OF SKETCHES WITH MOVIE BILLBOARD, ca. 1990s
Pen and ink
11 × 14⅞ inches (27.9 × 37.8 cm)
From the artist's studio

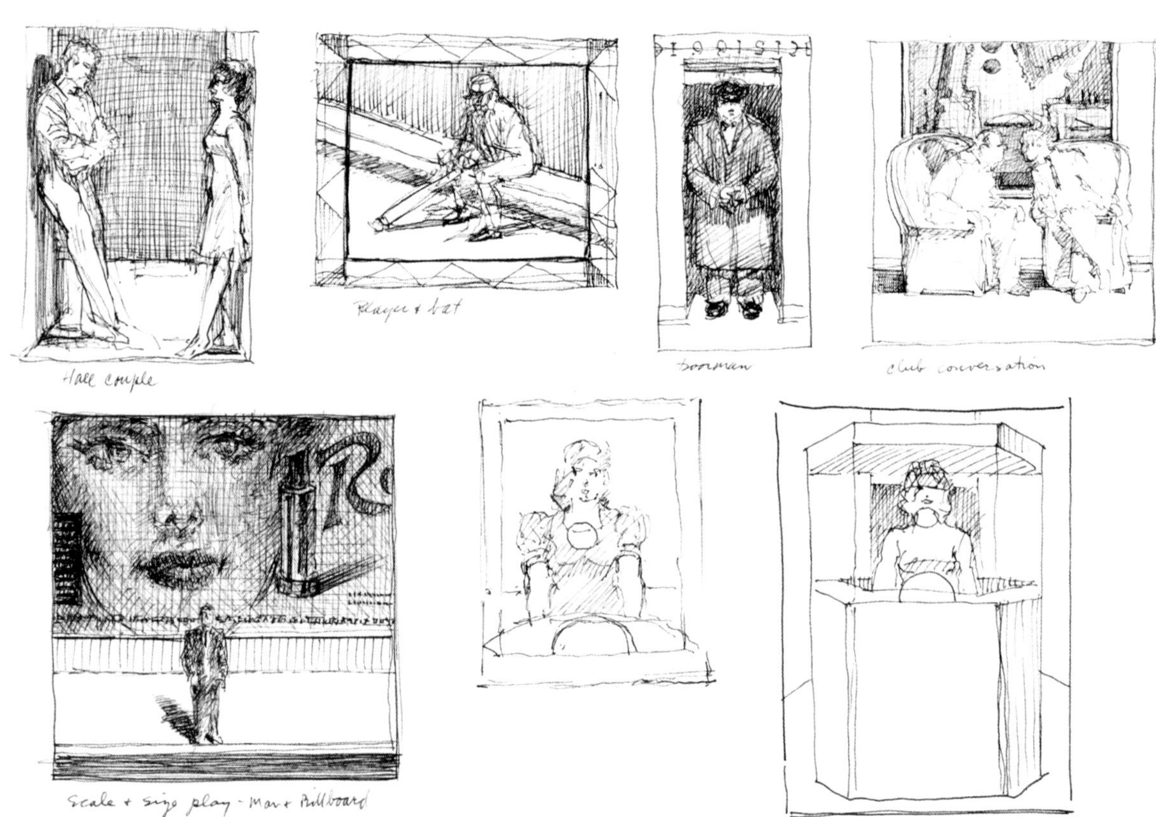

 PAGE OF SKETCHES WITH CITYSCAPES, ca. 1990s
Pen and ink
11 × 15 inches (27.9 × 38.1 cm)
From the artist's studio

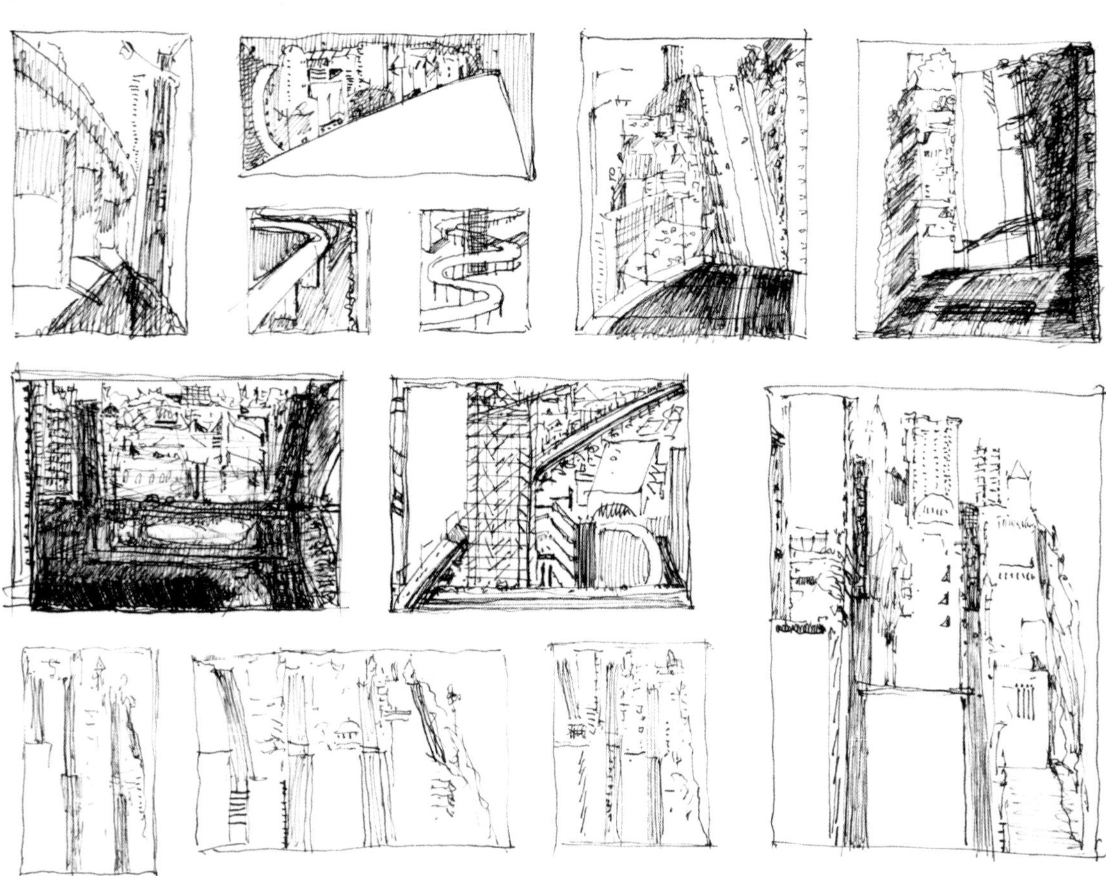

77. **PAGE OF SKETCHES WITH
    MAN DRAWING ON STUDIO FLOOR**, ca. 1990s
Pen and ink
10¾ × 15 inches (27.3 × 38.1 cm)
From the artist's studio

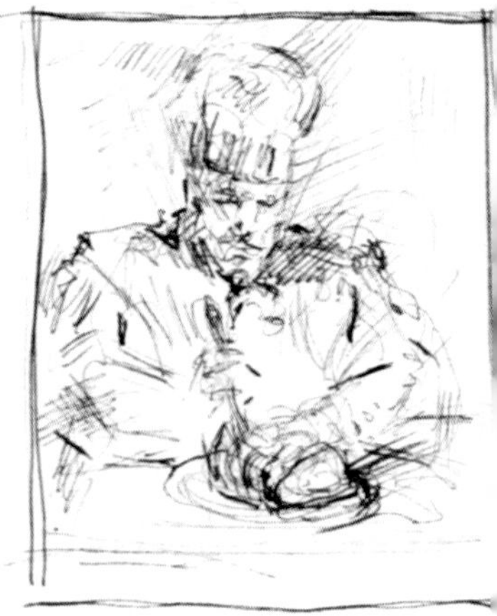

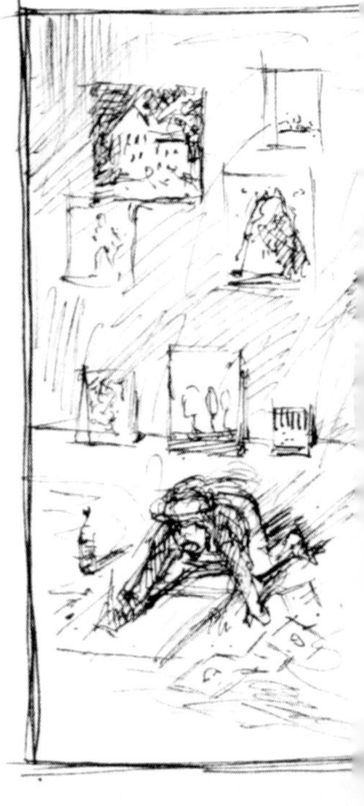

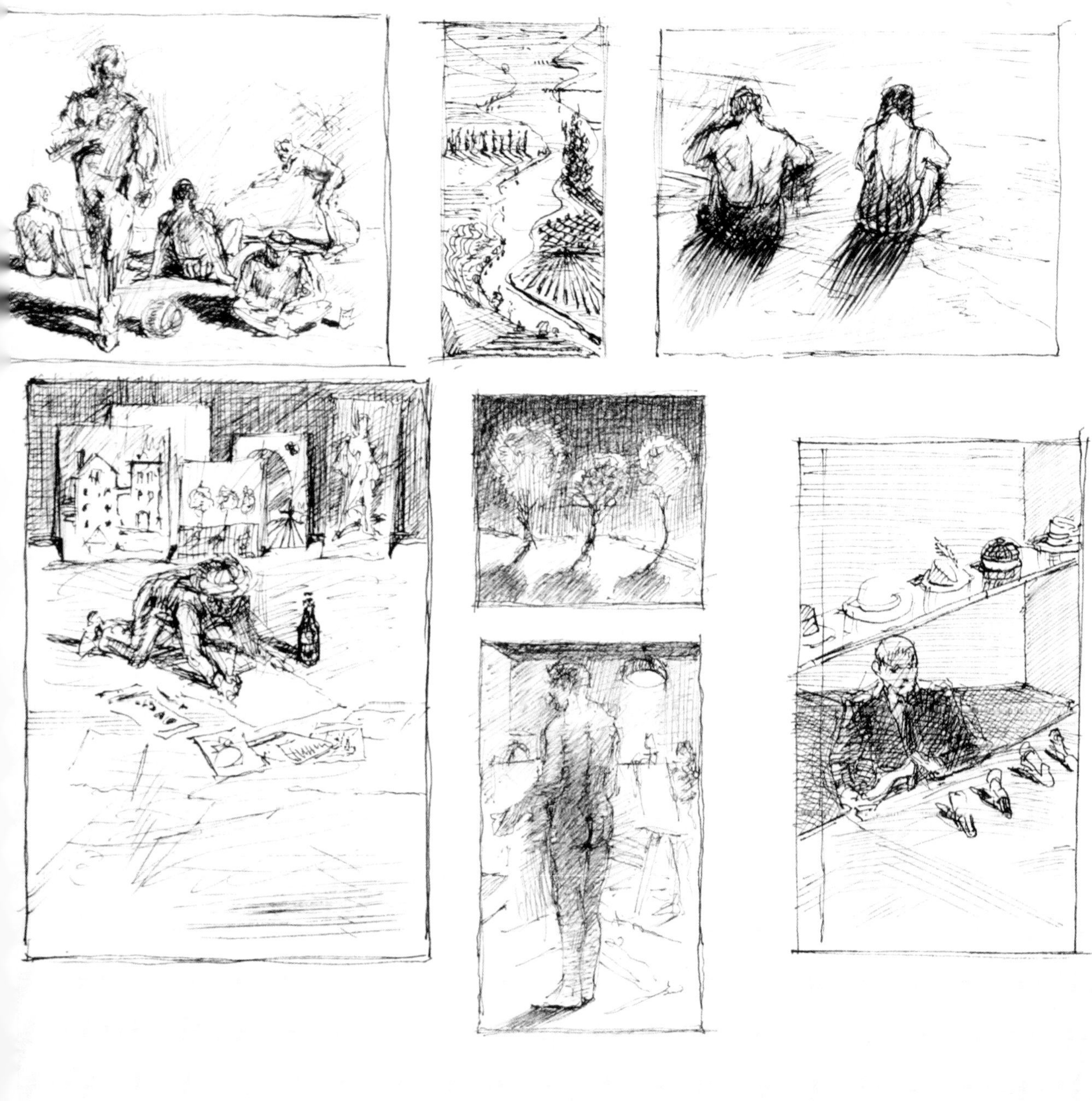

 PAGE OF SKETCHES WITH PAINT CANS, ca. 1989
Pen and black and red ink
11¼ × 14¾ inches (28.6 × 37.5 cm)
From the artist's studio

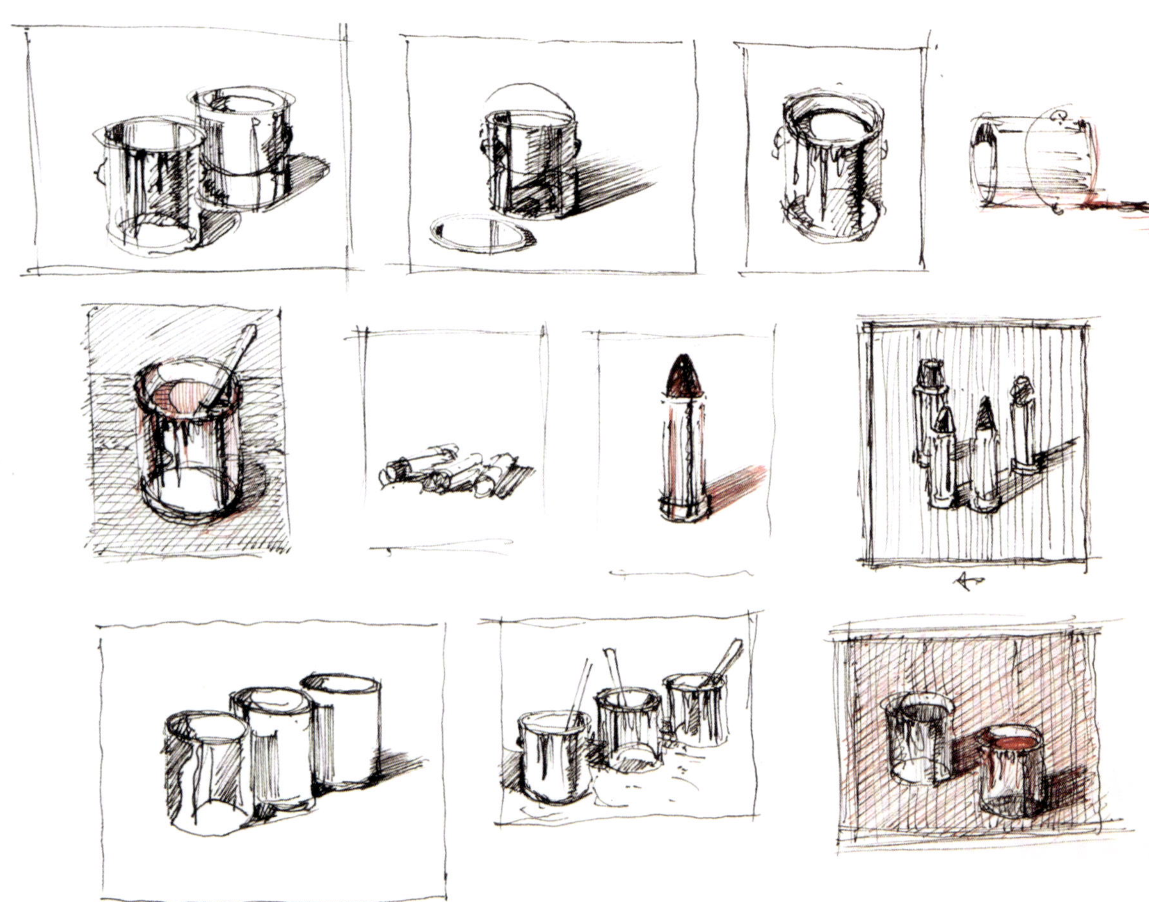

79. **PAGE OF SKETCHES WITH ICE CREAM CONES
AND TWO CAKES**, ca. 1990s
Pen and ink
11 × 15 inches (27.9 × 38.1 cm)
From the artist's studio

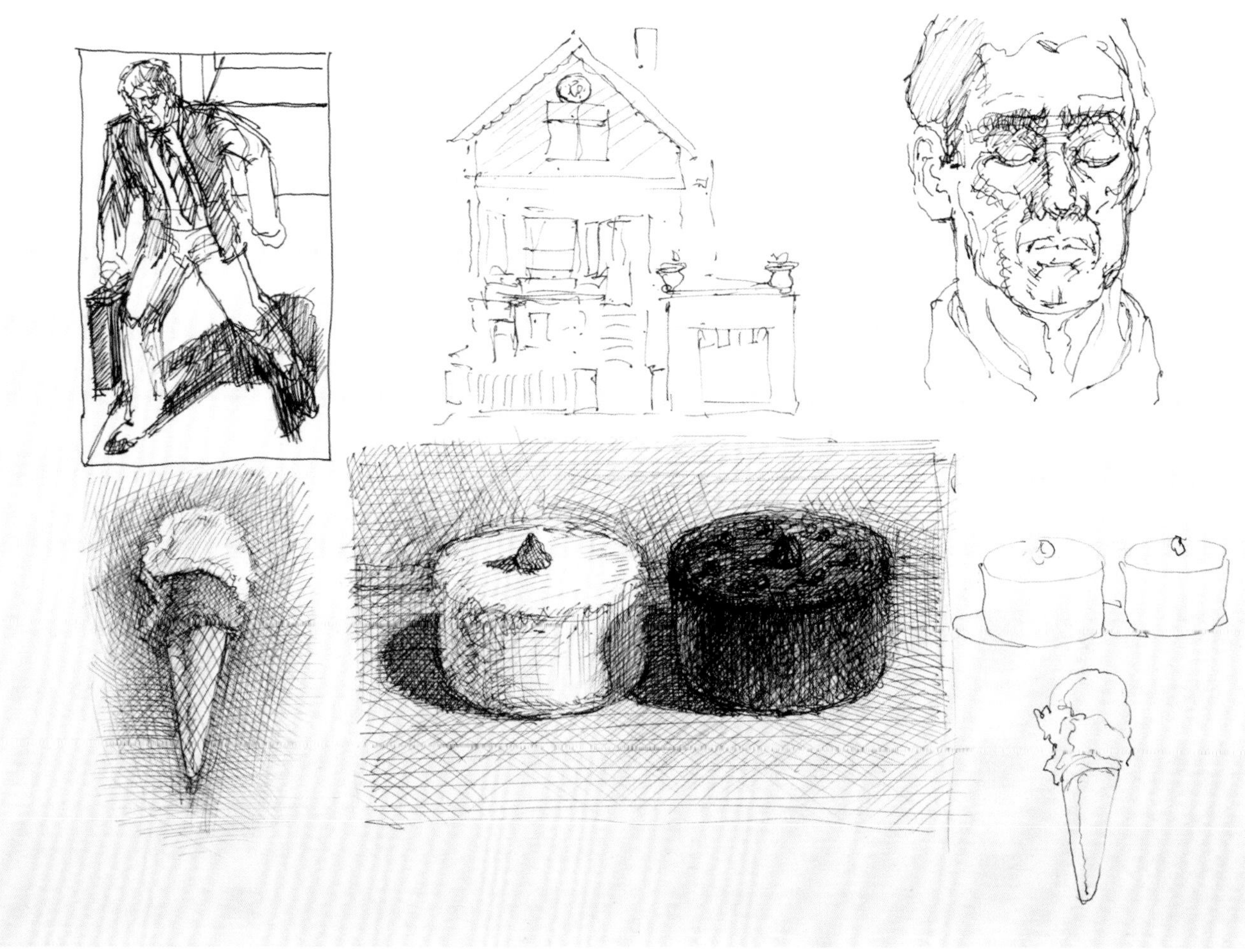

80. **PAGE OF SKETCHES "FLASH LITE ON,"** ca. 1990s
Pen and ink
10⅞ × 15 inches (27.6 × 38.1 cm)
From the artist's studio

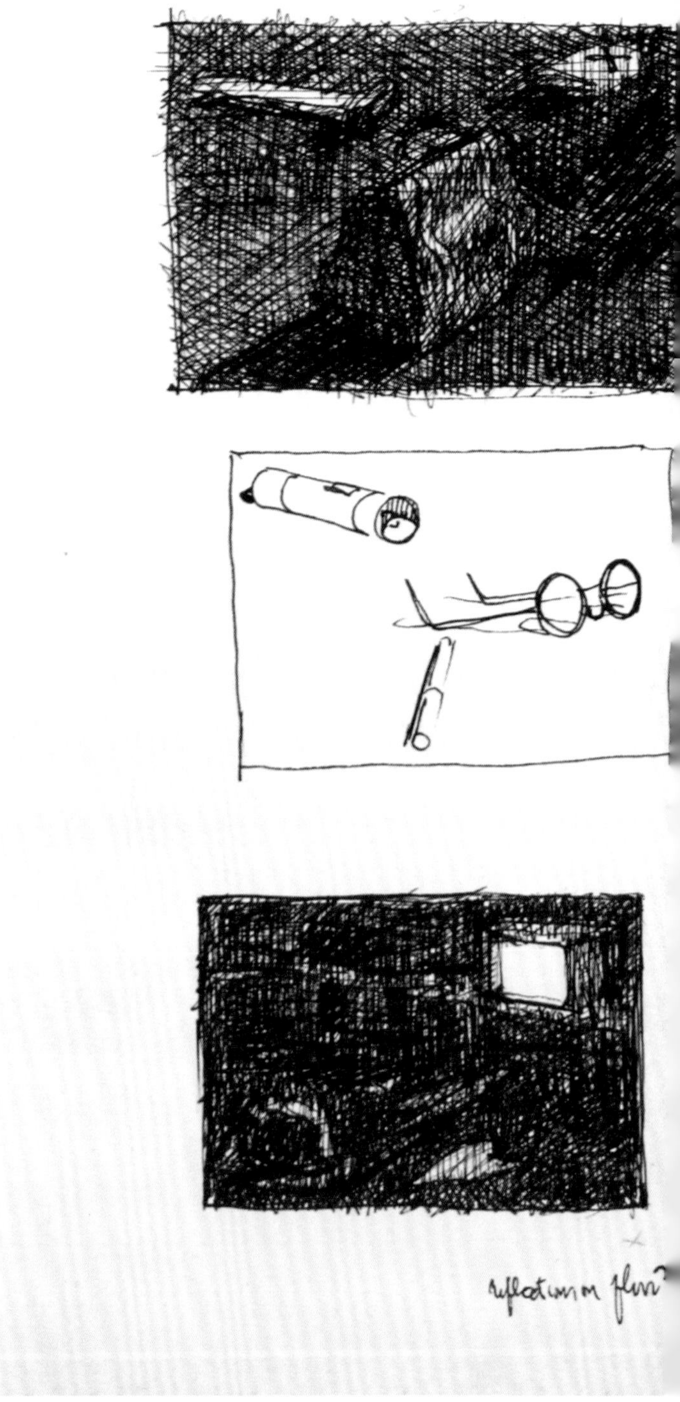

FLASH LITE ON

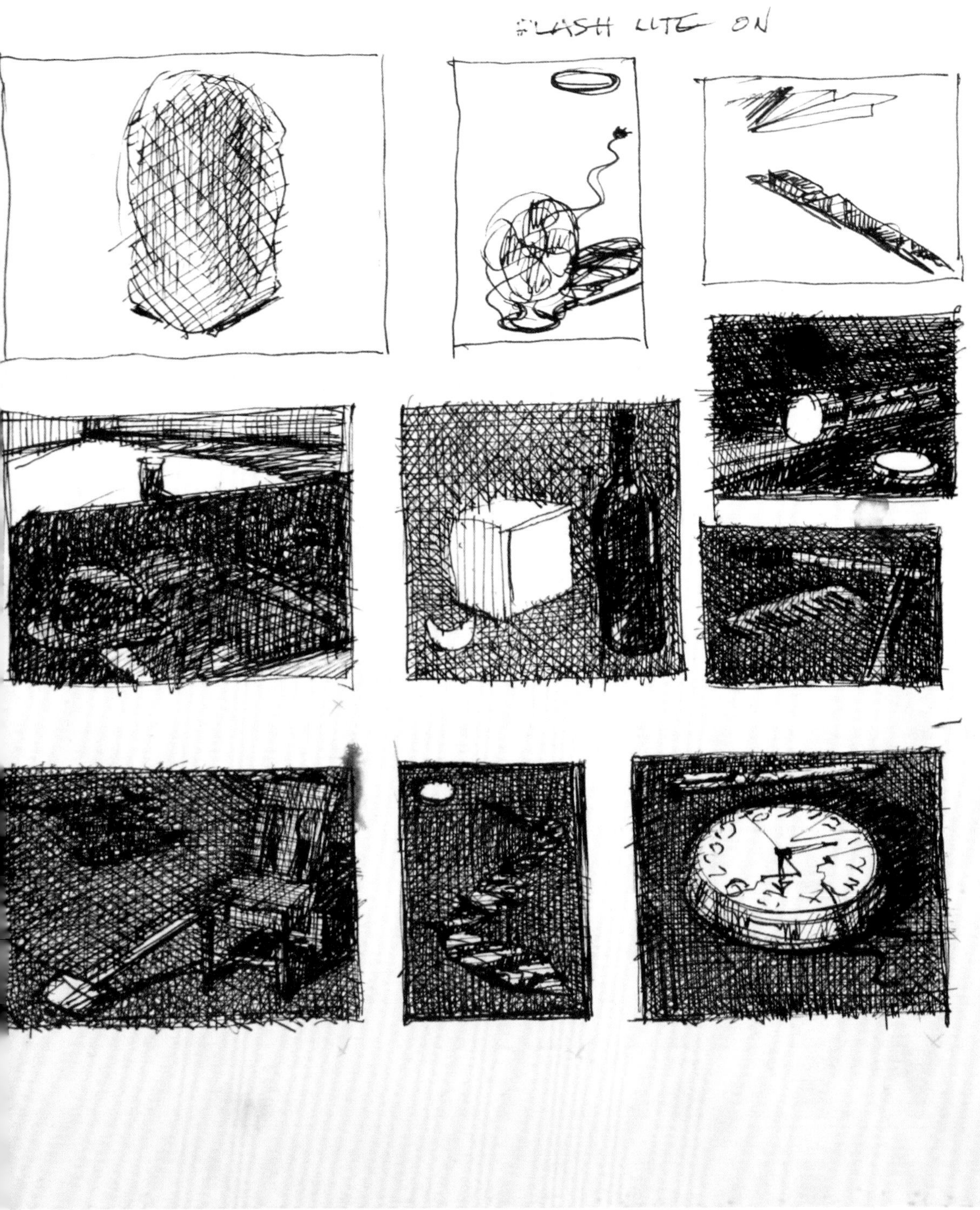

81. **BAGUETTES**, 1979
Brush and ink
6¼ × 4 inches (15.9 × 10.2 cm)
From the artist's studio

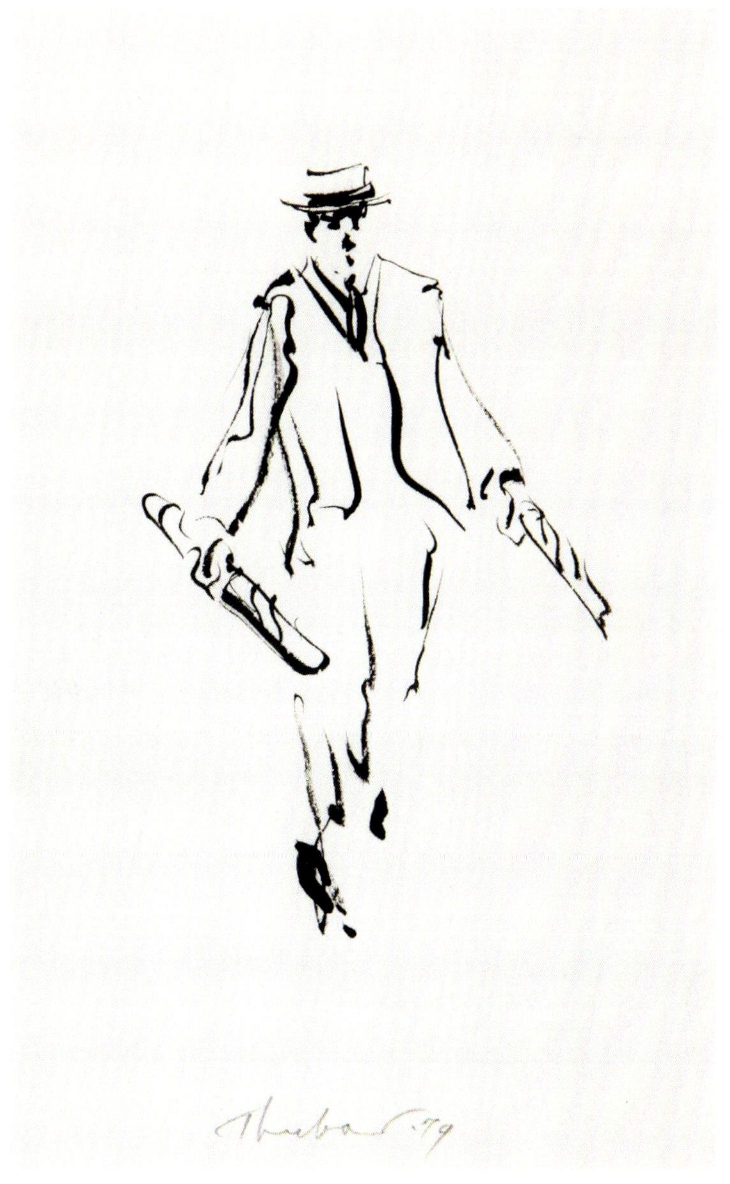

 **PAGE OF SKETCHES FOR BRILLAT-SAVARIN BOOK,
WITH FISHERMAN**, 1990s
Pen and ink
11⅛ × 15 inches (28.3 × 38.1 cm)
From the artist's studio

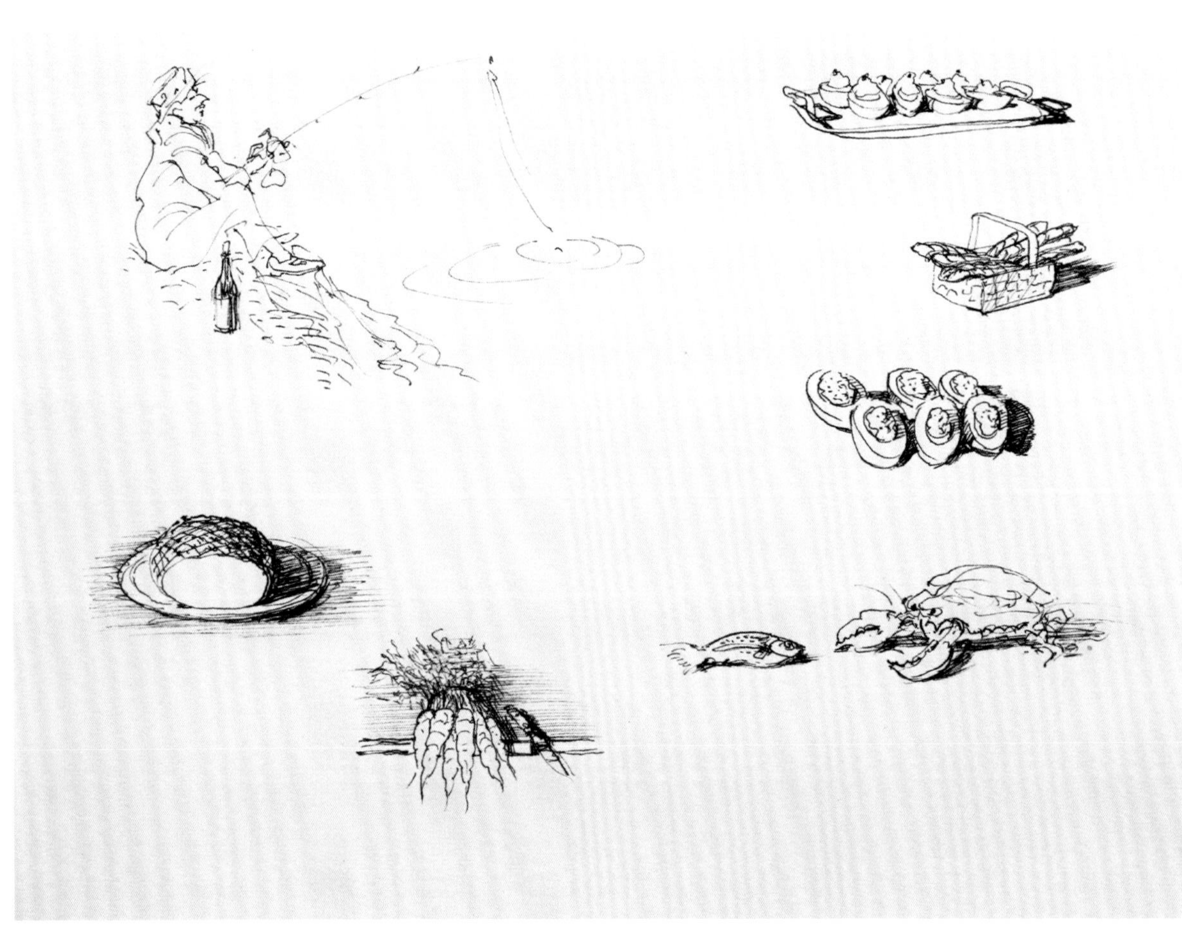

83. **PAGE OF SKETCHES FOR BRILLAT-SAVARIN BOOK,
WITH TURKEY, CHICKENS, AND FARMER**, 1990s
Pen and ink
11⅛ × 15 inches (28.3 × 38.1 cm)
From the artist's studio

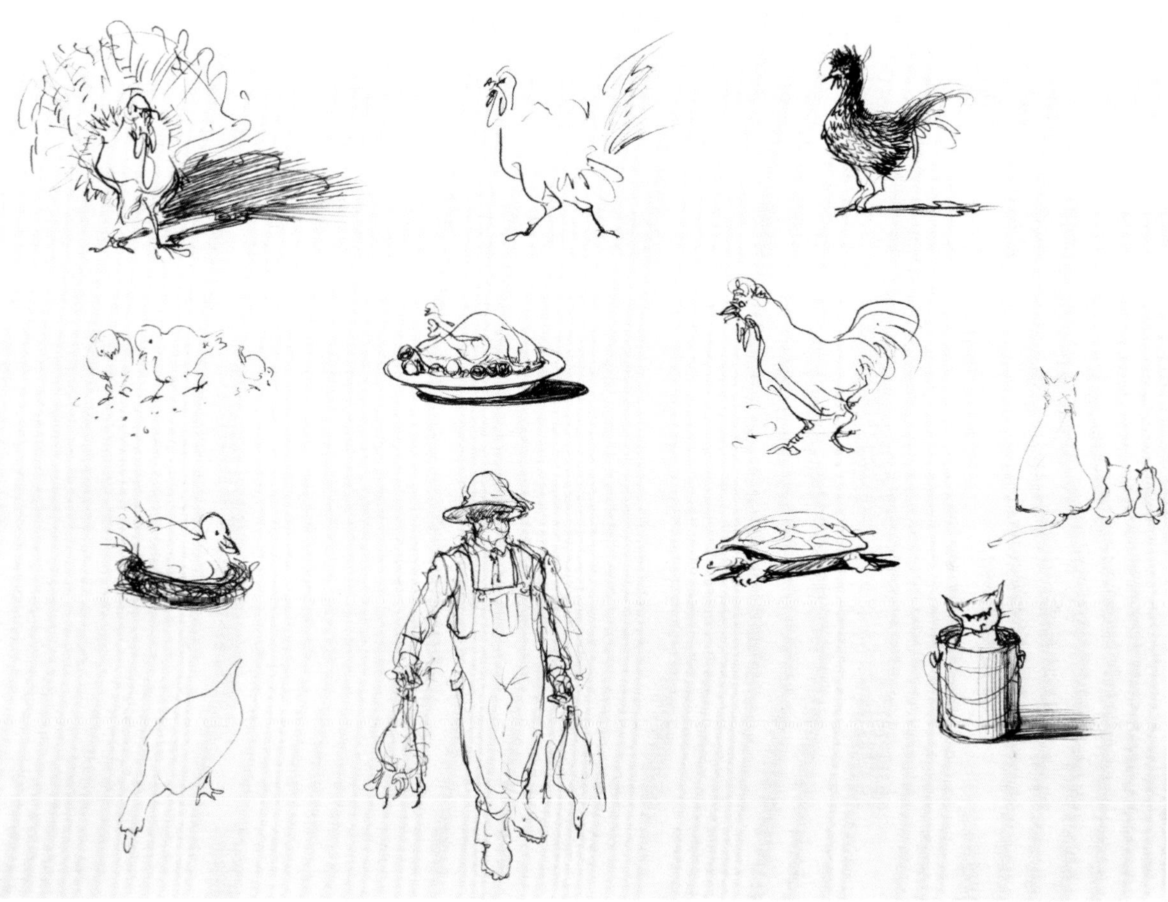

The Fastest Pencil in the West

A Conversation with Wayne Thiebaud

ISABELLE DERVAUX *You have been teaching drawing for most of your life and have often said that it was an important experience for you. How do you teach drawing?*

WAYNE THIEBAUD Um, what was my first art instruction experience? I saw someone demonstrate. A nice man, who was a father of a chum of mine in southern California, had a frame shop and he had some of his paintings there, and he asked me one day, because he saw me drawing: "How would you like to go and watch me paint?" He drove me down to Palm Springs, when it was just a little out-of-the-way place. (This was in the 1930s.) He set up a little French easel and started painting. He had a curious start at the top, made a sky, mountain, and then it's like he pulled down a picture shade. I was just bewitched. I said to him, "How do you do that?" He said, "You just start and do it."

Well, later on, when I had my first teaching job, they admonished us as students of art education not to demonstrate for students, not to touch their work. The committee on art education from the Museum of Modern Art had a recommended program, and it was basically a kind of do-it-yourself approach, with lots of interest in self-taught artists. That's the way I was told to teach. Well, it didn't work for me. And that's when I started doing demonstrations like that fellow did for me.

So that's the way I teach. I teach by example. I try to not make it my way but, in the old academic sense, to try to inquire after those things which become basic tools in drawing. Those tools are specified by what is needed to make a three-dimensional world on a two-dimensional surface. Basically, that primary process, if we face it correctly, can be like a study of any other academic subject. The big problem of having art schools in universities is that it doesn't work very well.

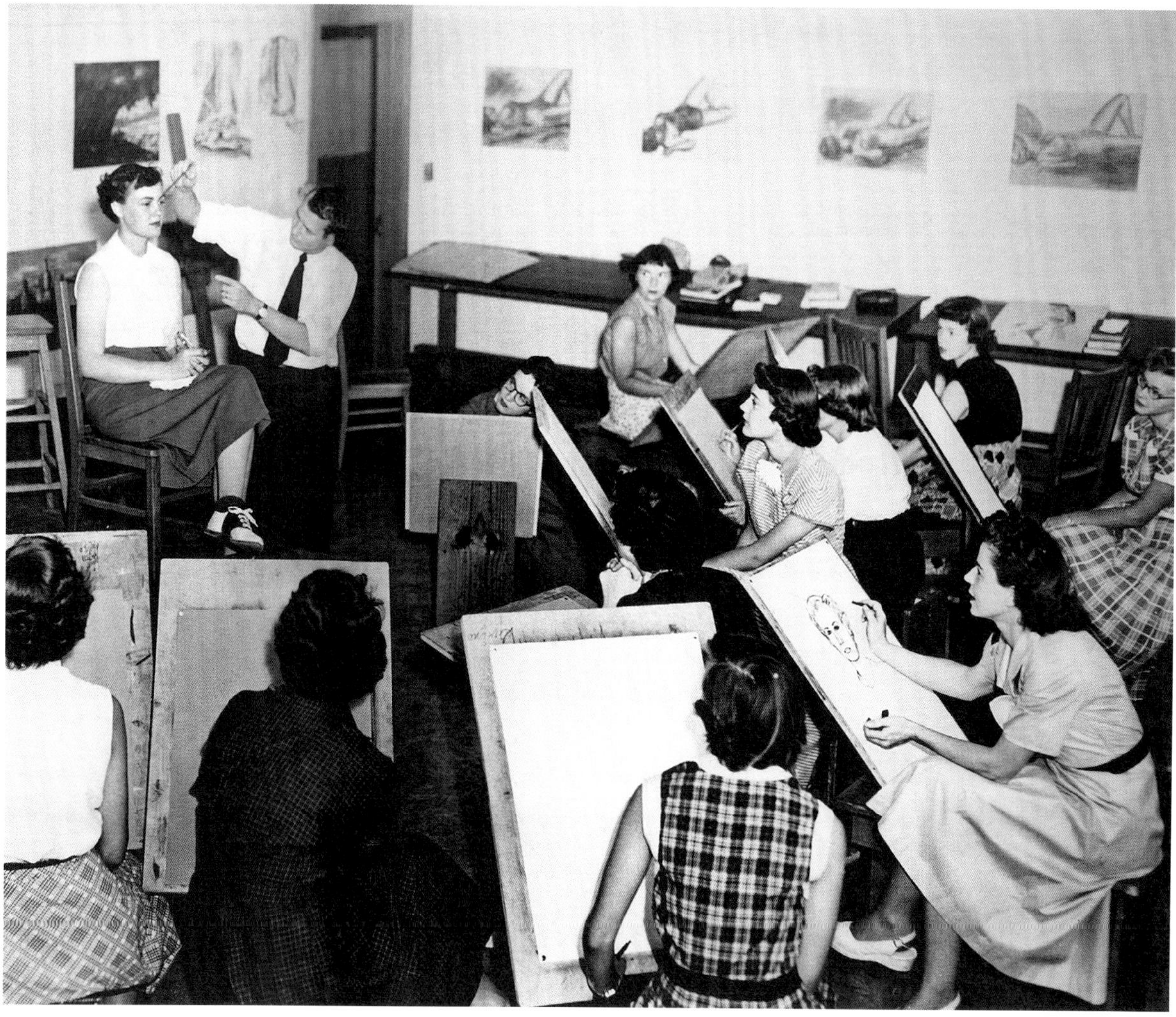

ID: *What doesn't work very well?*

WT: Trying to teach a very difficult drawing skill that must require long hours of practice under instructors with knowledge of how to import the ideas and tools necessary to produce such awareness. Also, it is an unnatural act because it is asking you to lie. To produce a fictional surface by drawing a volume on a flat plane. And it requires many hours of intense focus for anyone to engage the mind and body in this kind of serious research. Basically, college and university art departments do not allow that amount of class time for such practices nor do they employ the kind of drawing masters that are required.

ID: *Do you think students should learn drawing before painting?*

FIG. 1.
Thiebaud teaching evening class at
Sacramento Junior College, 1950.

WT: That depends upon what they wish to accomplish. University art departments do offer alternate art experiences. This is the great attraction, like Gombrich says, "the desire for the primitive."[1] It's a much more natural human proclivity, I think. "If I want to draw, I'll get some charcoal and what will I draw? Well, I'll trace my hand and I'll have a hand there. If I draw some feet and legs on an interesting lump or protuberance, it looks like the body of a bison." That's the secret of the beginnings of painting, isn't it? The seeing-in process. So you need to decide what it is you want to do and obtain the tools that allow you to do it. They can be very minimal. For example, spit and soot were enough to allow James Castle to make his expressive little worlds.[2]

It's all about your aim—what it is you want in drawing. You don't need much. I mean— it depends if you want to be an apprentice, a journeyman, or a master. What do you choose? Do you want to extend and make noble a tradition of volumetric drawing, classical drawing? What is it you want to try to do? At the center, or at the core of that—those desires, those interests—you are obliged to concern yourself with getting those tools which will allow you to do it, and that requires a critical awareness and a capacity for critical interrogation of what the work is, what it needs, what it can be. So teaching for me is that kind of challenge in many various ways.

ID: *More practically, how do you teach drawing?*

WT: I teach drawing in the old-fashioned draftsman's way. When I watched those drawing masters at the [École des] Beaux-Arts and the [Académie de la] Grande Chaumière, the drawing instructor would come in, and you would set up a model in the middle of the room. It doesn't have to be a live model, it can be a still life. A drawing instructor will go around from student to student and point out to the student what's wrong with his perception and his drawing, and even make drawing corrections on it. You learn many things from students along that line, but what you're obliged to do is to circle that class and go to every student and confer with him or her what needs to be done. So that's the way I teach.

ID: *Do you correct the students' drawings?*

WT: Yes. And I have additional methods. I have the students work on each other's works, and change positions to see if they can have a sense of critical interrogation, learn how to do it formally. Of course I have left out another important aspect, and that's demon- strating, as we talked about a little earlier. Usually what I'll do in the very early days of the class, when they get their materials going and they do some quick drawings and things like that, is to stop and make a rather complete drawing for them to see how I go about it.

ID: *You draw while they watch you drawing?*

WT: Exactly. And it can be two- or three-hour drawing or whatever. I don't let them ask questions while I'm drawing, but I stop every twenty minutes or so and say, "Now are there any questions about what I've been doing?" And they'll ask simple things like, "Why did you sand your charcoal?" I say, "Well, I just brought it to a point, that's all."

"Why do you look so much longer than you draw?" "Well, to make assessments. You want to train your eyes so that they move constantly, so that when you're drawing the eye you want to also suddenly look at the toe, and you learn then to scan just like any kind of scanning device so that you graphically make notes on where those crucial areas are." We call them checkpoints or points of reference. It's a manner I also saw William Coldstream use—a teacher at the Slade School in England. You'll see often the little marks left over. And one of his students, Euan Uglow, took that as his style.[3] So anyway, that's the way the class goes along.

ID: *Now, in your own career, you didn't start by learning drawing the academic way.*

WT: No. I bought a book called *The Natural Way to Draw*, by Nicolaïdes.[4] It's standard in America, particularly in the universities, because it's a good quick type book in a way, i.e., gesture drawings, contour drawings. He was very good about it, this fellow Nicolaïdes. He taught at the New York Art Students League.

ID: *When did you buy this book?*

WT: When I needed help. So then I did what he told me and practiced doing this for so-and-so. . . . Before that, I had been doing mostly cartoons.

ID: *A way of drawing very different from the academic way.*

WT: Well, the academy uses gesture and contour sketching also. They don't talk much about it, but if you look at an Ingres drawing, the first thing you'll see in his academic teaching is a quick overall gesture. He'll look at you, and he'll go [*making swift gestures in the air*]. So that he's got very early on a general—almost a hallucinatory, very pale sketch, and then he'll begin his checkpoints and drawing and changes. He is also, of course, working for the ideal so that those drawings become standardized and they're actually sort of goofy drawings.

ID: *What do you call goofy drawings?*

WT: Caricature. . . . Always longer second toe, patrician toe as opposed to a peasant toe. . . . When van Gogh went to class—you know that story? They said, "You can't draw in here." They looked at that toe. "You want to have a patrician toe. Instead you have a big stubby toe, a peasant's toe." So he went and took plaster casts, taught plaster cast drawing for a few weeks in order to get some skill of his own, and he got that Bargue book—that big standard drawing book. . . .

ID: *Charles Bargue?*[5]

WT: Yes.

ID: *What is the relationship between your drawings and your paintings?*

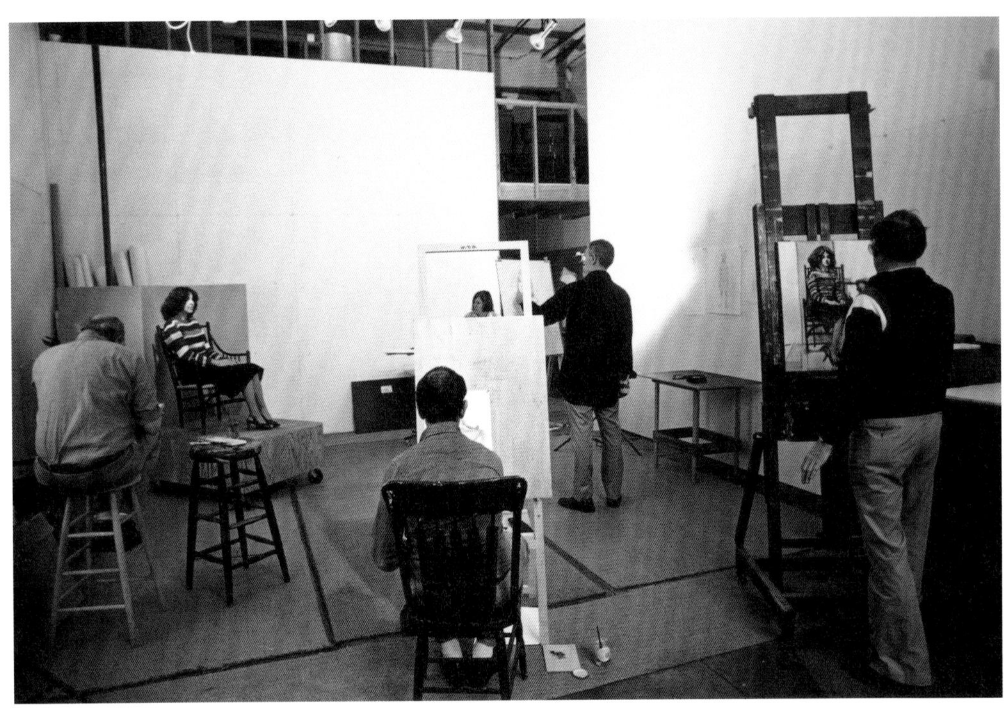

WT: Well, painting . . . that's another whole thing from drawing. Now you're getting into painting and the consolidation of various forces that allow you to paint. That's a very difficult change for a lot of students to go from drawing to painting. A lot of them never go. They don't want to go. They just love drawing. You have to really become very vulnerable to go from drawing to painting.

What do I mean by that? In painting you have to juggle six or eight things at once: color, material, drawing of course, layering, a number of factors which are just almost too much to handle at one time. Painting is—this will sound absolutely idiotic—but painting for me, great painting is maybe even more complex than the most elaborate mathematical theory or any high human achievement—not so much mental as a mind/body complex. That's a very interesting matter! And hard for people to feel or know about or experience until one has an opportunity to try to do it.

ID: *Let's talk about your process. . . . You start your paintings with small "notes" as you call them.*

WT: Thumbnails. Actually those are little proposed paintings, little compositions.

ID: *How do you go from the thumbnail to the final painting? Other drawings?*

WT: Well, your drawing skills I suppose are centrally responsible to do that. . . . What is the difference between drawing and painting? You're drawing with a brush, aren't you? Drawing is a most primary, most important thing of all. Nothing, I think, goes without that, does it?

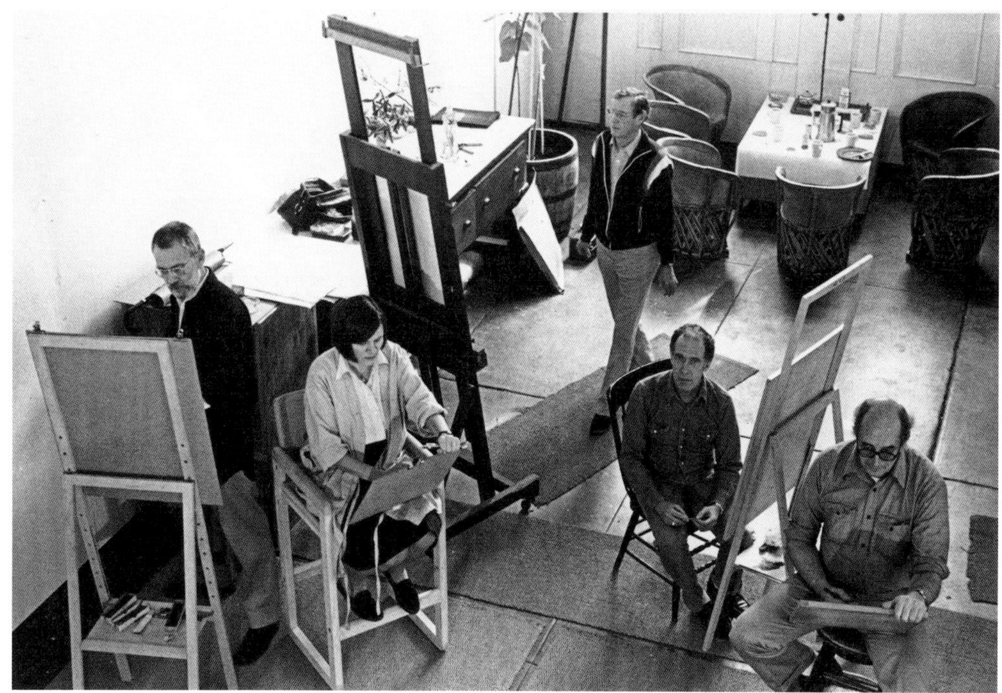

ID: *Your cityscapes and later landscapes, with their complex compositions, seem to involve a lot more drawing than your earlier works. . . .*

WT: It is because I am attempting to combine several different projective systems into one overall integrated composition. The earlier works involved a different kind of drawing that comes out of caricature. Caricature is a wonderful tool. What I am referring to is some measure of exaggeration of sizes, color, space, light that will enhance or redefine ordinary actions or things.

In a conversation with de Kooning in 1956, he asked me what I was presently painting, and I said, "You know, I don't know what to do. I am just . . . " He said, "Well you shouldn't be painting then. One has to love something. You gotta love something. It can be a brushstroke if you want it to be. But, you got to have something that you feel is real, that you live in. And then when you start that, start looking at the best possible paintings from every kind of historical period you can." Very good advice.

So when I came back from being that year with those heroes of mine, going to the Club and talking with the critics and all that—that was a great opportunity for me.[6] So I came back and sat down: What am I going to paint? I decided since I'd been using every mannerism I could think of, and all this . . . why don't I just try to get a composition as basic as I can, see if I can get the planes to sit properly, the space to work properly. What shall I paint? Well, I am going to take basic shapes: a triangle, a rectangle, some squares or parallelograms or whatever architecture I can think of, and I made these ovals thinking I am going to put something on those and see if I can make them sit on those things. And triangles went on them and I thought to myself, "Let's see, I have worked in a lot of restaurants and I've seen rows of pies and things." So when I got these ovals and put these triangles, I made sort of basic pies. I just made it very plain at first, and I had not realized what I had done. . . . I ended up with this row of pie paintings and stupefied myself. I mean, I virtually said to myself, "That would be the end of a serious painter." And I could not from then on leave that subject matter alone, and it was because the drawing and the painting was coming together in this very interesting way, which is really like cartooning. It felt wonderful but I thought I would never be taken seriously in the "fine art world."

You see, I didn't go to art school. I had these wonderful people in commercial art and sign painting and old cartoonists and lettering men. They are the ones who showed me how to do things. There is a language of form—I would call it a kind of Esperanto of advertising art— where, if you are going to do a lipstick, for instance, you find a way of making it very clear graphically. If you look at retail advertising, that diamond ring is made out of this construct. A shoe is done a certain way, all kinds of jewelry, all kinds of household goods. . . . You learn very quickly this kind of language of form. And you can make ads as an art director very quickly because of this. That kind of drawing was what I began to use when I started doing these very simple shapes, because that's what I was doing as a layout man. They are graphic caricatures that come out of advertising.

ID: *So your drawing comes from that commercial background. At the same time you have mentioned the influence of someone like de Kooning. . . .*

WT: I'm very much influenced by de Kooning, Richard Diebenkorn, and many other contemporary painters. They were very helpful to me and very influential. I live out of their work, but also out of historical antecedents that I'm very interested in, Morandi and—well you know all of those. It really is a mix. What you hope is, and this is pretty presumptuous but interesting. Let's take van Gogh. Take French tapestry, Monticelli, Millet, Seurat, on and on, and explain van Gogh! . . . What happened? A new visual species that is remarkably singular. You hope you can get your painting to have, if you can, that singular characteristic. That's why the mixture for me is so important and working from memory is an important aid.

ID: *The mixture of?*

WT: Mixture of as many feelings and visual memory awareness as possible.

ID: *Let's get back to your drawing practice. Do you draw from observation?*

WT: Yes, at drawing sessions with other people. I do that a lot. I did that for seven years with a group (Figs. 2–3).[7]

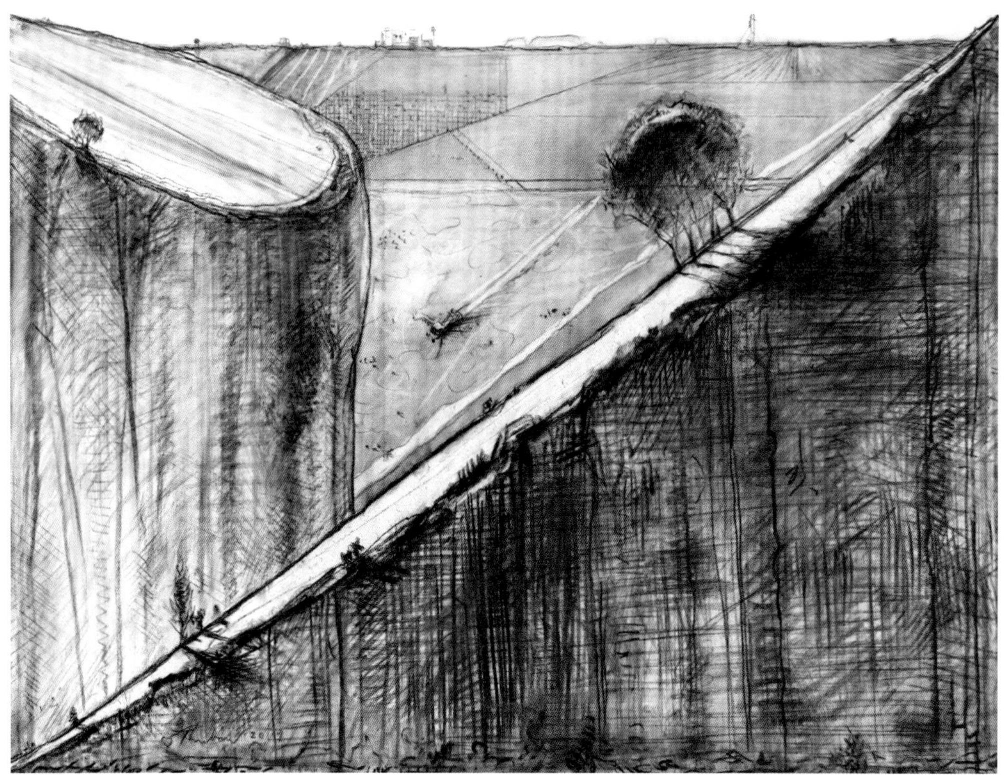

ID: *And that was mostly figure drawing?*

WT: All figures. Yes.

ID: *What about the other subjects: still life, cityscape, landscape?*

WT: The charcoal drawings of objects are all from observation (Nos. 35–37).

ID: *Those were done in connection with your teaching?*

WT: Yes.

ID: *But don't you also sketch outdoors?*

WT: Yes, I do. Quite a bit. I was given a nice reference from Brian O'Doherty. He looked at some of my drawings—those I was doing outside—and he said "[Edward] Hopper made all those kinds of drawings also, but his paintings are from the studio, you know? Most of those are not done outside. They're made up in the studio by putting together all these parts." So he was suggesting to me that that's what I should be doing, and that's what I did.

ID: *I wonder if you could talk about the drawings on canvas that you did very recently (Fig. 4). How did they come about?*

WT: I often start with charcoal before I paint—that's a usual thing that painters do—and at one point I kept drawing, and for some reason it was sort of entrancing, what was going on. It seemed nice and I decided to continue on, thinking maybe I'll get it further along than usual and then paint later. I left to go to lunch or something, figuring I'd come back to paint. I came in and I liked it. I thought, "I think that looks better than what I've been painting," [*laughs*] and I just kept it, and we showed it in conjunction with some later works.

ID: *That was a Sacramento River scene?*

WT: Yes, and the Sacramento fields, bluffs, and farmlands. The little river, but not the irrigation river.

ID: *Did you do a whole group of those drawings on canvas?*

WT: No, not very many, but I like doing them. I might do more.

ID: *You like the surface of the canvas as opposed to paper?*

WT: Yes. It's so . . . it's a little more sensuous, like handmade paper. It's a very beautiful surface.

ID: *Have you drawn on handmade paper?*

WT: A little bit, not much. One time someone gave me a very pale blue paper. He said, "That's very rare French paper." That tells me right away, "Don't draw on it! Keep the paper!" He told me that it was made from rags from French army uniforms. No. Too good. Still too good. I'm of the Depression, so that's hard for me to use really expensive things.

ID: *Are you the kind of artist who always has a little sketchbook in his pocket and draws all the time?*

WT: Yes.

ID: *From memory or observation?*

WT: Lots from memory but also from observation, in the airports and cafes and while traveling.

ID: *You mentioned also that you draw in front of the TV?*

WT: Yes. That's very difficult but very good for you. You make mostly gesture drawings, but every once in a while you can draw a commentator, or fashion, women posing, or animals— great nature programs! I still do it, and the students do it too. That's one of their homework assignments.

ID: *What are some of the others?*

WT: To draw twenty-five things that you've never drawn and wouldn't think of drawing. Draw a used car lot. Go out and draw traffic. Draw in restaurants. Anything that will give them more and more experience and get them more and more exposed to looking at things.

For students especially I continue to be very interested in the need as much as possible to learn to specify problems and work on them. In other words, to think of something to do that'll help them see better and develop better facilities. For instance, a wonderful assignment book would be to take George Seurat's process, get some good paper like that with texture or canvas, and then use that process. That's an actual process that you can use, learn from, find out something about light, about generality and so on. In other words, I think too much classroom activity is way too much laissez-faire and undisciplined. I mean, it's kind of entertaining and keeps people busy, but it's not a process that is useful, you know. You don't learn things from that, I don't think. Well, a little bit; you learn something about how to mess around [*laughs*] and the joy of that, and that's pretty good, but—I sound so old-fashioned when I thought I was a modern painter!

ID: *You have the firm conviction that drawing is primarily a trade that one has to learn.*

WT: Absolutely, yes. It can be done in a lot of ways and with a lot of joys, I think. I'm making it sound like it's awful. . . . It has a high fatigue factor if it's focused to a degree where you prove that you can stand up to that discipline, but the next day you can make the most lyrical, wild, expressive drawings that become like de Kooning, the fastest pencil in the West!

Notes

This conversation was recorded in Sacramento on 31 January 2017.

1. Ernst Gombrich, *The Preference for the Primitive: Episodes in the History of Western Taste and Art*, London, 2002.

2. James Castle (1899–1977) was a self-taught artist who made drawings on found materials, such as packaging cardboards, using soot mixed with saliva and applied with a stick or other found instruments.

3. Sir William Coldstream (1908–1987), who developed a painstaking method, involving a system of descriptive marks, to paint as accurately as possible from observation, was a highly influential teacher at the Slade School of Fine Arts. His student Euan Uglow (1932–2000) worked in a related style.

4. Kimon Nicolaïdes, *The Natural Way to Draw: A Working Plan for Art Study*, Boston, 1941.

5. Charles Bargue (1826/27–1883) was a French painter and lithographer who published, in collaboration with academic artist Jean-Léon Gérôme (1824–1904), a popular drawing course between 1868 and 1871. Vincent van Gogh and Pablo Picasso are known to have studied from it.

6. In 1956–57, Thiebaud lived for a year in New York, where he was in contact with many artists associated with Abstract Expressionism, notably Willem de Kooning and Franz Kline. "The Club" refers to the Eight-Street Club, where these artists met regularly.

7. From 1976 to 1984, Thiebaud met regularly with four other artists—Mark Adams, Theophilus Brown, Gordon Cook, and Beth Van Hoesen—to draw from a model.

Selected Bibliography

ARTIST'S STATEMENTS AND INTERVIEWS

Albright, Thomas. "Wayne Thiebaud: Scrambling Around with Ordinary Problems." *Art News* 77, no. 2 (February 1978), pp. 82–86.

Arthur, John, ed. *Realists at Work.* New York, 1983; "Wayne Thiebaud," pp. 114–29.

Aschheim, Eve, and Chris Daubert. *Episodes with Wayne Thiebaud: Four Interviews 2009–2011.* New York, 2014.

Benson, A. LeGrace G., and David H. R. Shearer. "Documents: An Interview with Wayne Thiebaud." *Leonardo 2*, no. 1 (1969), pp. 65–72.

Berkson, Bill. "Thiebaud on the Figure: An Interview with Bill Berkson." In *Wayne Thiebaud: Figurative Works, 1959–1994.* Exhibition catalogue, The Wiegand Gallery, College of Notre-Dame, Belmont, California, 1994, n.p.

Butterfield, Jan. "Wayne Thiebaud: 'A Feast for the Senses.'" *Arts Magazine* 51 (October 1977), pp. 132–37.

Demand, Thomas. "Elements of Painting: Wayne Thiebaud in Conversation with Thomas Demand." *Frieze Masters* 3 (October 2014).

Gettings, Frank, ed. *Drawings 1974–1984.* Exhibition catalogue, Hirshhorn Museum and Sculpture Garden, Washington, DC, 1984; "Wayne Thiebaud," pp. 230–32.

Glenn, Constance W. "Artist's Dialogue: A Conversation with Wayne Thiebaud." *Architectural Digest* 39, no. 9 (September 1982), pp. 62, 68.

Larsen, Susan. Oral history interview with Wayne Thiebaud, 17–18 May 2001. Archives of American Art, Smithsonian Institution.

Lewallen, Constance. "Wayne Thiebaud: Interview." *View* (Point Publications, San Francisco) 6, no. 6 (Winter 1990), pp. 1–23.

Maréchal-Workman, Andrée. "Wayne Thiebaud: Beyond the Cityscapes." *Smithsonian Studies in American Art 1*, no. 2 (Fall 1987), pp. 35–51.

Masi, Alessia. "Interview to Wayne Thiebaud." In *Wayne Thiebaud at Museo Morandi.* Exhibition catalogue, Museo Morandi, Bologna, 2011, pp. 29–57.

McGough, Stephen C. "An Interview with Wayne Thiebaud." In *Thiebaud Selects Thiebaud: A Forty-Year Survey from Private Collections.* Exhibition catalogue, Crocker Art Museum, Sacramento, 1996, pp. 7–15.

Stone, Gwen. "Wayne Thiebaud: In Conversation with Gwen Stone." *Visual Dialog* (Winter 1977–78), pp. 12–15.

Strand, Mark, ed. *The Art of the Real: Nine Contemporary Figurative Painters*. New York, 1983; "Wayne Thiebaud," pp. 181–97.

Thiebaud, Wayne. "As Far as I'm Concerned, There Is Only One Study and that Is the Way in Which Things Relate to One Another." *Untitled* (Friends of Photography, Carmel, California), no. 7/8 (1974), pp. 23–25.

—— "A Fellow Painter's View of Giorgio Morandi." *The New York Times*, 15 November 1981, pp. D37–D38.

—— "Matisse—A Personal View." In *Henri Matisse: An Exhibition of Drawings*. Exhibition catalogue, John Berggruen Gallery, San Francisco, 1982, pp. ix–x.

—— Introduction. In *Figure Drawings: Five San Francisco Artists*. Exhibition catalogue, Charles Campbell Gallery, San Francisco, 1983.

—— "Artist's Choice: Four Contemporary Painters—Wayne Thiebaud, Helen Frankenthaler, Sam Messer, and Pat Steir—pick their favorites of the Christmas crop of new books." *Art & Antiques* (December 1986), p. 101.

—— Foreword. In *Drawn to Excellence: Masters of Cartoon Art*. Exhibition catalogue, Cartoon Art Museum, San Francisco, 1988.

—— Foreword. In Beverly Hennessey, ed. *On Art and Artists: Essays by Thomas Albright*. San Francisco, 1989.

—— "Forum: Balthus's *Study for 'The Guitar Lesson*.'" *Drawing* 16, no. 1 (May/June 1994), pp. 9–10.

Tooker, Dan. "Wayne Thiebaud Interviewed by Dan Tooker." *Art International* 18 (November 1974), pp. 22–25, 33.

Wollheim, Richard. "On Thiebaud and Diebenkorn: Richard Wollheim Talks to Wayne Thiebaud." *Modern Painters* 4, no. 3 (Autumn 1991), pp. 64–68.

—— "An Interview with Wayne Thiebaud." In *Wayne Thiebaud: Cityscapes*. Exhibition catalogue, Campbell-Thiebaud Gallery, San Francisco, 1993, n.p.

—— "Matisse at MOMA: Richard Wollheim Talks to Wayne Thiebaud." *Modern Painters* 6, no. 3 (Autumn 1993), pp. 56–61.

**BOOKS AND
EXHIBITION CATALOGUES**

Baker, Kenneth, Nicholas Fox Weber, Karen Wilkin, and John Yau. *Wayne Thiebaud*. New York, 2015.

Beal, Graham W. J. *Wayne Thiebaud: Paintings*. Exhibition catalogue, Walker Art Center, Minneapolis, 1981.

Coplans, John. *Wayne Thiebaud*. Exhibition catalogue, Pasadena Art Museum, 1968.

Figures: Thiebaud. Exhibition catalogue, Stanford University Art Museum, 1965.

Glenn, Constance, and Jack Glenn, eds. *Wayne Thiebaud: Private Drawings, The Artist's Sketchbook*. New York, 1987.

Kimmelman, Michael. "Wayne Thiebaud." In *Portraits: Talking with Artists at the Met, the Modern, the Louvre, and Elsewhere*. New York, 1998, pp. 157–73.

McGough, Stephen C. *Thiebaud Selects Thiebaud: A Forty-Year Survey from Private Collections*. Exhibition catalogue, Crocker Art Museum, Sacramento, 1996.

Nash, Steven A. *Wayne Thiebaud: A Paintings Retrospective*. Exhibition catalogue, Fine Arts Museums of San Francisco, 2000. Essay by Adam Gopnik.

Tsujimoto, Karen. *Wayne Thiebaud*. Exhibition catalogue, San Francisco Museum of Modern Art, San Francisco, 1985.

Vision and Revision: Hand Colored Prints by Wayne Thiebaud. San Francisco, 1991. Introduction by Wayne Thiebaud. Texts by Bill Berkson and Robert Flynn Johnson.

Wayne Thiebaud. Exhibition catalogue, Allan Stone Gallery, New York, 1967.

Wayne Thiebaud at Museo Morandi. Exhibition catalogue, Museo Morandi, Bologna, Italy, 2011. Essay by Alessia Masi.

Wayne Thiebaud: Charcoal Still Lifes 1964–1974. Exhibition catalogue, Lawrence Markey, San Antonio, Texas, and Paul Thiebaud Gallery, San Francisco, 2010. Essay by Bill Berkson.

Wayne Thiebaud: Cityscapes. Exhibition catalogue, Campbell-Thiebaud Gallery, San Francisco, 1993.

Wayne Thiebaud: Creations on Paper.
Exhibition catalogue, Visual Art
Gallery, College of Saint Catherine,
Saint Paul, Minnesota, 1977. Essay by
Philip Larson.

*Wayne Thiebaud: Drawings, Graphics
1961–1983.* Exhibition catalogue, The
Trout Gallery, Emil R. Weiss Center
for the Arts, Dickinson College,
Carlisle, Pennsylvania, 1983. Essay by
David Alan Robertson.

Wayne Thiebaud: Figure Drawings.
Exhibition catalogue, Campbell-
Thiebaud Gallery, San Francisco, 1993.
Essay by Victoria Dalkey.

Wayne Thiebaud: In Black and White.
Exhibition catalogue, Allan Stone
Projects, New York, 2014. Essay by
Carter Ratcliff.

*Wayne Thiebaud: Landscapes & City
Views.* Exhibition brochure, Crocker
Art Museum, Sacramento, 1983.

*Wayne Thiebaud: Paintings and Works
on Paper.* Exhibition catalogue, John
Berggruen Gallery, San Francisco,
2012.

*Wayne Thiebaud: Paintings, Pastels,
Drawings, and Prints.* Exhibition
catalogue, John Berggruen Gallery,
San Francisco, 1980.

Wayne Thiebaud: Pastels 1960–2000.
Exhibition catalogue, Campbell-
Thiebaud Gallery, San Francisco, 2000.

*Wayne Thiebaud: Prints and Works on
Paper.* Exhibition catalogue, Simms
Reed Gallery, London, 2015.

Wayne Thiebaud: Recent Drawings.
Exhibition catalogue, Eloise Pickard
Smith Gallery, University of
California, Santa Cruz, 1982.

Wayne Thiebaud: Riverscapes.
Exhibition catalogue, Paul Thiebaud
Gallery, San Francisco, 2002.

Wayne Thiebaud: Still Lifes & Landscapes.
Exhibition catalogue, Associated
American Artists, New York, 1993.
Essay by Kathleen Bahet.

Wayne Thiebaud: Survey 1947–1976.
Exhibition catalogue, Phoenix Art
Museum, 1976. Essay by Gene Cooper.

*Wayne Thiebaud: Works on Paper from
the Collection of the Artist.* Exhibition
catalogue, Arts Club of Chicago,
1987. Text by Bill Berkson.

Zakian, Michael. *Wayne Thiebaud:
Works on Paper, 1948–2004.*
Frederick R. Weisman Museum of
Art, Pepperdine University, Malibu,
California, 2014.

ARTICLES

Berkson, Bill. "Thiebaud's Vanities." *Art in America* 73, no. 12 (December 1985), pp. 111–20.

—— "Wayne Thiebaud, Stanford Art Gallery." *Artforum* 27, no. 3 (November 1988), p. 154.

—— "Wayne's World." *Modern Painters* 11, no. 2 (Summer 1998), pp. 18–19.

Brown, Christopher. "New Drawings by Wayne Thiebaud." *Artweek* 8, no. 19 (7 May 1977), p. 20.

Gopnik, Adam. "The Art World: Window Gazing." *The New Yorker* 67, no. 10 (29 April 1991), pp. 78–80.

Hurwitz, Laurie S. "Wayne Thiebaud's Studied Sensuality." *American Artist* 57, no. 615 (October 1993), pp. 26–33, 77.

Kimmelman, Michael. "Wistful Joy in Soda-Fountain Dreams." *The New York Times*, 29 June 2001, pp. E31, E33.

Morch, Al. "5 Artists Drawn Together." *San Francisco Examiner*, 10 January 1983, p. B14.

Parks, John A. "Thiebaud's World." *Drawing* 1, no. 1 (Fall 2003), pp. 16–27.

Stein, Ruthe. "Artist Designs Sets for 'Krazy Kat' Ballet." *San Francisco Chronicle*, 23 January 1990, pp. B3, B5.

Stowens, Susan. "Wayne Thiebaud: Beyond Pop Art." *American Artist* 44, no. 458 (September 1980), pp. 48–51, 102–4.

Waldman, Diane. "Thiebaud: Eros in Cafeteria." *ArtNews* 65, no. 2 (April 1966), pp. 39–41, 55–56.

Wollheim, Richard. "A Painter's Alchemy." *Modern Painters* 11, no. 2 (Summer 1998), pp. 20–24.

Workman, Carol. "Wayne Thiebaud's Cityscapes." *Images & Issues* (Winter 1981–82), pp. 67–70.

Every effort has been made to trace copyright owners and photographers. The Morgan apologizes for any unintentional omissions and would be pleased in such cases to add an acknowledgment in future editions.

PHOTOGRAPHIC COPYRIGHT
All artwork by Wayne Thiebaud © Wayne Thiebaud / Licensed by VAGA, New York, NY; image courtesy Acquavella Galleries, Nos. 10, 13, 17, 22–23, 26, 54; collection of Harry W. and Mary Margaret Anderson, No. 48; Architectural Digest © Condé Nast, p. 111, Fig. 1; collection of Gretchen and John Berggruen, San Francisco. Photography courtesy of the Morgan Library & Museum, Nos. 21, 55; photo © Christie's Images / Bridgeman Images © 2017 C. Herscovici / Artists Rights Society (ARS), New York, p. 114, Fig. 4; Alfredo Dagli Orti / Art Resource, NY, p. 28, Fig. 12 left; © The Richard Diebenkorn Foundation, p. 35, Fig. 17; © the estate of Philip Guston, courtesy Hauser & Wirth, p. 20, Fig. 7 top; © King Features Syndicate, p. 18, Fig. 6 top; Alan Meckler Collection, NY, photography courtesy of the Morgan Library & Museum, Nos. 24, 27, 31, 35, 38; © 2017 Mondrian / Holtzman Trust, p. 115, Fig. 5; Museo Morandi Istituzione Bologna Musei © 2017 Artists Rights Society (ARS), New York / SIAE, Rome, p. 31, Fig. 15 left; photography courtesy of the Morgan Library & Museum, Nos. 3, 7, 24, 31, 35, 38; © RMN-Grand Palais / Art Resource, NY, p. 30, Fig. 14 left; Smithsonian American Art Museum, Washington, DC, U.S.A. / Art Resource, NY, p. 21, Fig. 8, p. 29, Fig. 13; Allan Stone Collection, courtesy: Allan Stone Projects, New York, p. 18, Fig. 6 bottom, p. 34, Fig. 16 right, Nos. 8, 11–12, 16, 19, 30, 32, 47, 49; image courtesy of Wayne Thiebaud studio, Nos. 1–2, 4–6, 9, 15, 20, 27–29, 33–34, 36–37, 39–41, 43–46, 50–53, 56–83, p. 13, Fig. 1, p. 20, Fig. 7 bottom, p. 22, Fig. 9, p. 25, Fig. 10, p. 27, Fig. 11, p. 28, Fig. 12 right, p. 30, Fig. 14 right, p. 31, Fig. 15 right, pp. 148–49, Figs. 2–3, p. 151, Fig. 4; Yale University Art Gallery, Nos. 14, 18.

PHOTOGRAPHY
Ben Blackwell, p. 35, Fig. 17; Janny Chiu, p. 18, Fig. 6 top, p. 34, Fig. 16 left; Steven H. Crossot, p. 113, Fig. 3; Tony De Camillo, No. 18; Lee Fatherree, No. 48; Graham S. Haber, Nos. 3, 7, 21, 24, 27, 31, 35, 38, p. 15, Figs. 2–3, p. 17, Figs. 4–5, p. 112, Fig. 2; Mary Nichols, p. 111, Fig. 1; Kent Pell, No. 17; John Wilson White, Studio Phocasso, No. 42, p. 25, Fig. 10 bottom.

Cover: Wayne Thiebaud, *Shelf of Pies*, 1960 (No. 7).

Published to accompany the exhibition *Wayne Thiebaud, Draftsman*
18 May–23 September 2018
organized by the Morgan Library & Museum

Wayne Thiebaud, Draftsman is made possible with lead funding from Acquavella Galleries, generous support from Allan Stone Projects and Agnes Gund, and assistance from The Meckler Foundation, the Wyeth Foundation for American Art, and Nancy Schwartz.

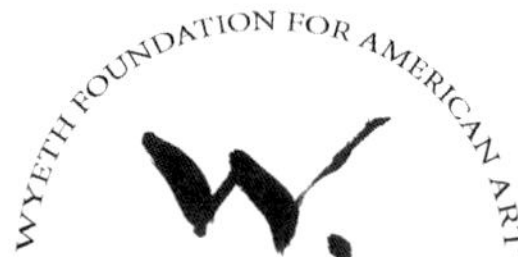

The Morgan Library & Museum
Karen Banks, *Publications Manager*
Patricia Emerson, *Senior Editor*
Eliza Heitzman, *Assistant Editor*

Project Staff
Marilyn Palmeri, *Imaging and Rights Manager*
Eva Soos, *Imaging and Rights Assistant Manager*
Kaitlyn Krieg, *Imaging and Rights Administrative Assistant*
Graham S. Haber, *Photographer*
Janny Chiu, *Assistant Photographer*

Designed by McCall Associates
Typeset in Austin and Brandon Grotesque
Printed on Kasadaka White

The Morgan wishes to thank Min Tian.

First published in the United Kingdom in 2018 by Thames & Hudson Ltd, 181A High Holborn, London WC1V 7QX, in association with The Morgan Library & Museum, 225 Madison Avenue, New York, NY 10016

Wayne Thiebaud, Draftsman © 2018 The Morgan Library & Museum, New York / Thames & Hudson Ltd, London

Texts © 2018 The Morgan Library & Museum

117 illustrations.

For image copyrights see p. 159.

British Library Cataloguing-in-Publication Data

A catalogue record for this book is available from the British Library

ISBN 978-0-500-02189-7

Printed and bound in China by C&C Offset Printing Co. Ltd

To find out about all our publications, please visit **www.thamesandhudson.com**. There you can subscribe to our e-newsletter, browse or download our current catalogue, and buy any titles that are in print.

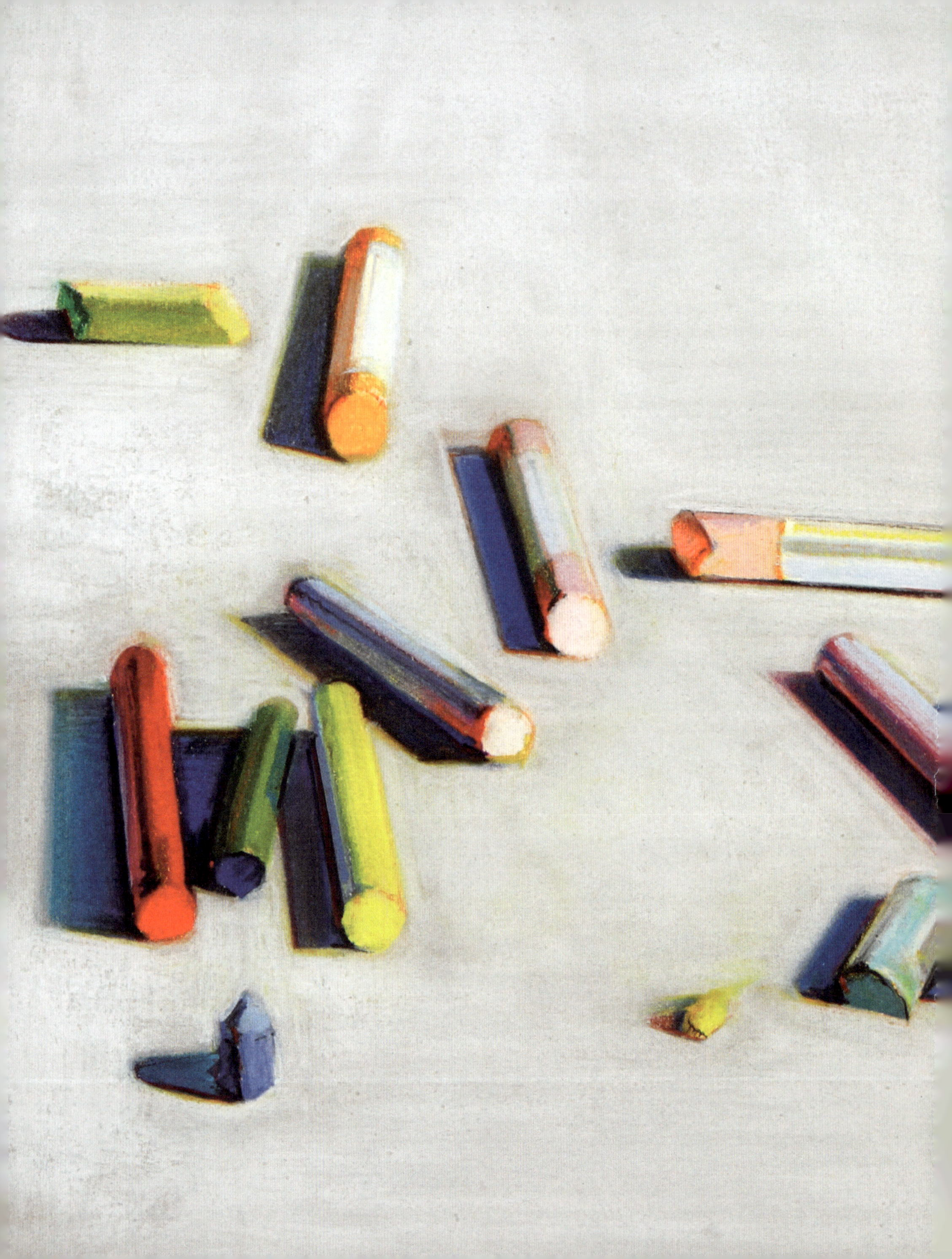